OTHER TITLES OF INTEREST FROM ST. LUCIE PRESS

The 90-Day ISO 9000 Manual and Implementation Guide
The Executive Guide to Implementing Quality Systems
Focused Quality: Managing for Results
Improving Service Quality: Achieving High Performance in the Public and Private Sectors
Introduction to Modern Statistical Quality Control and Management
ISO 9000: Implementation Guide for Small to Mid-Sized Businesses
Organization Teams: Continuous Quality Improvement
Organization Teams: Facilitator's Guide
Principles of Total Quality
Quality Improvement Handbook: Team Guide to Tools and Techniques
The Textbook of Total Quality in Healthcare
Total Quality in Higher Education
Total Quality in Managing Human Resources
Total Quality in Marketing
Total Quality in Purchasing and Supplier Management
Total Quality in Radiology: A Guide to Implementation
Total Quality in Research and Development
Total Quality Management for Custodial Operations
Total Quality Management: Text, Cases, and Readings, 2nd Edition
Total Quality Service

For more information about these titles call, fax or write:

St. Lucie Press
100 E. Linton Blvd., Suite 403B
Delray Beach, FL 33483
TEL (407) 274-9906 • FAX (407) 274-9927

S_{L}^{t}

Total Quality in
MARKETING

The St. Lucie Press
Total Quality Series™

BOOKS IN THE SERIES:

Total Quality in HIGHER EDUCATION

Total Quality in PURCHASING and SUPPLIER MANAGEMENT

Total Quality in INFORMATION SYSTEMS

Total Quality in RESEARCH AND DEVELOPMENT

Total Quality in MANAGING HUMAN RESOURCES

Total Quality in ORGANIZATIONAL DEVELOPMENT

Total Quality in MARKETING

MACROLOGISTICS IN STRATEGIC MANAGEMENT

For more information about these books call St. Lucie Press at (407) 274-9906

Series Editor • *Frank Voehl*
Series Development Editor • *Sandy Pearlman*

Total Quality in

MARKETING

By
William C. Johnson
School of Business and Entrepreneurship
Nova Southeastern University
Fort Lauderdale, Florida

Richard J. Chvala
Senior Consultant
Sales and Marketing
Ethyl Corporation
Richmond, Virginia

S^t_L

St. Lucie Press
Delray Beach, Florida

658.8
Jnt

Printed and bound in the U.S.A. Printed on acid-free paper.
10 9 8 7 6 5 4 3 2 1

ISBN 1-884015-13-1

Phone: (407) 274-9906
Fax: (407) 274-9927

S^t_L

Published by
St. Lucie Press
100 E. Linton Blvd., Suite 403B
Delray Beach, FL 33483

DEDICATION

*This book is dedicated to our parents before us,
who knew quality as a way of life
and imparted it to their children*

CONTENTS

SERIES PREFACE

The St. Lucie Press Series on Total Quality originated in 1993 when some of us realized that the rapidly expanding field of quality management was neither well defined nor well focused. This realization, coupled with America's hunger for specific, how-to examples, led to the formulation of a plan to publish a series of subject-specific books on total quality, a new direction for books in the field to follow.

The essence of this series consists of a core nucleus of seven new direction books, around which the remaining books in the series will revolve over a three-year period:

- Education Transformation: *Total Quality in Higher Education*

- Respect for People: *Total Quality in Managing Human Resources*

- Speak with Facts: *Total Quality in Information Systems*

- Customer Satisfaction: *Total Quality in Marketing*

- Continuous Improvement: *Total Quality in Research and Development*

- Supplier Partnerships: *Total Quality in Purchasing and Supplier Management*

- Cost-Effective, Value-Added Services: *Measuring Total Quality*

We at St. Lucie Press have been privileged to contribute to the convergence of philosophy and underlying principles of total quality, leading to a common set of assumptions. One of the most important deals with the challenges facing the transformation of the marketing process for the 21st century. This is a particularly exciting and turbulent time in this field, both domestically and globally, and change may be viewed as either an opportunity or a threat. As such, the principles and practices of total quality can aid in this transformation or, by flawed implementation approaches, can bring an organization to its knees.

As the authors of this text explain, the total quality orientation to marketing redefines line managerial roles and identifies new responsibilities for the traditional function to come to grips with. The marketing practitioner's role now includes strategic input and continual development of the strategic planning system to increase customer satisfaction both now and in the future. The full meaning of these changes is fully explored in light of the driving forces reshaping the marketing environment. The focus is both academic and business oriented, exploring long-range marketing policy-making and models and showing the integration of total quality principles and Kotler's model of the three types of strategic orientation for the marketing function.

As Series Editor, I am pleased with the manner in which the series is coming together. Its premise is that excellence can be achieved through a singular focus on customers and their interests as a number one priority, a focus that requires a high degree of commitment, flexibility, and resolve. The new definition of the degree of satisfaction will be the total experience of the interaction—which will be the determinant of whether the customer stays a customer. However, no book or series can tell an organization how to achieve total quality; only the customers and stakeholders can tell you when you have it and when you do not. High-quality goods and services can give an organization a competitive edge while reducing costs due to rework, returns, and scrap. Most importantly, outstanding marketing quality performance generates satisfied customers, who reward the organization with continued patronage and free word-of-mouth advertising.

In the area of abstracts, we are indebted to Richard Frantzreb, President of Advanced Personnel Systems, who has granted permission to incorporate selected abstracts from their collection, which they independently publish in a quarterly magazine called *Quality Abstracts*. This feature is a sister publication to *Training and Development Alert*. These journals are designed to keep readers abreast of literature in the field of quality and to help readers benefit from the insights and experience of experts and practitioners who are implementing total quality in their organizations. Each journal runs between 28 and 36 pages and contains about 100 carefully selected abstracts of articles and books in the field. For further information, contact Richard Frantzreb (916-781-2900).

We trust that you will find this book both usable and beneficial and wish you maximum success on the quality journey. If it in some way makes a contribution, then we can say, as Dr. Deming often did at the end of his seminars, "I have done my best."

Frank Voehl
Series Editor

AUTHORS' PREFACE

Yogi Berra once said, "When you come to a fork in the road, take it." We believe that companies today are at a "fork in the road" where they either improve their competitiveness or risk extinction. It is widely accepted among today's business executives that quality in products and services is essential to survival in the fiercely competitive global marketplace. Moreover, there is mounting evidence to indicate that quality is a powerful strategy for raising return on investment. Jack Welch, chairman of General Electric, echoes this view on quality by saying, "The value decade is on us. If you can't sell a top-quality product at the world's lowest price, you're going to be out of the game."

We have discovered, however, that despite the acknowledged benefits of quality, few companies see its value in achieving a long-term competitive advantage. In fact, a recent study by Arthur D. Little surveyed 500 companies using total quality management (TQM) and found that only 36 percent believed it was significantly boosting their competitiveness.

We are not suggesting that TQM is a panacea for solving an organization's problems. Yet it offers a rich library of tools that support more "fact-based" management decision making. Many of these tools can be taught and utilized not just by managers, but by workers and teams as well. These tools are also useful in both identifying and isolating problems as well as solving them.

We wrote this book to show the compatibility that exists between TQM and marketing and how marketing practitioners can use these tools to enhance their marketing practices. For example, the very definitions of TQM are anchored in the concept of customer satisfaction. Moreover, the central premise of TQM is to view an organization as an interrelated collection of processes rather than in interacting set of functional units and to optimize the flow of such activities as order fulfillment, reduced cycle time, or service delivery. These goals are also at the heart of marketing.

This book was written with both the academician and the practitioner in mind. For instructors, the book is well suited to be used as a supplement or stand-alone text in a quality or service management course. Instructors in particular will find the cases and discussion questions useful as supplements to the text material. The book can also be used by practitioners in a training and development context. Hand-on exercises along with profiles of companies that have successfully integrated quality into their marketing practices are provided to assist trainers in presenting the various total quality principles.

The organization of the book begins by laying the groundwork for the importance of quality practices and how quality and marketing are related. The next two chapters deal with a historical perspective of quality and a look at the quality gurus, followed by a foundational chapter on the House of Quality. Once the foundation of the House of Quality is laid, the next four chapters deal with building blocks of the structure, namely the management system, the role of vision and quality, quality and strategy, using quality teams, and implementing quality practices in marketing processes. The concluding chapter deals with adopting quality standards by examining various award criteria such as Baldrige, Deming, and ISO 9000.

SERIES EDITOR

Frank Voehl has had a twenty-year career in quality management, productivity improvement, and related fields. He has written more than 200 articles, papers, and books for international business journals, publications, and conferences worldwide on the subject of quality. Mr. Voehl has consulted on quality and productivity issues, as well as measurement system implementation, for hundreds of companies (many *Fortune* 500 corporations). As general manager of FPL Qualtec, he was influential in the FPL Deming Prize process, which led to the formation of the Malcolm Baldrige Award, as well as the National Quality Award in the Bahamas. He is a member of Strategic Planning committees with the ASQC and AQP and has assisted the IRS in quality planning as a member of the Commissioner's Advisory Group.

An industrial engineering graduate from St. John's University in New York City, Mr. Voehl has been a visiting professor and lecturer at NYU and the University of Miami, where he helped establish the framework for the Quality Institute. He is currently president and CEO of Strategy Associates, Inc. and a visiting professor at Florida International University.

On the local level, Mr. Voehl served for ten years as vice chairman of the Margate/Broward County Advisory Committee for the Handicapped. In 1983, he was awarded the Partners in Productivity award by Florida Governor Graham for his efforts to streamline and improve the Utilities Forced Relocation Process, which saved the state some $200 million over a seven-year period.

AUTHORS

William C. Johnson is a Full-Professor of Marketing in Nova Southeastern University's School of Business & Entrepreneurship. He teaches several marketing courses at both the master's and doctoral levels. He received his Ph.D. in business from Arizona State University in 1985.

Dr. Johnson has consulted extensively with the soft drink as well as industrial chemical industries. He has also worked with a variety of small businesses in Broward County in dealing with their marketing problems. In addition, he has had experience in international education, giving seminars to businesspersons from Taiwan, Thailand, and Indonesia.

During his more than 11 years teaching in higher education, Dr. Johnson has published widely in such journals as *The Journal of Applied Management and Entrepreneurship, The Journal of Marketing in Higher Education, Marketing News, International Business Chronicle, Arizona Business Education Journal, The Marketing Connection, Broward Daily Business Review,* and *Beverage World.*

Rich Chvala is Senior Consultant, Sales and Marketing Training, for Ethyl Corporation, a *Fortune* 500 company based in Richmond, Virginia. He received an undergraduate degree in biochemistry, with a minor in psychology, from Michigan Technological University and a master's in educational/ organizational administration from Michigan in 1976.

Mr. Chvala serves on the national board of the American Marketing Association and was the keynote speaker at the AMA's First International Congress on Customer Satisfaction. He has 15 years experience as a national sales manager and marketing executive for both capital goods and service companies and consults and trains in strategy and creating value for the customer with several *Fortune* 500 companies in the United States, Europe, and the Far East.

CHAPTER 1

WHY TOTAL QUALITY IN MARKETING

Every time we travel in a car, fly in an airplane, or have surgery in the hospital we are reminded how critical quality has become in our lives. At today's prices, no one wants a car that falls short of perfect, an airline flight that is an hour late (or, worse, not 100 percent safe), or a surgical procedure that is not done exactly right. We are also painfully aware of how a bad education can hurt not just our kids but our country as well. Thus, with more choices among product and service providers than ever before, we as consumers can be much more selective about who we patronize. In short, quality may become the biggest competitive issue of the 1990s and beyond.

Today's companies are experiencing vicious competition as never before. Much of this competition since the late 1970s has focused on quality. And quality competition has gone global. What started as a quality race between the United States and Japan now includes many Pacific Rim countries as well as Western European countries. Many American companies such as Motorola, Hewlett-Packard, 3M, AT&T, and Milliken have introduced various quality programs with startling success. Yet more firms need to adopt quality prac-

1

tices to survive the fierce global competition. A recent survey of 100 top executives of the country's largest companies found that 79 percent equated quality with business survival, 92 percent agreed that companies have no choice but to produce quality products because of fierce competition, and 96 percent felt that quality is one of the most important criteria their customers use. In another survey, 57 percent of U.S. executives polled considered quality more important than profit or cost. A retired vice-president of corporate quality for Ford Motor Company sums it up best by saying, "What we need is an **American total quality renaissance** [emphasis added]."

At a 1990 conference in Tokyo, J.M. Juran, the noted American quality guru, made a startling prediction. He stated that "America is about to bounce back...and in the 1990s 'Made-in-America' will again become a symbol of world-class quality." Juran continued by saying that "when 30 percent of U.S. products were failures vs. 3 percent for Japan, the difference was enormous. But at failures of 0.3 percent and 0.03 percent, it will be difficult for anyone to tell."

It is still too early to tell whether Juran's vision was accurate. Yet quality efforts begun in such U.S. industries as autos, semiconductors, telecommunications equipment and office equipment are approaching the quality standards set by world-class competitors in Japan and Western Europe. Until recently, many such efforts were delayed by the misguided notion that quality costs more. The common perception of the relationship between cost and quality is illustrated in Figure 1.1. This conventional wisdom suggested that there was a "trade-off" between improving quality and costs.[1]

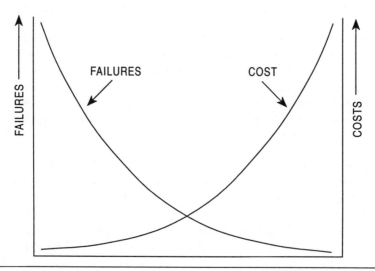

Figure 1.1 Common Business Wisdom on the Quality–Cost Relationship.

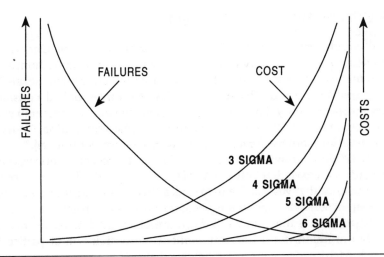

Figure 1.2 Actual Quality–Cost Relationship.

The Japanese, following the advice of Deming and Juran, demonstrated that preventing instead of fixing defects was less costly over time. Murray Weidembaum, former chairman of the President's Council of Economic Advisors, has said, "The key to improving American quality is to do it right the first time. Finding and correcting mistakes is extremely time-consuming and expensive." Some experts say that only 20 percent of the defects occur on the assembly line. The rest are due to design flaws or purchasing policies that stress low price over materials quality.

Motorola's Six Sigma process changed the relationship between quality and cost. In fact, a "family" of relationships rather than a single relationship best represents the quality/cost relationship. As Figure 1.2 clearly reveals, the more quality increases, the more costs go down.[2] Improving quality reduces the so-called "hidden plant" costs such as people, floor space, and equipment that are used to find and fix things that should have been done right the first time.

Moreover, we learned from the Japanese that there are no easy answers when it comes to quality programs. Total quality is not attained by using a "cookbook" approach, but rather involves a cultural transformation of the entire organization.

The trends of the 1990s make a culture that fosters quality and satisfaction a matter of survival in business markets. Scarcer resources, the accelerating speed of business, persistent environmental concerns, and a shortage of skilled labor will contribute to slow and no-growth markets. Satisfying customer quality demands will represent a key competitive advantage. (For additional information, see Abstract 1.1 at the end of this chapter.)

THE COMPETITIVENESS PROBLEM

Although over 26 studies have been completed in the United States during the last decade on ways to improve our international competitiveness, a minority of firms have actually adapted the recommendations.[3] U.S. products still lag behind those of Japan and Germany, according to a poll recently conducted by Bozell-Gallup Worldwide Quality (see Figure 1.3).[4] According to John F. Welch, Jr., "Quality is our best assurance of customer allegiance, our strongest defense against foreign competition, and the only path to sustained growth and earnings."[5] Allen F. Jacobsen, chairman of the board and chief executive officer of 3M Company, says, "I'm convinced that the winners of the '90s will be companies that make quality and customer service an obsession in every single market [in which] they compete."[6]

The problem is that many U.S. firms are playing a defensive game these days by shrinking, reducing employment, downsizing, and paring back business. Many economists today believe that without a serious turnaround in competitiveness, another 10 to 15 percent devaluation in the dollar would be needed to erase the merchandise trade deficit.

QUALITY PAYS

In examining the effect of quality on cost, the relationship is compelling, especially when one consideres product failure rates. Specifically, reducing field failures means lower warranty costs and reducing factory defects cuts expenditures on rework and scrap. In a study of U.S. and Japanese air conditioner manufacturers, David Garvin, an assistant professor at the Harvard Business School, found that the failure rates of products from the highest quality producers were between 500 and 1000 times less than those of products from the lowest.[7]

Quality also pays in the form of customer retention. Customer defections represent a significant cost to companies. In fact, according to a 1985 TARP study, it is five times more expensive to get a new customer than it is to keep an existing one.[8] Moreover, it is estimated that 65 percent of all business comes from existing customers.

Research also shows a relationship between quality, market share, and return on investment (ROI). The exhaustive database from the Profit Impact of Market Strategy (PIMS) unequivocally documents these relationships. Higher quality yields a higher ROI for any given market share. Among businesses with less than 12 percent of the market, those with inferior quality averaged a ROI of 4.5 percent, those with average product quality averaged a ROI of 10.4 percent, and those with superior product quality averaged a ROI of 17.4 percent. The positive relationship between relative perceived quality and return on sales or ROI is graphically illustrated in Figure 1.4.[9] (For additional information, see Abstract 1.2 at the end of this chapter.)

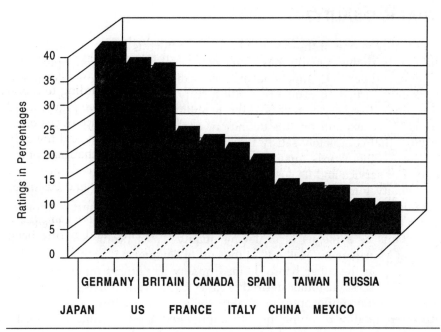

Figure 1.3 International Competitiveness: Excellent/Very Good Respondent Rating.

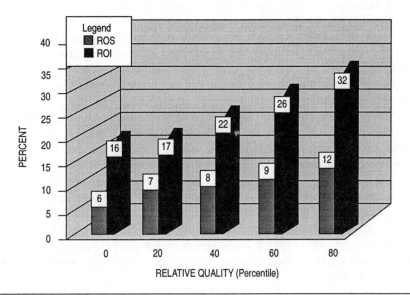

Figure 1.4 Quality/Profit Relationship.

WHAT IS QUALITY?

Quality is one of those elusive concepts which is easy to visualize but difficult to define. Quality has many definitions, ranging from specific to general, and varies by functional area. For example, Philip Kotler, a leading marketing guru, defines quality as "the totality of features and characteristics of a product or service that bear on its ability to satisfy stated or implied needs."[10] To expand on this definition, quality must provide goods and services that completely satisfy the needs of both *internal* and *external* customers. In other words, quality serves as a "bridge" between the producer of a good or service and its customer.

Quality gurus such as Deming viewed quality as reducing variation. Deming's quality philosophy can be summarized in his Fourteen Points, which include such topics as "creating a constancy of purpose" and "ending inspections as a means of achieving quality." (See profile entitled "The Deming Management Method" at the end of Chapter 4.)

Juran, on the other hand, defined quality as "fitness for use," where products possess customer-desired product features and are free of deficiencies. The Juran philosophy of quality centers around three basic quality processes: quality planning, quality improvement, and quality control. In *Juran on Quality by Design*, he makes the distinction between "Big Q" and "Little Q" in defining quality, as shown in Table 1.1. Until recently, most managers associated quality with manufactured goods and production. However, during the 1980s there emerged a broader definition of quality to include services as well as goods. This broadened definition, represented by the content of "Little Q," includes *all* processes within a firm, not just production. The customers described under "Little Q" are *all* who are impacted in helping to create value-added exchanges, both external and internal. Finally, "Big Q" quality is based on the Juran Universal Trilogy of quality planning, quality control, and quality improvement vs. a more limited functional approach under "Little Q."[11]

Crosby, another leading quality guru, defines quality as "conformance to requirements, not as goodness." Crosby believes that quality is created by a system of prevention, not appraisal, where the performance standard is "zero defects" or meeting specifications 100 percent of the time.

Garvin takes a more aggressive and strategic approach to defining quality. He views quality as a means of pleasing customers, not just protecting annoyances. He eschews the defensive quality posture practiced by many U.S. companies in favor of a more strategic approach based on a combination of eight quality dimensions including product performance, features, reliability, conformity, durability, serviceability, aesthetics, and perceived quality.[12]

Sparks and Legault take Garvin's eight dimensions of quality and apply

Table 1.1 Contrasting Big Q and Little Q

Topic	Content of Little Q	Content of Big Q
Products	Manufactured goods	All products, goods, and services, whether for sale or not
Processes	Processes directly related to manufacture of goods	All processes: manufacturing, support, business, etc.
Industries	Manufacturing	All industries: manufacturing, service, government, profit, and not-for-profit
Quality viewed as:	A technological problem	A business problem
Customer	Clients who buy the products	All who are impacted, external and internal
How to think about quality	Based on culture of functional departments	Based on the Universal Trilogy
Quality goals are included:	Among factory goals	In company business plan
Cost of poor quality	Costs associated with deficient manufactured goods	All costs that would disappear if everything were perfect
Improvement is directed at:	Departmental performance	Company performance
Evaluation of quality is based mainly on:	Conformance to factory specifications, procedures	Responsiveness to customer needs
Training in managing quality is:	Concentrated in the Quality Department	Company-wide
Coordination is by:	The quality manager	A quality council of upper managers

them to a firm's value chain. The elements of the quality process as viewed by the customer as well as those that the customer never sees but which help define quality from the manufacturer's viewpoint are illustrated in Figure 1.5. The importance of each dimension varies by product (or service). For example, aesthetics would be less important for certain industrial products.[13]

What quality is and how it is defined also changes over time. Marketers

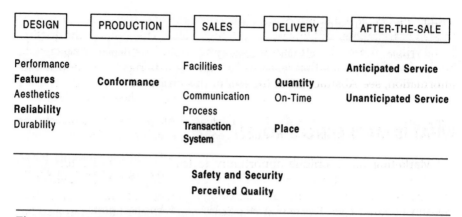

Figure 1.5 A Practical Definition of Quality for Products.

need to realize that quality is a "moving target." For example, the changes in the cues customers have used to define quality in automobiles over the past 20 years are indicated in Table 1.2.[14] Note that whereas styling was the most important quality indicator in 1970, safety assumed this position in 1990.

It should be emphasized that quality is more than simply meeting specifications and that the customer's point of view on quality is key. That is, *quality is what the customer says it is.* A recent study found that consumers

Table 1.2 Characteristics of Quality in Automobiles
(Ranked by Consumers in Order of Importance)

1970	1975	1980	1985	1990
Styling	Fuel economy	Reliability	Value for the money	Safety
Value for the money	Styling	Fuel economy	Ease of handling	Reliability
Ease of handling	Prior experience with the make	Value for the money	Fuel economy	Trouble-free maintenance
Fuel economy	Size and weight	Riding comfort	Reliability	Ease of handling
Riding comfort	Ease of handling	Prior experience with the make	Safety	Fuel economy

define quality as reliability, durability, easy maintenance, easy to use, a trusted brand name, and low price with high value. The losers in the quality battle will be those who attempt to "do things right," while the winners will be those organizations that learn to "do the right things." (For additional information, see Abstract 1.3 at the end of this chapter.)

WHAT IS MARKETING'S ROLE?

Marketing has a unique opportunity to lead current and future total quality efforts. In fact, marketing can act as the driving force in achieving the primary objective of total quality: maximizing customer satisfaction at the lowest delivered cost. Firms that practice a market orientation can also be leaders in total quality. An integrated model showing the interrelationships between market orientation, total quality, and business profitability is provided in Figure 1.6. The model proposes that a more market-oriented business yields a better total quality offering, which in turn produces superior business performance.[15] (For additional information, see Abstract 1.4 at the end of this chapter.)

Firms that are more market oriented seek to create superior value for buyers by increasing benefits relative to the cost of delivering those benefits. A market orientation also requires an understanding of a firm's value

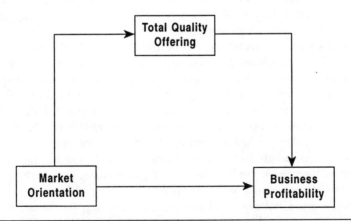

Figure 1.6 An Integrated Model of Total Quality and Market Orientation. (Source: Chang, Tung-Zong and Chen, Su-Jane. "The Impact of a Market Orientation on Total Quality Offering and Business Profitability." *Marketing Theory and Application*, Vol. 5, AMA Winter Educator's Proceedings, 1994, p. 59. Reprinted with permission.)

chain—the discrete set of activities performed by the firm and its suppliers (such as delivery, packaging, sales and technical support, etc.) that contribute value to the product/service offering. A firm must also understand its buyers' buyers. For example, a chemical manufacturer such as BASF must understand not only the needs of the carpet manufacturer, but the needs of consumers of such product (i.e., a homeowner or a builder).

Becoming market oriented in the short run may temporarily reduce profitability as firms may be required to make significant investments in order to better respond to customer needs. In the long run, however, market orientation should lead to better profits through superior quality, which should produce higher productivity and stronger customer loyalty.

MISCONCEPTIONS/CONTRADICTIONS REGARDING TQM

Consider the following prescriptions of the three leading quality gurus previously discussed: Juran advocates setting quality objectives and managing the quality plan according to those objectives. Deming, on the other hand, is opposed to objectives as well as the so-called merit system, which he views as a "destroyer of people." Deming believes that you cannot measure performance and that appraisal of people is "ruinous." Crosby is also against using material rewards but recommends recognizing contributions toward the quality effort. Crosby also recommends zero defects as a quality objective. Juran and Deming believe that such an objective is unrealistic given the inherent variability in all processes.

How does one reconcile these different views? Clearly, the quality approach used will be dictated by the particular situation. What may work in one organization may not be suitable in another. Further, no one approach can guarantee success in every organization. Thus, instead of following a "one size fits all" prescription, companies introducing TQM should follow common *principles*, as no particular recipe can guarantee success in all situations. Further, there is also a need to identify the necessary *conditions* that will allow TQM efforts to succeed. However, before examining the conditions that will increase the likelihood of TQM success, let's look at some of the misconceptions based on the conclusions offered above.

According to Chatterjee and Yilmaz, the following are common misconceptions regarding TQM:

1. **Quality is conformance to requirements:** Quality involves more than just conformance to design requirements. It also includes other relevant attributes such as performance, reliability, durability, serviceability, and aesthetics.

2. **Quality is free:** The cost of quality is not simply the cost of nonconformance. There is also the cost associated with the resources devoted to quality assurance, including the costs of prevention and appraisal.

3. **Quality improves the bottom line:** In the long run, this is certainly true. Yet there are a variety of other factors such as changes in the economy, changes in consumer demand, or competitive rivalry that can influence profitability.[16]

For additional information, see Abstract 1.5 at the end of this chapter.

IS TQM SUCCESSFUL?

According to many business writers and academicians. TQM is all but dead and buried. For those companies that have embraced TQM as a philosophy and long-term business strategy as opposed to a one-shot cure-all approach, there are sizable payoffs. The findings of a study conducted jointly by *Industry Week,* the Quality and Productivity Management Association (QPMA), and Development Dimensions International are presented in Table 1.3. Of the 536 participating North American organizations that have implemented TQM, 78 percent reported "highly or moderately successful" operational results (i.e., cycle time, improved productivity, fewer defects). The majority of those surveyed also reported higher payoffs of TQM initiatives in the areas of customer retention and satisfaction. In fact, 85 percent of the companies experienced either high or moderate success when TQM was implemented in this area. Finally, organizational climate was favorably affected by the introduction of quality programs. Of the businesses surveyed, 82 percent reported that TQM was either highly or moderately successful. (For additional information, see Abstract 1.6 at the end of this chapter.)

Table 1.3 Success in Implementing TQM

	Highly successful	Moderately successful	Low level of success	Don't know
Operational results	38%	40%	15%	7%
Customer retention and satisfaction	47%	38%	6%	9%
Organizational climate	44%	38%	14%	4%

COMMON PRINCIPLES FOR TQM SUCCESS

Firms that want to successfully implement TQM would do well to manage the areas over which they have the most control: human resources, training, organizational structure, and commitment. Beginning with commitment, this means a single-minded devotion to quality in all areas of the company, including production, design, sales and marketing, logistics, service, etc. Marketing becomes everyone's responsibility, That is, each employee should think and act like the customers that he or she serves. Employees must understand that customers pay their salaries and must do whatever it takes to please the customer.

Organizational structure is another important principle in developing a successful TQM program. The organization should be organized around the flow of value-added processes. Task-oriented jobs in today's world of customers, competition, and changes are obsolete. Adam Smith's division of labor paradigm is passe.

Training is also key in developing successful TQM programs. Management as well as employees need to be trained in the principles of quality and how to use its tools. Specifically, the training needs to show the relationship between TQM-initiated efforts and selected marketing behaviors, such as profitability per customer and customer retention rates.

Finally, human resource management plays a significant role in designing a successful TQM program. For example, the key aspects of this principle include employee selection, job promotion, and job enrichment as well as reward and recognition programs. In short, employees need to be treated as an important resource. Yet it is widely reported that many quality programs fail. The reasons why many TQM efforts fail are discussed in the next section. (For additional information, see Abstract 1.7 at the end of this chapter.)

WHY TQM EFFORTS FAIL

According to Juran, the most frequent reason why TQM programs fail is the failure of upper management to be personally involved in their company's efforts toward quality. There are nondelegable responsibilities that managers often try to delegate. For example, if there is a quality council in the company, the CEO should sit in on its meetings or perhaps even chair the council. The CEO should also be personally involved by initiating quality goals and helping to create means of measurement in order to fulfill the quality programs.

A second reason why TQM efforts fail is because they are mounted as stand-alone programs, unconnected to marketing strategies, rigidly and narrowly applied, and expected to produce a miraculous transformation of the company. When done right, TQM is a "way of life" as opposed to a program. TQM needs to become institutionalized as an organizing logic and culture of a firm.

A third reason why TQM programs fail is that they often are not customer focused but rather are run as internal programs by technocrats. Ultimately, the business must be designed around the goal of customer satisfaction. Every employee, whether serving the customer or assisting those who serve the customer, must view every activity, every procedure, and every process through the perspective of: "How does this contribute to serving our customers?" Nothing happens in marketing until somebody buys something.

Finally, TQM programs fail when a company attempts to do too much too quickly. Quality efforts work best when companies start with a few highly focused practices and add more sophisticated ones later. (For additional information, see Abstract 1.8 at the end of this chapter.)

SUMMARY

A customer is the most important visitor on our premises.
He is not dependent on us. We are dependent on him.
He is not an interruption of our work. He is the purpose of it.
He is not an outsider on our business. He is part of it.
We are not doing him a favor by serving him.
He is doing us a favor by giving us an opportunity to do so.

Mahatma Gandhi
(speech given to immigrant Indians
Johannesburg, South Africa, 1890)

The rapidly changing economic landscape in the United States includes more discerning consumers who desire the highest quality products at the lowest delivered cost. The relative openness of U.S. markets to foreign firms means that U.S. firms will face intense competition from emerging economies which enjoy lower wage rates and lower costs of capital. American mangers are going to be forced to rethink the way in which they do business.

Competing in a global economy is going to require firms to understand what "world-class" quality means. Constantly pushing the boundaries for productivity will be the price of the ticket in the door. William F. Galvin, president of Babson College and former vice-chairman of Xerox Corporation, commented, "We are going to have multiple countries competing in the same businesses. Fulfilling customer requirements with lower costs will be the driving factor in successes. And the people who spend their time looking at how to do things differently, more cost-effectively, and right the first time are the ones most likely to succeed...In the future, the concept of quality will involve focusing increasingly on enhancing customer value, forcing companies to take a much more proactive stance toward their customers."

Marketing will play an even more important role in total quality programs in the future, as companies try to make sure that the quality they offer is the quality that their customers want. Quality efforts should be focused on improving customer satisfaction at a reasonable cost. In fact, many companies today will only consider quality programs if there is a return on their investment. Thus, companies will need to determine the link between their investment in quality initiatives and its effect on customer retention and market share. (For additional information, see Abstract 1.9 at the end of this chapter.)

DISCUSSION QUESTIONS

1. Why has quality become such a high priority for businesses today?

2. What are some of the "common denominators" in the definition of quality?

3. How do the views of quality of Deming, Juran, Crosby, and Garvin differ?

4. What impact does quality have on selected business performance measures such as profitability, cost reductions, or market share?

5. How do total quality and marketing complement one another?

6. Is total quality management successful? Discuss.

7. What are some of the reasons why total quality efforts fail in some companies?

8. How has Maytag used total quality to achieve a sustainable competitive advantage?

ENDNOTES

1. Belohlav, James. "Quality, Strategy, and Competitiveness." *California Management Review*, Spring 1993, p. 60.
2. Belohlav, James. "Quality, Strategy, and Competitiveness." *California Management Review*, Spring 1993, pp. 61–62.
3. Tenner, Arthur and DeToro, Irving. *Total Quality Management*, Addison-Wesley, Reading, Mass.
4. Bozell-Gallup Worldwide Quality Poll, 1993.

5. "Quality: The U.S. Drives to Catch Up." *Business Week*, November 18, 1982, p. 68.
6. Rienzo, Thomas F. "Planning Deming Management for Service Organizations." *Business Horizons*, May–June 1993, p. 19.
7. Galvin, David A. "Quality on the Line." *Harvard Business Review*, September–October 1983, p. 1.
8. Technical Assistance and Research Program (TARP), White House Office of Consumer Affairs, 1985.
9. Buzzell, Robert D. and Gale, Bradley T. *The PIMS Principles*, The Free Press, New York, 1987, p. 107.
10. Kotler, Philip. *Marketing Management*, 8th ed., Prentice-Hall, Englewood Cliffs, N.J., p. 56.
11. Juran, J. M. *Juran on Quality by Design*, The Free Press, New York, 1992, p. 12.
12. Garvin, David A. "Competing on the Eight Dimensions of Quality." *Harvard Business Review*, November–December 1987.
13. Sparks, Richard E. and Legault, Richard D. "A Definition of Quality for Total Customer Satisfaction: The Bridge between Manufacturer and Customer." *SAM Advanced Management Journal*, Winter 1993, p. 17.
14. Vavra, T. *Aftermarketing*, Richard D. Irwin, Burr Ridge, Ill., 1992.
15. Chang, Tung-Zong and Chen, Su-Jane. "The Impact of a Market Orientation on Total Quality Offering and Business Profitability." *Marketing Theory and Application*, Vol. 5, AMA Winter Educator's Proceedings, 1994, p. 59.
16. Chatterjee, S. and Yilmaz, M. "Quality Confusion: Too Many Gurus, Not Enough Disciples." *Business Horizons*, May–June 1993.

PROFILES

EASTMAN CHEMICAL

Eastman Chemical, a 1993 Malcolm Baldrige National Quality Award winner, initiated its quality management process in 1982, then called "Customers and Us." It was through this program that Eastman opened its plants to customers for the first time and its people actually met their customers. Eastman also sent some of its people to its customers' plants.

Eastman's quality process is decidedly home grown and deceptively simple. It begins with a review and assessment of customer relationships (including supplier relationships) and then identifies opportunities for improvement, initiates projects to make those improvements, and reports those improvements back to the customer.

Sales plays a very prominent role in Eastman's quality model. The sales organization contracts with the company's ten separate and diverse business organizations, ranging from packaging plastics to coatings to fine chemicals—each with its own specific set of business strategies. The sales organization is charged with implementing those strategies. Eastman's sales organization is responsible for $4 billion in sales and often serves in the capacity of coordinating many of Eastman's 18,000 employees in team efforts focused on improving customer relations.

Sales is the linkage to Eastman's quality improvement efforts. In fact, Eastman use the phrase "linking in" to describe how the salespeople identify specific customer problems and put together cross-functional teams to study problems. Input gathered by the salesperson often comes from call reports and nonsales contacts with customers. These data, along with data obtained from Eastman's complaint process and customer satisfaction survey, represent a powerful tool for building customer relationships. The sales organization manages the process for administering the customer satisfaction survey by delivering and collecting the surveys directly to and from the customer. The salespeople are also responsible for implementing improvements suggested on the customer satisfaction surveys. Eastman's philosophy is "An improvement is not an improvement until your customer knows about it."

MAYTAG

Maytag was building top-quality appliances long before the concept of total quality was born. In fact, top-quality home appliances have been the hallmark of Maytag's success since the early 1900s. The "lonely Maytag repairman" communicates this point in the company's advertising.

Maytag defines quality in a very basic way: a product that works properly and dependably without repairs for a significant portion of its expected life. Maytag takes a proactive view toward quality by providing a continual, up front, company-wide commitment from the design phase to purchasing, and from manufacturing to servicing. Its approach to quality is summed up in six basic principles:

1. **Keep it simple.** Design products with as few components as possible. Simplifying design contributes a great deal to the overall dependability of Maytag's products. The fewer parts there are, the fewer parts there are to malfunction.

2. **Respect and listen to your people.** Maytag uses a team approach in implementing quality initiatives. Its philosophy is that the workers' minds are just as important as their hands.

3. **Hire only the best workers possible and involve them.** Maytag workers are involved in the manufacturing and decision-making process of their products.

4. **Manufacture your own components.** Maytag ensures product quality and keeps its costs down by producing most of its own components.

5. **Effective capital spending is critical to maintaining quality.** Maytag believes wise capital investments play a major role in keeping the company's products at the forefront of a changing marketplace.

6. **Use common sense.** Maytag recognizes that success in its business is based on continuing customer satisfaction. It understands that to achieve long-term success, you must retain existing customers.

ABSTRACTS

ABSTRACT 1.1
KEIRETSU IN AMERICA

Kinni, Theodore B.
Quality Digest, December 1992, pp. 24–31

The author is a well-known business writer who presents a concise and intriguing look at one of the key features of Japan's success— an integrated marketing and sales/purchasing/supplier quality management system: *keiretsu*. The opening frame sets the stage with a simple well-directed statement: "Corporate Communism? Industrial war machines? As U.S. business comes to terms with dealing with Japan Inc. on home turf, it's time we understood how our new neighbors do business." The reason, according to Kinni, is that Japanese business interests hold a sizable stake in over 1500 U.S. factories, a fact which is confirmed by the Japan External Trade Organization.

Keiretsu is the Japanese system of conglomerates which cross-market and trade heavily with one another, dating back to the Meiji Restoration of 1868. The author quotes Robert Kearns in describing how an American *keiretsu* structured along the lines of the Mitsubishi or Sumitomo group might operate: "Such a group would be worth close to a trillion dollars. Each of the 30 or so lead companies would own a piece of each other, would do business among themselves and meet once a month for lunch and discuss matters." *Keiretsu* members share in the economies of large-scale operation, says the author, such as low-cost capital at rates of 0.5 percent to 1.5 percent interest. Membership in a *keiretsu* virtually guarantees a market for one's goods, since other member companies own large stakes in each other's companies, and the value of their investments depends on the long-term success and growth of the member firms. According to Kinni, "the *keiretsu* system is an ideal structure for rapid and secure economic growth and a major reason for Japan's economic success since World War II." After describing how the system operates, the author turns to examples of the *keiretsu* way, which means allowing a foreign group to eventually own about 30 percent of one's company stock and, to some extent, dictate the organization's future. Some U.S. companies, like Timken Co., are building structures reminiscent of the *keiretsu* on their own, such as the "supplier city" in Perry Township, Ohio, which will bring its suppliers within arm's reach. What does the future hold?

Invasion or evolution? The author uses observers and "experts" to sum up the final arguments. "As the Japanese investments in this country mature, their plants and equipment will age, their employees will grow more expensive, and the playing field will level. Perhaps the *keiretsu* will learn a new respect for the individual and will begin to temper its authoritarian structures." On the other hand, he believes that U.S. corporations can learn much from the business practices of the *keiretsu*, with its efficient cross-marketing and supplier relationships. The best way to come to terms with *keiretsu*, he concludes, is to think of it as an immigrant, not an invader, with gifts to offer and lessons to learn—for those wise and gracious enough to know how to use them.

Overall, this is a most worthwhile article on an often misunderstood topic. As America moves further along in its understanding of the "extended enterprise," businesses will see themselves as members of a global network, whose aim will be to optimize the value chain through mutual relationships built on trust. Illustrations and models are provided, although the citations are from 1978 and 1986 material.

ABSTRACT 1.2
SELLING QUALITY

Schaaf, Dick
Training Magazine, June 1992, pp. 53–59

"Salespeople have often been left behind when the quality train pulls out of the station," while total quality management actually needs to *begin* with salespeople, says the author. For salespeople not trained in TQM, quality is perceived as just another component part of the company's standard offering, or not seen as part of the sales process itself. Moreover, the system of incentives works against quality efforts—rewarding finding new customers, not retaining old ones and encouraging sales quotas rather than customer partnerships. The author details the difficulties of emphasizing quality techniques in sales training, but he notes that quality has the potential *internally* of improving the sales process and *externally* of forming stronger relationships between salespeople and customers. Controlling variation, however, in a process which is known for its endless variation is difficult. Nevertheless, according to the author, sales training should create a two-way information flow: not only describing company offerings to the customer, but getting feedback on customer needs and the way they do business. The article includes two sidebars: "Training with Feedback" and "Quality in Three Dimensions." (©*Quality Abstracts*)

ABSTRACT 1.3
BUYERS AND DISTRIBUTORS: IT'S TIME FOR TEAMWORK

Forbes, Christine
Industrial Distribution, August 1991, pp. 20–24

Although written in 1991, this message is just as timely for the reader in today's world—1995 through the turn of the century. The call from sales professionals to purchasing managers and distributors is unanimous. The sales, purchasing, and distribution field has changed from one of inventory management and sales to a more holistic, value-added approach, featuring total quality management and value chain management. The change that has had the greatest impact on the industry has been the shift toward a smaller supplier base, limiting the number of vendors for each product and working more closely with suppliers. This new movement is called Total Cost, because it takes into account the total cost to the customer over and above the initial price. Late delivery, poor service, and faulty parts are looked on as part of the price of a product. Thus, industry leaders who have embraced Total Cost are willing to pay a higher initial purchase price when total cost benefits are guaranteed.

Therefore, organizations on the brink of Total Cost breakthrough are selecting the "best and the brightest" distributors. The primary benefits brought on by this change are improved efficiency and cost, more conclusive performance tracking, and stronger supplier relationships (or partnering). Distributors and sales and purchasing professionals all agree that many factors led to these changes, but the main catalyst has been an emphasis on value-added services. These services are generally a physical adaptation to a product such as an optional stereo for a car.

Whereas the most important demand that customers have for a product is for quality, their quality requirements vary sharply according to the customer's size, needs, and the extent to which the customer's own quality system has developed. For example, Amoco demands quality from its distributors by monitoring distributor nonconformance through such variables as delivery, product quality, and administrative errors. Several priorities must be constantly looked at by purchasing and distribution organizations in order for them to successfully embrace the changes around them.

Communication is a priority area where improvement is needed and new technological channels can help. Sales and marketing professionals, as well as purchasing agents, have also noted that distributors have fallen behind in education and technical ability. More specifically, purchasers want more new product information, better knowledge of the product, and most importantly, they want distributors to do their own screening to determine the best, most cost-efficient products. Limited graphs and no references are provided.

ABSTRACT 1.4
REINVENTING THE SALES FORCE

Wood, Wally
Across the Board, April 1994

The article opens with a dramatic premise: "The only way to keep mature firms on track is to reinvent, not reorganize; reinvent, not reengineer. While reengineering often focuses on taking costs out of the sales and marketing cycle, argues the author, reinventing means making the right investments in the sales function at precisely the right point in the life cycle. A survey by the Alexander Group of 53 companies on value-added sales services showed that the biggest area for improvement is analyzing costs because too many sales reps still function as "product pushers" and not "consumer advocates."

The author deals with the issues of knocking down walls between sales and marketing, as well as the business of team-based compensation. He deals with being customer-centric and the death of the mass market. The mistaken notion that computers come first in the reinventing process is dealt with: "If you automate a mess, all you'll have is the ability to make mistakes more quickly," argues Wood. He closes with the admonition that the single biggest obstacle to successful reinvention of the sales organization is past success. "Why do we have to change? Why should we do it this way? Roll the words 'sales relic' over your tongue a few times and you'll probably have the answer." This is a provocative article, although limited charts and references are provided.

ABSTRACT 1.5
HOW TO AVOID FAILURE WHEN IMPLEMENTING A QUALITY EFFORT

Numerof, Rita E. and Abrams, Michael N.
Tapping the Network Journal, Winter 1992–1993, pp. 10–14

Quality is dead at ABC Corporation, say the authors, despite the official line that "Quality was now going back to the line. Quality was no longer a separate function but once again part of 'everyone's' job." The authors analyze the reasons for failure of the seven-year quality initiative at this nameless *Fortune* 500 company, and they discuss seven reasons for TQM's demise there:

1. Quality was established as a parallel process to the existing organization rather than as an integral part of it.

2. Quality activities, such as training and building employee involvement, were seen as the measure of success, rather than a means to a specifically defined end.

3. The company failed to define a narrow range of strategic business issues to address systematically, leaving teams to charge off on their own.

4. They failed to see quality improvement as a continuous process with a myriad of internal and external customer interfaces managed as a strategic process.

5. They failed to define a specific role for the company's management team beyond creating vision and awareness.

6. They failed to see improved relations with the employee as the foundation for improved relations with the customer.

7. They failed to understand the complex process of organizational change and manage it carefully.

But TQM is not the "mystical, time-consuming, resource-intensive process that it's made out to be," the authors insist. "In fact, the steps involved are fairly straightforward." They conclude with a brief listing of 8 steps involved in a quality effort and 13 key questions to address for successful quality implementation. (©*Quality Abstracts*)

ABSTRACT 1.6
WHY QUALITY PROGRAMS AREN'T—AND HOW THEY COULD BE

Boyce, Graham W.D.
Business Quarterly, Autumn 1992, pp. 57–64

Too often, TQM lacks strategic alignment with the rest of the organization, and in too many instances, says the author, quality initiatives have stalled or failed. In surveying 32 Canadian-based companies involved with quality, the author observed three elements of quality programs which need to be carefully considered, and he explains seven related principles, with illustrations drawn from the companies surveyed:

- **Philosophy**—The underlying reasons for focusing on quality. Define what it is you want to achieve as an organization. Make the connection between quality and strategic goals explicit. Use the term "quality" carefully, and only when it is meant.

- **Process**—The approach adopted. Start with facts—the same ones and all of them. Prepare thoroughly—then act.

- **Results**—The measurement and utilization of outcomes. Ensure a clear focus to all quality initiatives, based on specific issues, rather than metrics.

One source of dissatisfaction with quality initiatives, says the author, is that people simply expect too much. He sees three factors at work here: (1) Quality has an intrinsic appeal: Who wants to do things badly? (2) Some feel that quality is the secret behind the Japanese success, and that if we adopt the Japanese approach to quality we will be equally successful. (3) Quality has an emotional, nationalistic appeal, something Americans exported to the Japanese and which is now being reclaimed by its rightful owners. "Taken together," he says, "these factors have served to boost quality into the realm of some magic elixir." In conclusion, the author observes, "Quality has to permeate the strategic process of the organization, the thinking and policy-making, as much as it has to be a fundamental part of its operations." (©*Quality Abstracts*)

ABSTRACT 1.7
THE LAW OF PRODUCING QUALITY

Wollner, George E.
Quality Progress, January 1992, pp. 35–40

Most large-scale efforts to bring TQ into organizations fail, says the author. Top leadership commitment is the key to success, he contends, and commitment is determined by appropriate incentives. The author expounds two important laws of producing quality:

- Achieving TQ is a matter of incentive.

- More quality is produced when it brings organizational leaders more of the success they desire.

He cites Soviet production policies as examples of disincentives. "While TQ can be an effective tool for redesigning or eliminating non-productive processes," he says, "the first step has to be in the elimination of the wrong incentives." Almost every failed TQ effort results from an organization's perception that the TQ process is not worth it, he concludes. The key is for the leader to "consistently and continuously measure the three TQ success objectives (increasing customer satisfaction, increasing employee satisfaction, and decreasing unit costs) and link employees' important rewards to their achievements." He mentions the power of noneconomic incentives such as employee empowerment, recognition, self-esteem, and pride in work, as well as monetary incentives. The author introduces the term "incentive controller" as the person or group who has the power to provide or withhold the prized incentives that an organization or individual seeks. "When the incentive controller and the end consumer are the same, and competitive conditions prevail, the market produces quality well," he says. But when incentive controllers are stockholders or politicians, for example, short-term gain can rob long-term advantage. The author discusses the role of TQ leaders in realigning the organizational incentive system. In every case of successful TQ, he says, three critical events occur:

1. The leaders of the organization experience an irresistible incentive to improve product quality.

2. They transform this challenge into a compelling vision that is attractive to the work force.

3. They make it in everyone's best interest to use TQ as the way to achieve the vision.

The article concludes with a simple "TQ Success Forecaster." (©*Quality Abstracts*)

ABSTRACT 1.8
MAKING TOTAL QUALITY WORK: ALIGNING ORGANIZATIONAL PROCESSES, PERFORMANCE MEASURES, AND STAKEHOLDERS

Olian, Judy D. and Rynes, Sara L.
Human Resources Management, Vol. 30 Issue 3, Fall 1991, pp. 303–333

Throughout this article, four survey sources are used: the KPMG survey of 62 companies, two Conference Board surveys of 149 firms and 158 *Fortune* 1000 companies, and the AQF/Ernst & Young study of 500 international organizations. The cornerstone of this 30-page article revolves around the authors' statement: "The goals of total quality can be achieved only if organizations entirely reform their cultures. Total quality (TQ) is increasingly used by companies as an organization-wide system to achieve fully satisfied customers through the delivery of the highest quality in products and services. In fact, TQ is the most important single strategic tool available to leaders to effect the transformation of their organizations. Traditional management, operations, finance and accounting systems are reviewed against changes that are needed in organizational processes, measurement systems, and the values and behaviors of key stakeholders to transform the status quo and shift to a total quality culture that permeates every facet of the organization."

Total quality must reflect a system-wide commitment to the goal of serving the strategic needs of the organization's customer bases, through internal and external measurement systems, information and authority sharing, and committed leadership. In this sense, the objectives are very similar to ISO 9000 readiness for registration. Therefore, the concepts presented by the authors are also valid for those sales-based TQM organizations that are seeking ISO 9000 certification. The article contains the following pertinent data: (1) organizational synergies critical to achieving a pervasive culture, whether it be for TQM, ISO 9000, or other types of quality assurance; (2) the essentials of TQ; (3) organizational processes that support TQ; (4) establishing quality goals, including a look at Six Sigma and benchmarking; (5) training for TQ; (6) recognition and rewards; (7) measuring customer reactions and satisfaction; (8) developing four areas of measurement: operation, financial, breakthrough, and employee contributions; and (9) getting stakeholder support. Of significant added value are over 60 references on the subjects discussed, which are reason enough to obtain a copy of this extremely worthwhile article, in spite of its formidable length. This is highly recommended reading for sales and marketing organizations seeking to implement total quality.

ABSTRACT 1.9
THE NEW BOUNDARIES OF THE "BOUNDARYLESS" COMPANY

Hirschhorn, Larry and Gilmore, Thomas
Harvard Business Review, May/June 1992, Vol. 70 Issue 3, pp. 104–115

The opening lines of the first two paragraphs clearly set the stage for this interesting and thought-provoking article on organizational boundaries which are meant to be defined in the eye of the beholders: the institutional leaders and sales support staff. "In an economy founded on innovation and change, one of the premier challenges of management is to design more flexible organizations. For many executives, a single metaphor has come to embody this managerial challenge and to capture the kind of organization they want to create: the corporation without boundaries." From this vision of Jack Welch to the "data feelings" of the alert marketing manager, a wide variety of challenging topics are covered: (1) challenges of flexible work; (2) remapping organizational boundaries of authority, tasks, politics, and identity; (3) the authority vacuum; and (4) downsizing with dignity.

The authors point out, however, that managers should not assume that boundaries may be eliminated altogether. Once the traditional boundaries of hierarchy, function, and geography disappear, a new set of boundaries become important and must be dealt with. These new boundaries are more psychological than organizational, and instead of being reflected in a company's structure, they must be enacted over and over again in a manager's *relationships* with bosses, subordinates, and peers. The four new important boundaries are the authority boundary, task boundary, political boundary, and identity boundary. The article ends with a plea for getting started and is enhanced by an interesting mini-study on "The Team that Failed." The implications for marketing and sales are for renewed networking within as well as outside of the enterprise. A shortcoming is that references are not provided.

CHAPTER 2

OVERVIEW of TOTAL QUALITY

Frank Voehl

WHAT IS TOTAL QUALITY?

Introduction

During the past five years, there has been an explosion of books in the field of total quality. Yet in all of the thousands of books and billions of words written on the subject, there is an absence of three essential ingredients: a good working definition, a comprehensive yet concise history, and a clear and simple systems model of total quality. This overview of total quality is intended to fill that void and provide some interesting reading at the same time.

Understanding the Concept of Total

Total quality is total in three senses: it covers every process, every job, and every person. First, it covers *every process*, rather than just manufacturing or production. Design, construction, R&D, accounting, marketing, repair, and every other function must also be involved in quality improvement. Second, total quality is total in that it covers *every job*, as opposed to only those involved in making the product. Secretaries are expected not to make typing errors, accountants not to make posting errors, and presidents not to make strategic errors. Third, total quality recognizes that *each person* is responsible for the quality of his or her work and for the work of the group.

Total quality also goes beyond the traditional idea of quality, which has been expressed as the degree of conformance to a standard or the product of workmanship. Enlightened organizations accept and apply the concept that quality is the degree of user satisfaction or the fitness of the product for use. In other words, *the customer determines whether or not quality has been achieved in its totality.*

This same measure—total customer satisfaction—applies throughout the entire operation of an organization. Only the outer edges of the company actually have contact with customers in the traditional sense, but each department can treat the other departments as its customers. The main judge of the quality of work is the customer, for if the customer is not satisfied, the work does not have quality. This, coupled with the achievement of corporate objectives, is the bottom line of total quality.

In that regard, it is important, as the Japanese say, to "talk with facts and data." Total quality emphasizes the use of fact-oriented discussions and statistical quality control techniques by everyone in the company. Everyone in the company is exposed to basic quality control ideas and techniques and is expected to use them. Thus, total quality becomes a common language and improves "objective" communication.

Total quality also radically alters the nature and basic operating philosophy of organizations. The specialized, separated system developed early in the 20th century is replaced by a system of *mutual feedback and close interaction of departments.* Engineers, for example, work closely with construction crews and storekeepers to ensure that their knowledge is passed on to workers. Workers, in turn, feed their practical experience directly back to the engineers. The information interchange and shared commitment to product quality is what makes total quality work. Teaching all employees how to apply process control and improvement techniques makes them party to their own destiny and enables them to achieve their fullest potential.

However, total quality is more than an attempt to make better products; it is also a search for better ways to make better products. Adopting the total quality philosophy commits the company to the belief that there is always a better way of doing things, a way to make better use of the company's resources, and a way to be more productive. In this sense, total quality relies heavily upon value analysis as a method of developing better products and operations in order to maximize value to the stakeholder, whether customers, employees, or shareholders.

Total quality also implies a different type of worker and a different attitude toward the worker from management. Under total quality, workers are generalists rather than specialists. *Both workers and managers are expected to move from job to job, gaining experience in many areas of the company.*

Defining Total Quality

First and foremost, total quality is a set of philosophies by which management systems can direct the efficient achievement of the objectives of the organization to ensure customer satisfaction and maximize stakeholder value. This is accomplished through the continuous improvement of the quality system, which consists of the social system, the technical system, and the management system. Thus, it becomes a way of life for doing business for the entire organization.

Central to the concept is the idea that a company should *design quality into its products*, rather than inspect for it afterward. Only by a devotion to quality throughout the organization can the best possible products be made. Or, as stated by Noriaki Kano, "Quality is too important to be left to inspectors."[1]

Total quality is too important to take second place to any other company goals. Specifically, it should not be subsidiary to profit or productivity. Concentrating on quality will ultimately build and improve both profitability and productivity. Failure to concentrate on quality will quickly erode profits, as customers resent paying for products they perceive as low quality.

The main focus of total quality is on *why*. It goes beyond the *how to* to include the *why to*. It is an attempt to identify the causes of defects in order to eliminate them. It is a continuous cycle of detecting defects, identifying their causes, and improving the process so as to totally eliminate the causes of defects.

Accepting the idea that the customer of a process can be defined as the next process is essential to the real practice of total quality. According to total quality, control charts should be developed for each process, and any errors identified within a process should be disclosed to those involved in the next process in order to raise quality. However, it has been said that it seems contrary to human nature to seek out one's own mistakes. People tend to find the errors caused by others and to neglect their own. Unfortunately, exactly that kind of self-disclosure is what is really needed.[2]

Instead, management too often tends to blame and then take punitive action. This attitude prevails from front-line supervisors all the way up to top management. In effect, we are encouraged to hide the real problems we cause; instead of looking for the real causes of problems, as required by total quality, we look the other way.

The Concept of Control

The Japanese notion of *control* differs radically from the American; that difference of meaning does much to explain the failure of U.S. management to adopt total quality. In the United States, control connotes someone or something that limits an operation, process, or person. It has overtones of a "police force" in the industrial engineering setting and is often resented.

In Japan, as pointed out by Union of Japanese Scientists and Engineers counselor and Japanese quality control scholar Noriaki Kano, *control* means "all necessary activities for achieving objectives in the long-term, efficiently and economically. Control, therefore, is doing whatever is needed to accomplish what we want to do as an organization."[1]

The difference can be seen very graphically in the Plan, Do, Check, Act (P-D-C-A) continuous improvement chart, which is widely used in Japan to describe the cycle of control (Figure 2.1). Proper control starts with planning, does what is planned, checks the results, and then applies any necessary corrective action. The cycle represents these four stages—Plan, Do, Check, Act—arranged in circular fashion to show that they are continuous.

In the United States, where specialization and division of labor are emphasized, the cycle is more likely to look like Fight, Plan, Do, Check.

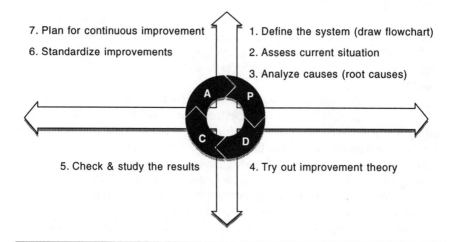

7. Plan for continuous improvement

6. Standardize improvements

1. Define the system (draw flowchart)

2. Assess current situation

3. Analyze causes (root causes)

A P

C D

5. Check & study the results

4. Try out improvement theory

Figure 2.1 P-D-C-A Chart. System improvement is the application of the Plan-Do-Check-Act cycle to an improvement project.

Instead of working together to solve any deviations from the plan, time is spent arguing about who is responsible for the deviations.

This sectionalism, as the Japanese refer to it, in the United States hinders collective efforts to improve the way things are done and lowers national productivity and the standard of living. *There need be nothing threatening about control if it is perceived as exercised in order to gather the facts necessary to make plans and take action toward making improvements.*

Total quality includes the control principle as part of the set of philosophies directed toward the efficient achievement of the objectives of the organization. Many of the individual components of total quality are practiced by American companies, but few practice total quality as a whole.

TOTAL QUALITY AS A SYSTEM

Introduction

Total quality begins with the redefinition of management, inspired by W. Edwards Deming:

> *The people work in a system. The job of the manager is to work on the system, to improve it continuously, with their help.*

One of the most frequent reasons for failed total quality efforts is that many managers are unable to carry out their responsibilities because they have not been trained in how to improve the quality system. They do not have a well-defined process to follow—a process founded on the principles of customer satisfaction, respect for people, continuous improvement, and speaking with facts. Deming's teachings, as amplified by Tribus,[3] focus on the following ten management actions:

1. Recognize quality improvement as a system.

2. Define it so that others can recognize it too.

3. Analyze its behavior.

4. Work with subordinates in improving the system.

5. Measure the quality of the system.

6. Develop improvements in the quality of the system.

7. Measure the gains in quality, if any, and link them to customer delight and quality improvement.

8. Take steps to guarantee holding the gains.

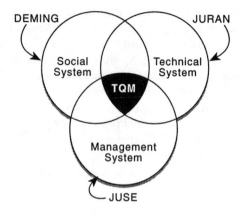

Figure 2.2 Implementing TQM—System Model.

9. Attempt to replicate the improvements in other areas of the system.

10. Tell others about the lessons learned.

Discussions with Tribus to cross-examine these points have revealed that the manager must deal with total quality as *three* separate systems: a social system, a technical system, and a management system. These systems are depicted as three interlocking circles of a ballantine,[4] as shown in Figure 2.2.

Overview of the Social System

Management is solely responsible for the transformation of the social system, which is basically the culture of the organization. It is the social system that has the greatest impact on teamwork, motivation, creativity, and risk taking. How people react to one another and to the work depends on how they are managed. If they enter the organization with poor attitudes, managers have to re-educate, redirect, or remove them. The social system includes the reward structure, the symbols of power, the relationships between people and among groups, the privileges, the skills and style, the politics, the power structure, the shaping of the norms and values, and the "human side of enterprise," as defined by Douglas McGregor.

If a lasting culture is to be achieved, where continuous improvement and customer focus are a natural pattern, the social system must be redesigned so as to be consistent with the vision and values of the organization. Unfortunately, the social system is always in a state of flux due to pressure from ever-changing influences from the external political and technological

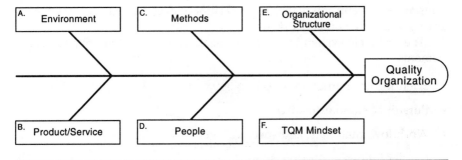

Figure 2.3 Strategic Areas for Cultural Transformation.

environments. The situation in most organizations is that the impact of total quality is not thought through in any organized manner. Change occurs when the pain of remaining as the same dysfunctional unit becomes too great and a remedy for relief is sought.

As shown in Figure 2.3, six areas of strategy must be addressed in order to change and transform the culture to that of a quality organization:

- Environment
- Product/service
- Methods
- People
- Organizational structure
- Total quality management mindset

Each of these areas will be covered in some detail in the chapters in this book. Of the six, however, structure is key in that total quality is about empowerment and making decisions at lower levels in the organization. Self-managing teams are a way to bring this about quickly.

The Technical System

According to Tribus,[5] "The technical system includes all the tools and machinery, the practice of quality science and the quantitative aspects of quality. If you can measure it, you can probably describe and perhaps improve it using the technical systems approach." The technical system thus is concerned with the flow of work through the organization to the ultimate customer. Included are all the work steps performed, whether by equipment, computers, or people; whether manual labor or decision making; or whether factory worker or office worker.

The technical system in most organizations contains the following core elements:

- Scientific accumulation of technology

- Pursuit of standardization

- Workflow, materials, and specifications

- Job definitions and responsibility

- Machine/person interface

- Number and type of work steps

- Availability and use of information

- Decision-making processes

- Problem-solving tools and process

- Physical arrangement of equipment, tools, and people

The expected benefits from analyzing and improving the technical system are to (1) improve customer satisfaction, (2) eliminate waste and rework, (3) eliminate variation, (4) increase learning, (5) save time and money, (6) increase employee control, (7) reduce bottlenecks and frustration, (8) eliminate interruptions and idle time, (9) increase speed and responsiveness, and (10) improve safety and quality of work life.

The three basic elements of every system are (1) suppliers who provide input, (2) work processes which add value, and (3) output to the customer. High-performing units and teams eliminate the barriers and walls between these three elements. A standard problem-solving process is often used by teams, such as the quality control story, business process analysis, etc.[6]

The Management System

The third system is the managerial system, which becomes the integrator. Only senior managers can authorize changes to this system. This is the system by which the other two systems are influenced. It is the way that practices, procedures, protocols, and policies are established and maintained. It is the leadership system of the organization, and it is the measurement system of indicators that tell management and the employees how things are going.

The actual deployment of the management system can be visualized in the shape of a pyramid. As shown in Figure 2.4, there are four aspects or

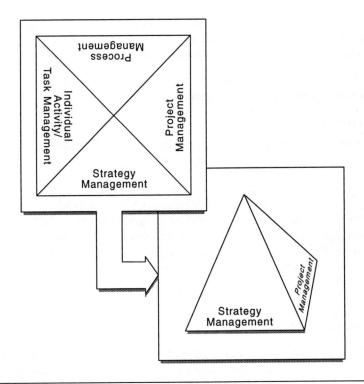

Figure 2.4 Management System Pyramid.

intervention points of deployment: strategy management, process management, project management, and individual activity management. A brief overview of these four aspects is as follows:

- **Strategy management:** Purpose is to establish the mission, vision, guiding principles, and deployment infrastructure which encourage all employees to focus on and move in a common direction. Objectives, strategies, and actions are considered on a three- to five-year time line.

- **Process management:** Purpose is to assure that all key processes are working in harmony to guarantee customer satisfaction and maximize operational effectiveness. Continuous improvement/problem-solving efforts are often cross-functional, so that process owners and indicator owners need to be assigned.

- **Project management:** Purpose is to establish a system to effectively plan, organize, implement, and control all the resources and activities needed for successful completion of the project. Various types of project teams are often formed to solve and implement both process-related as well as policy-related initiatives. Team activities should be linked to business objectives and improvement targets.

- **Individual activity management:** Purpose is to provide all employees with a method of implementing continuous improvement of processes and systems within each employee's work function and control. Flow-charting key processes and individual mission statements are important linkages with which all employees can identify. A quality journal is often used to identify and document improvements.

Various types of assessment surveys are used to "audit" the quality management system. Examples include the Malcolm Baldrige assessment, the Deming Prize audit, and the ISO 9000 audit, among others. Basic core elements are common to all of these assessments. Their usefulness is as a yardstick and benchmark by which to measure improvement and focus the problem-solving effort. Recent efforts using integrated quality and productivity systems have met with some success.[7]

The House of Total Quality

The House of Total Quality (Figure 2.5) is a model which depicts the integration of all of these concepts in a logical fashion. Supporting the three systems of total quality described in the preceding section are the four principles of total quality: customer satisfaction, continuous improvement, speaking with facts, and respect for people. These four principles are inter-related, with customer satisfaction at the core or the hub.

As with any house, the model and plans must first be drawn, usually with some outside help. Once the design has been approved, construction can begin. It usually begins with the mission, vision, values, and objectives which form the cornerstones upon which to build for the future. The pillars representing the four principles must be carefully constructed, well positioned, and thoroughly understood, because the success of the total quality system is in the balance. As previously mentioned, many of the individual components of total quality are practiced by American companies, but few practice total quality as a whole.

HISTORY OF TOTAL QUALITY

In the Beginning

About the year one million B.C., give or take a few centuries, man first began to fashion stone tools for hunting and survival.[8] Up until 8000 B.C.,

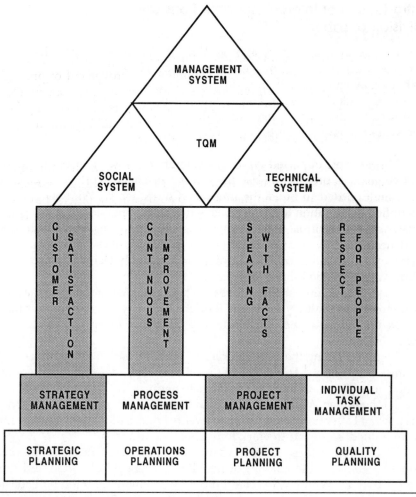

Figure 2.5 House of Quality.

however, very little progress was made in the quality control of these tools. It was at this time that man began assembling instruments with fitting holes, which suggests the use of interchangeable parts on a very limited basis. Throughout this long period, each man made his own tools. The evidence of quality control was measured to some extent by how long he stayed alive. If the tools were well made, his chances of survival increased. A broken axe handle usually spelled doom.

Introduction of Interchangeable Parts and Division of Labor

A little over 200 years ago, in 1787, the concepts of interchangeable parts and division of labor were first introduced in the United States. Eli Whitney, inventor of the cotton gin, applied these concepts to the production of 10,000 flintlock rifles for the U.S. military arsenal. However, Whitney had considerable difficulty in making all the parts exactly the same. It took him ten years to complete the 10,000 muskets that he promised to deliver in two years.

Three factors impacted Whitney's inability to deliver the 10,000 muskets in two years as promised. First, there was a dramatic shortage of qualified craftsmen needed to build the muskets. Consequently, Whitney correctly identified the solution to the problem—machines must do what men previously did. If individual machines were assembled to create each individual part needed, then men could be taught to operate these machines. Thus, Whitney's application of division of labor to a highly technical process was born. Whitney called this a *manufactory.*

Next, it took almost one full year to build the manufactory, rather than two months as Whitney originally thought. Not only did the weather inflict havoc on the schedule, but epidemics of yellow fever slowed progress considerably.

Third, obtaining the raw materials in a timely, usable manner was a hit-or-miss proposition. The metal ore used was often defective, flawed, and pitted. In addition, training the workers to perform the actual assembly took much longer than Whitney imagined and required a considerable amount of his personal attention, often fifteen to twenty hours a day. Also, once the men were trained, some left to work for competing armories.[9]

To compound these factors, his ongoing cotton gin patent lawsuits consumed a considerable amount of his highly leveraged attention and time. Fortunately for Whitney, his credibility in Washington granted him considerable laxity in letting target dates slip. War with France was no longer imminent. Thus, a quality product and the associated manufacturing expertise were deemed more important than schedule. What was promised in 28 months took almost 120 months to deliver.

Luckily for Whitney, the requirement of "on time and within budget" was not yet in vogue. What happened to Whitney was a classic study in the problems of trying to achieve a real breakthrough in operations. Out of this experience, Whitney and others realized that creating parts exactly the same was not possible and, if tried, would prove to be very expensive. This concept of interchangeable parts would eventually lead to statistical methods of control, while division of labor would lead to the factory assembly line.

The First Control Limits

The experiences of Whitney and others who followed led to a relaxation of the requirements for exactness and the use of tolerances. This allowed for a less-than-perfect fit between two (or more) parts, and the concept of "go–no-go" tolerance was introduced between 1840 and 1870.[10]

This idea was a major advancement in that it created the concept of upper and lower tolerance limits, thus allowing the production worker more freedom to do his job with an accompanying lowering of cost. All he had to do was stay within the tolerance limits, instead of trying to achieve unnecessary or unattainable perfection.

Defective Parts Inspection

The next advancement centered around expanding the notion of tolerance and using specifications, where variation is classified as either meeting or not meeting requirements. For those pieces of product that every now and then fell outside the specified tolerance range (or limits), the question arose as to what to do with them. To discard or modify these pieces added significantly to the cost of production. However, to search for the unknown causes of defects and then eliminate them also cost money. The heart of the problem was as follows: how to reduce the percentage of defects to the point where (1) the rate of increase in the *cost of control* equals the rate of *increase* in *savings*, which is (2) brought about by *decreasing the number of parts rejected.*

In other words, inspection/prevention had to be cost effective. Minimizing the percent of defects in a cost-effective manner was not the only problem to be solved. Tests for many quality characteristics require destructive testing, such as tests for strength, chemical composition, fuse blowing time, etc. Because not every piece can be tested, use of the statistical sample was initiated around the turn of the century.

Statistical Theory

During the early part of the 20th century, a tremendous increase in quality consciousness occurred. What were the forces at work that caused this sudden acceleration of interest in the application of statistical quality control? There were at least three key factors.

The first was a rapid growth in standardization, beginning in 1900. Until 1915, Great Britain was the only country in the world with some type of national standardization movement. The rate of growth in the number of industrial standardization organizations throughout the world, especially between 1916 and 1932, rose dramatically.[11] During that 15-year period, the movement grew from one country (Great Britain) to 25, with the United States coming on line about 1917, just at the time of World War I.

The second major factor ushering in the new era was a radical shift in ideology which occurred in about 1900. This ideological shift was away from the notion of exactness of science (which existed in 1787 when interchange-ability of parts was introduced) to probability and statistical concepts, which developed in almost every field of science around 1900.

The third factor was the evolution of division of labor into the factory system and the first assembly line systems of the early 20th century. These systems proved to be ideal for employing an immigrant work force quickly.

Scientific Management and Taylorism

Frederick Winslow Taylor was born in 1856 and entered industry as an apprentice in the Enterprise Hydraulics Shop in 1874. According to popular legend, the old-timers in the shop told him: "Now young man, here's about how much work you should do each morning and each afternoon. Don't do any more than that—that's the limit."[12]

It was obvious to Taylor that the men were producing below their capacity, and he soon found out why. The short-sighted management of that day would set standards, often paying per-piece rates for the work. Then, when a worker discovered how to produce more, management cut the rate. In turn, management realized that the workers were deliberately restricting output but could not do anything about it.

It was Taylor's viewpoint that the whole system was wrong. Having studied the writings and innovations of Whitney, he came to realize that the concept of division of labor had to be revamped if greater productivity and efficiency were to be realized. His vision included a super-efficient assembly line as part of a management system of operations. He, more than anyone at the time, understood the inability of management to increase individual productivity, and he understood the reluctance of the workers to produce at a high rate. Because he had been a working man, it was apparent to him that there was a tremendous difference between *actual* output and *potential* output. Taylor thought that if such practices applied throughout the world and throughout all industry, the potential production capacity was at least three or four times what was actually being produced. When he became a foreman, Taylor set out to find ways to eliminate this waste and increase production.

For more than 25 years, Taylor and his associates explored ways to increase productivity and build the model factory of the future. The techniques they developed were finally formalized in writing and communicated to other people. During the early years of this experimentation, most who knew about it were associated with Taylor at the Midvale Steel Company and Bethlehem Steel.

Other famous names began to enter the picture and contribute to the body of science of the new management thinking. Among them were Carl G.L. Barth, a mathematician and statistician who assisted Taylor in analytical work, and Henry L. Gantt (famous for the Gantt chart), who invented the slide rule. Another associate of Taylor's, Sanford E. Thompson, developed the first decimal stopwatch.[12] Finally, there was young Walter Shewhart, who was to transform industry with his statistical concepts and thinking and his ability to bridge technical tools with a management system.

At the turn of the century, Taylor wrote a collection of reports and papers that were published by the American Society of Mechanical Engineers. One of the most famous was *On the Art of Cutting Metals*, which had worldwide impact. With Maunsel White, Taylor developed the first high-speed steel. Taylor was also instrumental in the development of one of the first industrial cost accounting systems, even though, according to legend, he previously knew nothing about accounting.

Frank G. and Lillian Gilbreth, aware of Taylor's work in measurement and analysis, turned their attention to mechanizing and commercializing Taylorism. For their experimental model, they chose the ancient craft of bricklaying. It had been assumed that production in bricklaying certainly should have reached its zenith thousands of years ago, with nothing more to be done to increase production. Yet Frank Gilbreth was able to show that by following his techniques and with proper management planning, production could be raised from an average of 120 bricks per hour to 350 bricks per hour, and the worker would be less tired than he had been under the old system.

The Gilbreths refined some of the studies and techniques developed by Taylor. They used the motion picture camera to record work steps for analyses and broke them down into minute elements called "therbligs" (Gilbreth spelled backwards). Their results were eventually codified into the use of predetermined motion–time measures which were used by industrial engineers and efficiency experts of the day.

By 1912, the efficiency movement was gaining momentum. Taylor was called before a special committee of the House of Representatives which was investigating scientific management and its impact on the railroad industry. He tried to explain scientific management to the somewhat hostile railroad hearings committee, whose members regarded it as "speeding up" work. He said:

> Scientific management involves a complete mental revolution on the part of the *working man* engaged in any particular establishment or industry...a complete mental revolution on the part of these men as to their duties toward their work, toward their fellow man, and toward their employers.
>
> And scientific management involves an equally complete

mental revolution on the part of those on *management's side*...the foreman, the superintendent, the owner of the business, and the board of directors. Here we must have a mental revolution on their part as to their duties toward their fellow workers in management, toward their workmen, and toward all of their daily problems. Without this complete mental revolution on both sides, scientific management does not exist!

I want to sweep the deck, sweep away a good deal of the rubbish first by pointing out what scientific management is not—it is not an efficiency device, nor is it any bunch or group of efficiency devices. It is not a new system of figuring costs. It is not a new scheme of paying men. It is not holding a stopwatch on a man and writing things down about him. It is not time study. It is not motion study, nor an analysis of the movements of a man. Nor is scientific management the printing and ruling and unloading of a ton or two of blank forms on a set of men and saying, "Here's your system—go to it."

It is not divided foremanship, nor functional foremanship. It is not any of these devices which the average man calls to mind when he hears the words "scientific management." I am not sneering at cost-keeping systems—at time-study, at functional foremanship, nor at any of the new and improved schemes of paying men. Nor am I sneering at efficiency devices, if they are really devices which make for efficiency. I believe in them. What I am emphasizing is that these devices in whole or part are *not* scientific management; they are useful adjuncts to scientific management, but they are also useful adjuncts to other systems of management.[12]

Taylor found out, the hard way, the importance of the cooperative spirit. He was strictly the engineer at first. Only after painful experiences did he realize that the human factor, the social system, and mental attitude of people in both management and labor had to be adjusted and changed completely before greater productivity could result.

Referring to his early experiences in seeking greater output, Taylor described the strained feelings between himself and his workmen as "miserable." Yet he was determined to improve production. He continued his experiments until three years before his death in 1915, when he found that human motivation, not just engineered improvements, could alone increase output.

Unfortunately, the human factor was ignored by many. Shortly after the railroad hearings, self-proclaimed "efficiency experts" did untold damage to scientific management. Time studies and the new efficiency techniques were used by incompetent "consultants" who sold managers on the idea of increasing profit by "speeding up" employees. Consequently, many labor unions, just beginning to feel their strength, worked against the new science and all efficiency approaches. With the passing of Taylor in 1915, the scientific management movement lost, for the moment, any chance of reaching its true potential as the catalyst for the future total quality management system. Still, the foundation was laid for the management system that was soon to become a key ingredient of organizations of the future.

Walter Shewhart—The Founding Father

Walter Shewhart was an engineer, scientist, and philosopher. He was a very deep thinker, and his ideas, although profound and technically perfect, were difficult to fathom. His style of writing followed his style of thinking—very obtuse. Still, he was brilliant, and his works on variation and sampling, coupled with his teachings on the need for documentation, influenced forever the course of industrial history.

Shewhart was familiar with the scientific management movement and its evolution from Whitney's innovation of division of labor. Although he was concerned about its evolution into sweatshop factory environments, his major focus was on the other of Whitney's great innovations—interchangeable parts—for this encompassed variation, rejects, and waste.

To deal with the issue of variation, Shewhart developed the control chart in 1924. He realized that the traditional use of tolerance limits was shortsighted, because they only provided a method for judging the quality of a product that had already been made.[13]

The control limits on Shewhart's control charts, however, provided a ready guide for acting on the process in order to eliminate what he called *assignable causes*[8] of variation, thus preventing inferior products from being produced in the future. This allowed management to focus on the future, through the use of statistical probability—a prediction of future production based upon historical data. Thus, the emphasis shifted from costly correction of problems to prevention of problems and improvement of processes.[14]

Like Taylor, Shewhart's focus shifted from individual parts to a systems approach. The notion of zero defects of individual parts was replaced with zero variability of system operations.

Shewhart's Control System

Shewhart identified the traditional act of control as consisting of three elements: the act of specifying what is required, the act of producing what is specified, and the act of judging whether the requirements have been met.

This simple picture of the control of quality would work well if production could be viewed in the context of an exact science, where all products are made exactly the same. Shewhart knew, however, that because variation is pervasive, the control of quality characteristics must be a matter of probability. He envisioned a statistician helping an engineer to understanding variation and arriving at the economic control of quality.[15]

Shewhart's Concept of Variation

Determining the *state of statistical control* in terms of degree of variation is the first step in the Shewhart control system. Rather than specifying what is required in terms of tolerance requirements, Shewhart viewed variation as being present in everything and identified two types of variation: *controlled* and *uncontrolled.*

This is fundamentally different from the traditional way of classifying variation as either acceptable or unacceptable (go–no-go tolerance). Viewing variation as controlled or uncontrolled enables one to focus on the causes of variation in order to improve a process (before the fact) as opposed to focusing on the output of a process in order to judge whether or not the product is acceptable (after the fact).

Shewhart taught that controlled variation is a consistent pattern of variation over time that is due to random or *chance causes*. He recognized that there may be many chance causes of variation, but the effect of any one of these is relatively small; therefore, which cause or causes are responsible for observed variation is a matter of chance. Shewhart stated that a process that is being affected only by *chance* causes of variation is said to be *in a state of statistical control.*

All processes contain chance causes of variation, and Shewhart taught that it is possible to reduce the chance causes of variation, but it is not realistic or cost effective to try to remove them all. The control limits on Shewhart's control charts represent the boundaries of the occurrence of chance causes of variation operating within the system.

The second type of variation—uncontrolled variation—is an inconsistent or changing pattern of variation that occurs over time and is due to what Shewhart classified as *assignable causes.* Because the effects of assignable causes of variation are relatively major compared to chance causes, they can and must be identified and removed.[16] According to Shewhart, a process is *out of statistical control* when it is being affected by assignable causes.

One of Shewhart's main problems was how to communicate this newfound theory without overwhelming the average businessman or engineer. The answer came in the form of staged experiments using models which demonstrated variation. His *ideal bowl experiment*[17] with poker chips was modeled by his protege, W. Edwards Deming, some 20 years later with his famous *red bead experiment.*

Another major contribution of Shewhart's first principle of control was recognition of the need for operational definitions that can be communicated to operators, inspectors, and scientists alike. He was fond of asking, "How can an operator carry out his job tasks if he does not understand what the job is? And how can he know what the job is if what was produced yesterday was O.K., but today the same product is wrong?" He believed that inspection, whether the operator inspects his own work or relies on someone else to do it for him, must have operational definitions. Extending specifications beyond product and into the realm of operator performance was the first attempt to define the "extended system of operations" which would greatly facilitate the production process.

The Shewhart System of Production

Shewhart's second principle—the act of producing what is specified— consists of five important steps (Shewhart's teachings are in italics):

1. **Outline the data collection framework:** *Specify in a general way how an observed sequence of data is to be examined for clues as to the existence of assignable causes of variability.*

2. **Develop the sampling plan:** *Specify how the original data are to be taken and how they are to be broken up into subsamples upon the basis of human judgments about whether the conditions under which the data were taken were essentially the same or not.*

3. **Identify the formulas and control limits for each sample:** *Specify the criterion of control that is to be used, indicating what statistics are to be computed for each subsample and how these are to be used in computing action or control limits for each statistic for which the control criterion is to be constructed.*

4. **Outline the corrective actions/improvement thesis:** *Specify the action that is to be taken when an observed statistic falls outside its control limits.*

5. **Determine the size of the database:** *Specify the quantity of data that must be available and found to satisfy the criterion of control before the engineer is to act as though he had attained a state of statistical control.*[8]

The Shewhart system became a key component of the technical system of total quality. The works of Deming, Juran, Feigenbaum, Sarasohn, Ishikawa, and others who followed would amplify Shewhart's concept of quality as a *technical system* into its many dimensions, which eventually led to the body of knowledge known as total quality.

The Shewhart Cycle: When Control Meets Scientific Management

From the "exact science" days of the 1800s to the 1920s, *specification, production,* and *inspection* were considered to be independent of each other when viewed in a straight line manner. They take on an entirely different picture in an inexact science. When the production process is viewed from the standpoint of the control of quality as a matter of probability, then specification, production, and inspection are linked together as represented in a circular diagram or wheel. *Specification and production* are linked because it is important to know how well the tolerance limits are being satisfied by the existing process and what improvements are necessary. Shewhart compared this process (which he called the Scientific Method) to the dynamic process of acquiring knowledge, which is similar to an experiment. Step 1 was formulating the hypothesis. Step 2 was conducting the experiment. Step 3 was testing the hypothesis.[18] In the Shewhart wheel, the successful completion of each interlocking component led to a cycle of continuous improvement. (Years later, Deming was to popularize this cycle of improvement in his famous Deming wheel.)

Shewhart Meets Deming

It was at the Bell Laboratories in New Jersey where Shewhart, who was leading the telephone reliability efforts during the 1930s, first met Deming. Shewhart, as discussed earlier, was developing his system for improving worker performance and productivity by measuring variation using control charts and statistical methods. Deming was impressed and liked what he saw, especially Shewhart's intellect and the *wheel*—the Shewhart cycle of control. He realized that with training, workers could retain control over their work processes by monitoring the quality of the items produced. Deming also believed that once workers were trained and educated and were empowered to manage their work processes, quality would be increased and costly inspections could once and for all be eliminated. He presented the idea that higher quality would cost less, not more. Deming studied Shewhart's teachings and techniques and learned well, even if at times he was lost and said that his genius was in knowing when to act and when to leave a process alone. At times he was frustrated by Shewhart's obtuse style of thinking and writing.[19]

In 1938, Shewhart delivered four lectures to the U.S. Department of Agriculture (USDA) Graduate School at the invitation of Deming. In addition to being in charge of the mathematics and statistics courses at the USDA Graduate School, Deming was responsible for inviting guest lecturers. He invited Shewhart to present a series of lectures on how statistical methods of control were being used in industry to economically control the quality of manufactured products. Shewhart spent an entire year developing the lectures, titled them *Statistical Method from the Viewpoint of Quality Control*, and delivered them in March of 1938. They were subsequently edited into book format by Deming and published in 1939.

In a couple of years, both Deming and Shewhart were called upon by the U.S. government to aid the war effort. As David Halberstam recounted, the War Department, impressed by Shewhart's theories and work, brought together a small group of experts on statistical process control (SPC) to establish better quality guidelines for defense contractors.[20] Deming was a member of that group and he came to love the work.

Origins of Deming

Who was Dr. W. Edwards Deming, the man who was to take Shewhart's teachings, popularize them, and even go beyond? He was born on October 14, 1900 and earned his Ph.D. in physics at Yale University in the summer of 1927, which is where he learned to use statistical theory. As a graduate student in the late 1920s, he did part-time summer work at the famous Western Electric Hawthorne plant in Chicago. It was at this plant that Elton Mayo some ten years later would perform his experiments later known as the Hawthorne Experiments. While working at Hawthorne, Deming could not help noticing the poor working conditions of this sweatshop environment, which employed predominantly female laborers to produce telephones. Deming was both fascinated and appalled by what he saw and learned. It was at Hawthorne where he saw the full effects of the abuses of the Taylor system of scientific management. He also saw the full effect of Whitney's second great innovation—division of labor—when carried to extreme by ivory tower management uncaring about the state of the social system of the organization. So what if the work environment was a sweatshop—the workers were paid well enough! "The women should be happy just to have a job" seemed to be the unspoken attitude.

When Deming Met Taylor(ism)

A couple of years before meeting Shewhart, when Deming encountered Taylorism at Hawthorne, he found a scientific management system with the following objectives:

- Develop a science for each element of work.

- Scientifically select a workman and train and develop him.

- Secure whole-hearted cooperation between management and labor to ensure that all work is done in accordance with the principles developed.

- Divide the work between management and labor. The manager takes over all work for which he is better suited than the workman.

It was the fourth point, which evolved out of the division of labor concept, that Deming found to be the real villain. In practice, this meant removing from the worker basic responsibility for the quality of the work. What Deming disliked was that workers should not be hired to think about their work. That was management's job. Errors will occur, but the worker need not worry—the inspector will catch any mistakes *before* they leave the plant. In addition, management could always reduce the per-piece pay to reflect scrap and rework. Any worker who produced too many inferior quality pieces would be fired.

The problem with Taylorism is that it views the production process mechanistically instead of holistically, as a system which includes the human elements of motivation and respect. Taylorism taught American industry to view the worker as "a cog in the giant industrial machine, whose job could be defined and directed by educated managers administering a set of rules."[21] Work on the assembly lines of America and at Hawthorne was simple, repetitive, and boring. Management was top-down. Pay per piece meant that higher output equals higher take-home pay. Quality of work for the most part was not a factor for the average, everyday worker.

This system found a friend in the assembly line process developed by Henry Ford and was widely incorporated into America's private and public sectors. Taylor's management system made it possible for waves of immigrants, many of whom could not read, write, or speak English (and at times not even communicate with one another), to find employment in American factories. Taylor's ideas were even introduced into the nation's schools.[22]

Edwards Deming had various colleagues at the time, one of whom was Joseph Juran, another famous quality "guru." They rebelled at the scientific management movement. They felt that the authoritarian Taylorism method of management was degrading to the human spirit and counterproductive to the interests of employees, management, the company, and society as a whole.[23] Mayo and his Hawthorne research team confirmed these feelings with their findings: good leadership leads to high morale and motivation, which in turn leads to higher production. Good leadership was defined as democratic, rather than autocratic, and people centered, as opposed to production centered. Thus began the human relations era.

Post-World War II

When the war ended, American industry converted to peacetime production of goods and services. People were hungry for possessions and an appetite developed worldwide for products "made in the U.S.A." The focus in the United States returned to quantity over quality, and a gradual deterioration of market share occurred, with billions of dollars in international business lost to Japanese and European competitors. These were the modern-day phoenixes rising from the ashes of war. America became preoccupied with the mechanics of mass production and its role as world provider to a hungry people. What followed was an imbalance between satisfying the needs of the worker and a lack of appreciation for and recognition of the external customer. America moved away from what had made it great! (For additional information, see Abstract 2.1 at the end of this chapter.)

The Japanese Resurrection

Japan first began to apply statistical control concepts in the early 1920s, but moved away from them when the war began.[24] In 1946, under General Douglas MacArthur's leadership, the Supreme Command for the Allied Powers (SCAP) established quality control tools and techniques as the approach to effect the turnaround of Japanese industry. Japan had sacrificed its industry, and eventually its food supply, to support its war effort. Subsequently, there was little left in post-war Japan to occupy. The country was a shambles. Only one major city, Kyoto, had escaped wide-scale destruction; food was scarce and industry was negligible.[24]

Against a backdrop of devastation and military defeat, a group of Japanese scientists and engineers—organized appropriately as the Union of Japanese Scientists and Engineers (JUSE)—dedicated themselves to working with American and Allied experts to help rebuild the country. Reconstruction was a daunting and monumental task. With few natural resources available or any immediate means of producing them, export of manufactured goods was essential. However, Japanese industry—or what was left of it—was producing inferior goods, a fact which was recognized worldwide. JUSE was faced with the task of drastically improving the quality of Japan's industrial output as an essential exchange commodity for survival.

W.S. Magill and Homer Sarasohn, among others, assisted with the dramatic transformation of the electronics industry and telecommunications. Magill is regarded by some as the father of statistical quality control in Japan. He was the first to advocate its use in a 1945 lecture series and successfully applied SPC techniques to vacuum tube production in 1946 at NEC.[25]

Sarasohn worked with supervisors and managers to improve reliability and yields in the electronics field from 40 percent in 1946 to 80–90 percent in 1949; he documented his findings for SCAP, and MacArthur took notice. He ordered Sarasohn to instruct Japanese businessmen how to get things done. The Japanese listened, but the Americans forgot. In 1950, Sarasohn's attention was directed toward Korea, and Walter Shewhart was asked to come to Japan. He was unable to at the time, and Deming was eventually tapped to direct the transformation.

In July 1950, Deming began a series of day-long lectures to Japanese management in which he taught the basic "Elementary Principles of Statistical Control of Quality." The Japanese embraced the man and his principles and named their most prestigious award for quality the Deming Prize. During the 1970s, Deming turned his attention back to the United States. He died at the age of 93, still going strong. His Fourteen Points go far beyond statistical methods and address the management system as well as the social system or culture of the organization. In many ways, he began to sound more and more like Frederick Taylor, whose major emphasis in later years was on the need for a *mental revolution*—a transformation. Deming's Theory of Profound Knowledge brings together all three systems of total quality.

The Other "Gurus" Arrive

What began in Japan in the 1950s became a worldwide quality movement, albeit on a limited basis, within 20 years. During this period, the era of the "gurus" evolved (Deming, Juran, Ishikawa, Feigenbaum, and Crosby). Beginning with Deming in 1948 and Juran in 1954, the movement was eventually carried back to the United States by Feigenbaum in the 1960s and Crosby in the 1970s. Meanwhile, Ishikawa and his associates at JUSE kept the movement alive in Japan. By 1980, the bell began to toll loud and clear in the West with the NBC White Paper entitled "If Japan Can Do It, Why Can't We?" The following are thumbnail sketches of the teachings of the other gurus.

Joseph Juran

Joseph Juran was the son of an immigrant shoemaker from Romania and began his industrial career at Western Electric's Hawthorne plant before World War II. He later worked at Bell Laboratories in the area of quality assurance. He worked as a government administrator, university professor, labor arbitrator, and corporate director before establishing his own consulting firm, the Juran Institute, in Wilton, Connecticut. In the 1950s, he was invited to Japan by JUSE to help rebuilding Japanese corporations develop management concepts. Juran based some of his principles on the work of Walter Shewhart and, like Deming and the other quality gurus, believed that management and the system are responsible for quality. Juran is the creator of statistical quality control and the author of *The Quality Control Handbook*, which has become an international standard reference for the quality movement.

Juran's definition of quality is described as "fitness for use as perceived by the customer." If a product is produced and the customer perceives it as fit for use, then the quality mission has been accomplished. Juran also believed that every person in the organization must be involved in the effort to make products or services that are fit for use.

Juran described a perpetual spiral of progress or continuous striving toward quality. Steps on this spiral are, in ascending order, research, development, design, specification, planning, purchasing, instrumentation, production, process control, inspection, testing, sale, service, and then back to research again. The idea behind the spiral is that each time the steps are completed, products or services would increase in quality. Juran explained that chronic problems should be solved by following this spiral; he formulated a breakthrough sequence to increase the standard of performance so that problems are eliminated. To alleviate sporadic problems, which he finds are often solved with temporary solutions, he suggests carefully examining the system causing the problem and adjusting it to solve the difficulty. Once operating at this improved standard of performance, with the sporadic problem solved, the process of analyzing chronic and sporadic problems should start over again.

Juran pointed out that companies often overlook the cost of producing low-quality products. He suggested that by implementing his theories of quality improvement, not only would higher quality products be produced, but the actual costs would be lower. His Cost of Quality principle was known as "Gold in the Mine."

Juran is known for his work with statistics, and he relied on the quantification of standards and statistical quality control techniques. He is credited with implementing use of the Pareto diagram to improve business systems as well.

Juran's concept of quality included the managerial dimensions of planning, organizing, and controlling (known as the Juran Trilogy) and focused on the responsibility of management to achieve quality and the need to set goals. His ten steps to quality are as follows:

1. Build awareness of opportunities to improve.

2. Set goals for improvement.

3. Organize to reach goals.

4. Provide training.

5. Carry out projects to solve problems.

6. Report progress.

7. Give recognition.

8. Communicate results.

9. Keep score.

10. Maintain momentum by making annual improvement part of the regular systems and processes of the company.

Ishikawa and the Japanese Experts

Kaoru Ishikawa studied under both Homer Sarasohn and Edwards Deming during the late 1940s and early 1950s. As President of JUSE, he was instrumental in developing a unique Japanese strategy for total quality: the broad involvement of the entire organization in its *total* sense—every worker, every process, and every job. This also included the complete life cycle of the product, from start to finish.

Some of his accomplishments include the success of the quality circle in Japan, in part due to innovative tools such as the cause-and-effect diagram (often called the Ishikawa fishbone diagram because it resembles a fish skeleton). His approach was to provide easy-to-use analytical tools that could be used by all workers, including those on the line, to analyze and solve problems.

Ishikawa identified seven critical success factors that were essential for the success of total quality control in Japan:

1. Company-wide total quality control and participation by *all* members of the organization

2. Education and training in all aspects of total quality, which often amounts to 30 days per year per employee

3. Use of quality circles to update standards and regulations, which are in constant need of improvement

4. Quality audits by the president and quality council members (senior executives) twice a year

5. Widespread use of statistical methods and a focus on problem prevention

6. Nationwide quality control promotion activities, with the national imperative of keeping Japanese quality number one in the world

7. Revolutionary *mental* attitude on the part of both management and workers toward one another and toward the customer, including welcoming complaints, encouraging risk, and a wider span of control

Ishikawa believed that Japanese management practices should be democratic, with management providing the guidelines. Mission statements were used extensively and operating policies derived from them. Top management, he taught, must assume a leadership position to implement the policies so that they are followed by all.

The impact on Japanese industry was startling. In seven to ten years, the electronics and telecommunications industries were transformed, with the entire nation revitalized by the end of the 1960s.

Armand Feigenbaum

Unlike Deming and Juran, Feigenbaum did not work with the Japanese. He was Vice President of Worldwide Quality for General Electric until the late 1960s, when he set up his own consulting firm, General Systems, Inc. He is best known for coining the term *total quality control* and for his 850-page book on the subject. His teachings center around the integration of people–machine–information structures in order to economically and effectively control quality and achieve full customer satisfaction.

Feigenbaum taught that there are two requirements to establishing quality as a business strategy: establishing customer satisfaction must be central and quality/cost objectives must drive the total quality system. His systems theory of total quality control includes four fundamental principles:

- Total quality is a continuous work process, starting with customer requirements and ending with customer satisfaction.

- Documentation allows visualization and communication of work assignments.

- The quality system provides for greater flexibility because of a greater use of alternatives provided.

- Systematic reengineering of major quality activities leads to greater levels of continuous improvement.

Like Juran and Deming, Feigenbaum used a visual concept to capture the idea of waste and rework—the so-called Hidden Plant. Based upon studies, he taught that this "Hidden Plant" can account for between 15 and 40 percent of the production capacity of a company. In his book, he used the concept of the "9 M's" to describe the factors which affect quality: (1) markets, (2) money, (3) management, (4) men, (5) motivation, (6) materials, (7) machines and mechanization, (8) modern information methods, and (9) mounting product requirements.

According to Andrea Gabor in "The Man Who Discovered Quality," Feigenbaum took a nut-and-bolts approach to quality, while Deming is often viewed as a visionary. Nuts and bolts led him to focus on the benefits and outcomes of total quality, rather than only the process to follow. His methods led to increased quantification of total quality program improvements during the 1970s and 1980s. (For additional information, see Abstract 2.2 at the end of this chapter.)

Philip Crosby

Unlike the other quality gurus, who were scientists, engineers, and statisticians, Philip Crosby is known for his motivational talks and style of presentation. His emergence began in 1961, when he first developed the concept of zero defects while working as a quality manager at Martin Marietta Corporation in Orlando, Florida. He believed that "zero defects" motivated line workers to turn out perfect products. He soon joined ITT, where he quickly moved up the ranks to Vice President of Quality Control Operations, covering 192 manufacturing facilities in 46 countries. He held the position until 1979, when he opened his own consulting company, which became one of the largest of its kind with over 250 people worldwide.

He established the Quality College in 1980 and used that concept to promote his teachings and writings in 18 languages. It has been estimated that over five million people have attended its courses, and his trilogy of books are popular and easy to read. It is in these works where he introduces the four absolutes of his total quality management philosophy:

1. The definition of quality is conformance to requirements.

2. The system of quality is prevention of problems.

3. The performance standard of quality is zero defects.

4. The measurement of quality is the price of nonconformance, or the Cost of Quality.

The fourth principle, the Cost of Quality, is similar to Feigenbaum's Hidden Plant and Juran's Gold in the Mine. Like Deming, he has 14 steps to quality improvement. Also like Deming, he has been very critical of the Malcolm Baldrige National Quality Award, although his influence (like Deming's) can be seen in virtually all seven categories.

He departs from the other gurus in his emphasis on performance standards instead of statistical data to achieve zero defects. He believes that identifying goals to be achieved, setting standards for the final product, removing all error-causing situations, and complete organizational commitment comprise the foundation for excellence.

ISO 9000 and the Quality Movement

At the turn of the century, England was the most advanced nation in the world in terms of quality standards. During World War I, England led the charge and during World War II was at least the equal of the United States—with one exception. England did not have Shewhart, Deming, and the other American quality gurus. It was not until the Common Market accepted the firm touch of Prime Minister Margaret Thatcher that the European movement was galvanized in 1979 with the forerunner of ISO 9000. It was Thatcher who orchestrated the transformance of the British ISO 9000 series for the European community. In less than 20 years, it has become the worldwide quality standard.

ENDNOTES

1. During the course of the Deming Prize examination at Florida Power & Light in 1988 and 1989, Dr. Kano consistently emphasized this point during site visits to various power plants and district customer service operations. The concept of worker self-inspection, while new in the United States, has been a practiced art in Japan over the past 20 years.

2. Whethan, C. D. *A History of Science*, 4th edition, Macmillan, New York, 1980.

3. Tribus, Myron. *The Systems of Total Quality*, 1990, published by the author.

4. The total quality ballantine was developed by Frank Voehl to illustrate the three-dimensional and interlocking aspects of the quality system. It is loosely based on the military concept of three interlocking bullet holes representing a perfect hit.

5. Tribus, Myron. *The Three Systems of Total Quality*, 1990, published by the author; referenced in Voehl, Frank. *Total Quality: Principles and Practices within Organizations*, Strategy Associates, Coral Springs, Fla., 1992, pp. IV, 20.

6. The use of a storyboard to document the various phases of project development was introduced by Dr. Kume in his work on total quality control and was pioneered in the United States by Disney Studios, where it was used to bring new movies to production sooner.

7. For details, see Voehl, F. W. *The Integrated Quality System*, Strategy Associates, Coral Springs, Fla., 1992.

8. Shewhart, W. A. *Economic Control of Quality of Manufactured Product*, Van Nostrand, New York, 1931.

9. Olmstead, Denison. *Memoir of Eli Whitney, Esq.*, Arno Press, New York, 1972.

10. Walter Shewhart on the "go–no-go" concept: If, for example, a design involving the use of a cylindrical shaft in a bearing is examined, interchangeability might be ensured simply by using a suitable "go" plug gauge on the bearing and a suitable "go" ring gauge on the shaft. In this case, the difference between the dimensions of the two "go" gauges gives the minimum clearance. Such a method of gauging, however, does not fix the maximum clearance. The production worker soon realized that a slack

fit between a part and its "go" gauge might result in enough play between the shaft and its bearing to cause the product to be rejected; therefore, he tried to keep the fit between the part and its "go" gauge as close as possible, thus encountering some of the difficulties that had been experienced in trying to make the parts exactly alike.

11.　Walter Shewhart was the first to realize that, with the development of the atomic structure of matter and electricity, it became necessary to regard laws as being statistical in nature. According to Shewhart, the importance of the law of large numbers in the interpretation of physical phenomena will become apparent to anyone who even hastily surveys any one or more of the following works: Darrow, K. K. "Statistical Theories of Matter, Radiation, and Electricity." *The Physical Review Supplement*, July 1992, Vol. I No. I (also published in the series of Bell Telephone Laboratories reprints, No. 435); Rice, J. *Introduction to Statistical Mechanics for Students of Physics and Physical Chemistry*, Constable & Company, London, 1930; Tolman, R. E. *Statistical Mechanics with Applications to Physics and Chemistry*, Chemical Catalog Company, New York, 1927; Loeb, L. B. *Kinetic Theory of Gases*, McGraw-Hill, New York, 1927; Bloch, E. *The Kinetic Theory of Bases*, Methuen & Company, London, 1924; Richtmeyer, F. K. *Introduction to Modern Physics*, McGraw-Hill, New York, 1928; Wilson, H. A. *Modern Physics*, Blackie & Son, London, 1928; Darrow, K. K. *Introduction to Contemporary Physics*, D. Van Nostrand, New York, 1926; Ruark, A. E. and Urey, H. C. *Atoms, Molecules and Quanta*, McGraw-Hill, New York, 1930.

12.　Matthies, Leslie. "The Beginning of Modern Scientific Management." *The Office*, April 1960.

13.　Walter Shewhart on the use of the control chart: Whereas the concept of mass production of 1787 was born of an *exact* science, the concept underlying the quality control chart technique of 1924 was born of a *probable* science, which has empirically derived control limits. These limits are to be set so that when the observed quality of a piece of product falls outside of them, even though the observation is still within the limits L_1 and L_2 (tolerance limits), it is desirable to look at the manufacturing process in order to discover and remove, if possible, one or more causes of variation that need not be left to chance.

14.　Shewhart noted that it is essential, however, in industry and in science to understand the distinction between a stable system and an unstable system and how to plot points and conclude by rational methods whether they indicate a stable system. To quote Shewhart, "This conclusion is consistent with that so admirably presented in a recent paper by S. L. Andrew in the *Bell Telephone Quarterly*, Jan., 1931, and also with conclusions set forth in the recent book *Business Adrift*, by W. B. Donham, Dean of the Harvard Business School. Such reading cannot do other than strengthen our belief in the fact that control of quality will come only through the weeding out of assignable causes of variation—particularly those that introduce lack of constancy in the chance cause system."

15. As the statistician enters the scene, the three traditional elements of control take on a new meaning, as Shewhart summarized: "Corresponding to these three steps there are three senses in which statistical control may play an important part in attaining uniformity in the quality of a manufactured product: (a) as a concept of a statistical state constituting a limit to which one may hope to go in improving the uniformity of quality; (b) as an operation or technique of attaining uniformity; and (c) as a judgment."

16. Deming refers to assignable causes as being "specific to some ephemeral (brief) event that can usually be discovered to the satisfaction of the expert on the job, and removed."

17. Shewhart used what he called the *Ideal Bowl Experiment* to physically characterize a state of statistical control. A number of physically similar poker chips with numbers written on them are placed in a bowl. Successive samples (Shewhart seems to prefer a sample size of four) are taken from the bowl, each time mixing the remaining chips. The chips removed from the bowl are drawn by chance—there are only chance causes of variation. In speaking of chance causes of variation, Shewhart proves, contrary to popular belief, that the statistician can have a sense of humor. "If someone were shooting at a mark and failed to hit the bull's-eye and was then asked why, the answer would likely be *chance*. Had someone asked the same question of one of man's earliest known ancestors, he might have attributed his lack of success to the dictates of fate or to the will of the gods. I am inclined to think that in many ways one of these excuses is about as good as another. The Ideal Bowl Experiment is an abstract means of characterizing the physical state of statistical control." A sequence of samples of any process can be compared mathematically to the bowl experiment and, if found similar, the process can be said to be affected only by random or chance causes of variation or can be characterized as being in a *state of statistical control*. Shewhart states: "It seems to me that it is far safer to take some one physical operation such as drawing from a bowl as a physical model for an act that may be repeated at random, and then to require that any other repetitive operation believed to be random shall in addition produce results similar in certain respects to the results of drawing from a bowl before we act as though the operation in question were random."

18. It may be helpful to think of the three steps in the mass production process as steps in the Scientific Method. In this sense, specification, production, and inspection correspond, respectively, to formulating a hypothesis, conducting an experiment, and testing the hypothesis. The three steps constitute the dynamic scientific process of acquiring knowledge.

19. The following story was related at one of Deming's now-famous four-day quality seminars: I remember him [Shewhart] pacing the floor in his room at the Hotel Washington before the third lecture. He was explaining something to me. I remarked that these great thoughts should be in his lectures. He said that they were already written up in his third and fourth

lectures. I remarked that if he wrote up these lectures in the same way that he had just explained them to me, they would be clearer. He said that his writing had to be foolproof. I thereupon remarked that he had written his thoughts to be so darn foolproof that no one could understand them.

20.   Halberstam, David. The War Effort during WWII, Lectures, Articles and Interview Notes, 1960.

21.   This is a general consensus feeling among many historians and writers as to the inherent "evil" of Taylorism—machine over man. Walter Shewhart, to his credit and genius, tries to marry quality control and scientific management. In the foreword to his 1931 master work referred to in Endnote 8, he writes, "Broadly speaking, the object of industry is to set up economic ways and means of satisfying human wants and in so doing to reduce everything possible to routines requiring a minimum amount of human effort. Through the use of the scientific method, extended to take account of modern statistical concepts, it has been found possible to set up limits within which the results of routine efforts must lie if they are to be economical. Deviations in the results of a routine process outside such limits indicate that the routine has broken down and will no longer be economical until the cause of trouble is removed."

22.   Bonstingal, John Jay. Schools of Quality. Free Press, New York, 1992.

23.   The Hawthorne Experiments, Elton Mayo, 1938.

24.   Voehl, F. W. "The Deming Prize." South Carolina Business Journal, 1990 edition, pp. 33–38.

25.   This was first pointed out by Robert Chadman Wood in an article about Homer Sarasohn, published in Forbes in 1990.

26.   Figure 2.2 ©1991 F. W. Voehl. Figure 2.3 ©1992 Strategy Associates, Inc.

ABSTRACTS

ABSTRACT 2.1
THE UPSIDE-DOWN DEMING PRINCIPLE

Rottenberger, Kerry and Kern, Richard
Sales & Marketing Management, June 1992, pp. 39–44

In its search for a quick-fix solution, say the authors, American business is attacking quality from the bottom up via sales and service. After reviewing the history of the quality movement, and outlining Deming's 14 points in a sidebar, the authors observe that the emphasis does not seem like a passing fad: 76 percent of human resource executives at *Fortune* 500 corporations reported that quality is a strategic goal at their companies, and another 17 percent showed interest in implementing TQM training. In the remainder of the article, the authors quote various sales managers describing some of the ways they are approaching TQM. Some of these approaches include:

- Understanding fully one's existing sales process and then using quality tools to bring about continuous improvement to the process

- Using salesperson contact with customers to provide a constant flow of feedback on customers' wants

- Changing compensation plans to integrate customer satisfaction levels with sales quotas

- Shifting the mindset from dramatic improvement to incremental gains based on production and process

- Eliminating isolation so that quality initiatives are supported by the entire corporation

- Shifting the sales manager's role to that of coach, teacher, and team member, working together with salespeople to develop a quality sales process

- Integrating the quality process into the whole fabric of how one operates   (©*Quality Abstracts*)

ABSTRACT 2.2
WHAT BUSINESS SCHOOLS AREN'T TEACHING

Bruzzese, Anita
Incentive, March 1991, Vol. 165 Issue 3, pp. 29–31

It was at the University of Chicago that Dr. Deming, as a graduate student in the late 1920s, first encountered the sweatshop working conditions at the famous Bell Labs that influenced forever the course of total quality history. After 60 years, it is finally coming full circle, as outlined in this provocative article by Bruzzese. The author argues that as total quality and teamwork replace traditional management methods in the real world, educators and executives are stressing the urgency for curricula teaching total quality management. Companies such as Motorola and Xerox charge that the majority of business schools do not immerse students in the concept of TQM or give them the people skills needed to motivate a U.S. work force reeling, at the time the article was written, from recession, layoffs, and tough foreign competition. One reason business schools have neglected TQM is that many consider it only a buzzword for traditional subject matter.

Of particular interest are the findings of a panel of business leaders, who recommended ten action items/strategies for introducing total quality in university business schools. Finally, with the advent of the Malcolm Baldrige National Quality Award and the proliferation of total quality seminars, some campuses are beginning to incorporate TQM into their sales and marketing curricula. At the University of Chicago, the LEAD (leadership, education, and development) teamwork program has some 500 students who work in ten groups called cohorts. These groups study and learn together, as well as function as a social network. Although written for business schools, this article has a timely application to the sales profession.

ARTICLE

THE DEMING PRIZE VS. THE BALDRIGE AWARD*

Joseph F. Duffy

The Deming Prize and the Baldrige Award. They're both named after Americans, both very prestigious to win, both standing for a cry for quality in business, both engaged by their share of critics. One is 40 years old; the other a mere four. One resides in an alluring, foreign land; the other on American soil. One is awarded to the paradigm of Japanese business, individuals and international companies; the other to the best of U.S. business. One has grown in what a psychologist might call a mostly safe, nurturing environment; the other amongst a sometimes sour, sometimes sweet, bipolar parental image of government officials, academia and business gurus who seem to critically tug every way possible. One represents a country hailed as the world leader in quality; the other is trying to catch up—trying very hard.

A battle between Japan's Deming Prize and the Malcolm Baldrige National Quality Award would be as good a making for a movie as *Rocky* ever was: You have the older, wiser Japanese, who emanates a wisdom that withstands time, against the younger, quickly maturing American who has an outstanding reputation for being a victorious underdog. Who would win? We took the two awards to center ring, made them don their gloves and have a go.

ROUND 1: HISTORY

Although residing almost half a world apart, the Deming Prize and the Malcolm Baldrige National Quality Award are bonded by influence. After the ravages unleashed during World War II took a ruinous toll on Japan, W. Edwards Deming came to aid this seemingly hopeless land. With his exper-

* This article is reproduced from *Quality Digest*, August 1991, pp. 33–53. In it, the author interviewed four individuals representing organizations with a reputation for being involved in the formation of the Baldrige Award. While no conclusions are drawn, the topics are central to total quality and worthy of debate.

tise in statistical quality control (SQC), Deming helped lift Japan out of the rubble and into the limelight by having Japanese businesses apply SQC techniques.

In 1951, the Union of Japanese Scientists and Engineers (JUSE) created an accolade to award companies that successfully apply companywide quality control (CWQC) based on statistical quality control. In honor of their American quality champion, JUSE named the award the Deming Prize.

Not until 31 years later did a similar prize take root in the United States, mainly due to the efforts of Frank C. Collins, who served as executive director of quality assurance for the Defense Logistics Agency and has formed Frank Collins Associates, Survival Twenty-One—a quality consulting firm; he also serves on the board of directors of the Malcolm Baldrige National Quality Award Consortium.

Collins, after many trips to Japan, based his U.S. quality award idea on the Deming Prize. "That's where I got the idea for the Malcolm Baldrige Award," he explains, "although I never in my wildest dreams expected it to be connected to Malcolm Baldrige."

Malcolm Baldrige, Secretary of Commerce in the Reagan administration, was killed in a rodeo accident in 1987. Reagan chose to honor Baldrige by naming the newly created award after him.

"The original concept was that it would be the National Quality Award," says Collins. "It would be strictly a private sector affair. The government would have no part in it other than the President being the awarder of the recognition."

ROUND 2: PROCESS

The Deming Prize has several categories: the Deming Prize for Individual Person, the Deming Application Prize and the Quality Control Award for Factory. Under the Deming Application Prize are the Deming Application Prize for Small Enterprise and the Deming Application Prize for Division. In 1984, another category was added: The Deming Application Prize to Oversea Companies, which is awarded to non-Japanese companies.

The Deming Application Prize has 10 examination items and is based on CWQC—the Prize's main objective.

A company or division begins the Deming Prize process by submitting an application form to the Deming Prize Committee, along with other pertinent information. Prospective applicants are advised to hold preliminary consultations with the secretariat of the Deming Prize Committee before completing and submitting the application.

After acceptance and notification, applicants must submit a description of quality control practices and a company business prospectus, *in Japanese.*

If successful, the applicant will then be subject to a site visit. If the applicant passes, the Deming Prize is awarded.

Sound easy? Sometimes the applicant's information can fill up to 1,000 pages, and the examination process for U.S. companies is expensive.

The Baldrige Award applicant must first submit an Eligibility Determination Form, supporting documents and $50. Upon approval, the applicant must then submit an application package—running up to 50 pages for small business, 75 pages for a manufacturing or service company—and another fee. Among seven categories, 1,000 points are awarded. No particular score guarantees a site visit.

Each of the three categories—manufacturing, service and small company—are allowed up to two winners only.

ROUND 3: PURPOSE

The American obsession for winning is enormous. From Watergate to Iran-Contra, the American Revolution to Desert Storm, Americans have shown that they love to win no matter what the cost. So it's no wonder that as soon as quality awards and prizes have an impact, they fall under scrutiny. But most critics of these two world-class quality awards think these coveted prizes are mostly pristine in purpose.

Frank Voehl, *Quality Digest* columnist and corporate vice president and general manager of Qualtec Inc., a Florida Power & Light Group company, oversees the implementation of the total quality management programs within Qualtec's client companies. In 1987, Florida Power & Light (FPL) became the first and only U.S. company to win the Deming Prize. Through his work with hundreds of Japanese and U.S. companies, Voehl feels that there are seven reasons why companies quest for the Deming Prize or the Baldrige Award.

"The first general comment that a number of companies that I've talked to in Japan that have applied for the Deming Prize said was, 'We did not apply for the Deming Prize to win but to drive us toward better quality control,'" says Voehl. "Second is applying for and receiving the examination had more meaning than did winning the Prize." Voehl's other five reasons are:

- The audit or the exam itself helped point out many areas of deficiencies and continuous improvement activities that they hadn't noticed.

- Since the Deming Prize dictates a clear goal and time limit, quality control advanced at an extremely rapid rate.

- The company going for the quality award was able to accomplish in one or two years what would normally have taken five or ten years.

- There was a unification of a majority of the employees.

- They were able to communicate with a common language to the whole company. This is where the cultural change takes place.

Robert Peach, who was project manager of the Malcolm Baldrige National Quality Award Consortium for three years and now serves as a senior technical advisor to the administrator, feels the Baldrige Award "is not an award for the sake of the award—it is the 200,000 guidelines and applications that go out that matter, not the handful that actually apply."

And the companies that experiment with and implement the Baldrige criteria, as well as the Deming criteria, can only learn from their endeavor. However, for the companies taking it a step further and committing to win the prize, it isn't Little League, where the profits extracted from learning and having fun are supposed to outweigh the benefits of scoring more points than the other team. The Deming and the Baldrige are the Majors, where going for the award may mean 80-hour work weeks, quick hellos and goodbyes to spouses and missing your child's Little League games.

ROUND 4: GOING TO WAR

So your boss comes up to you and says, "Get ready—we're going for it." How you react may depend on the attitude of your senior-level management and the present quality state of your company. Ken Leach, a senior examiner for the Baldrige Award and founder of Leach Quality Inc., implemented the quality system at Globe Metallurgical—1988 winner of the Baldrige Award's small company category. He says winning the Baldrige was easy because its quality system was in place well before the birth of the Baldrige Award criteria.

"We got into it before Baldrige was even heard of, and we got into it at the impetus of our customers—Ford and General Motors in particular," explains Leach. "So we implemented a number of specific things to satisfy the customer, and you don't have a choice with them—you have to go through their audit system. We did that and did it very well. So that gave us the base to apply for the Baldrige and win it the very first year without trying to redo what we were already doing."

Leach says that because Globe was in such a readied state before the inception of the Baldrige Award, the company did not add any people or spend large sums of money on the implementation of a quality system. In fact, Globe was so advanced in its quality system that Leach claims he took the Baldrige Award application home after work on a Friday and returned it complete by the following Monday.

But even Leach agrees that Globe was exceptional and that not all companies can implement the Baldrige criteria as smoothly as Globe did.

Yokogawa-Hewlett-Packard (YHP) won the Deming Prize in 1982. Unlike Globe and its easy conquest of the Baldrige, YHP claims the quest for the Deming was no Sunday stroll. The company released the following statement in *Measure* magazine:

"Japanese companies compete fiercely to win a Deming Prize. Members of a management team typically work several hundred extra hours each month to organize the statistical charts, reports and exhibits for judging."[1] YHP also says that "audits had all the tension of a championship sports event."[2]

Voehl calls these extra hours and added stresses "pain levels and downside effects" and found that they were typical of most companies going for the Deming Prize. And because the Baldrige Award is a "second generation" of the Deming Prize, Voehl says the Baldrige Award is no exception to possible disruption. He explains that the quest for winning becoming greater than the quest for quality is a "natural thing that occurs within these organizations that you can't really prevent. Senior management focuses in on the journey and the overall effects that will happen as a result of going for the examination and the prize."

Voehl adds, "Getting ready for the examination and the site exams brings a tremendous amount of pressure upon the organizations, whether it's the Deming or the Baldrige, because of the implications that you should be the one department that results in the prize not being brought home."

William Golomski, who is the American Society for Quality Control's representative to JUSE, says deadline time for the award may be a time of pressure.

In the case of the Baldrige, there have been a few companies that hired consultants to help them get ready for a site visit after they've gone through an evaluation by examiners and senior examiners," recalls Golomski. "So I can understand that people who are still being asked to go through role playing for a site visit might get to the point where they'll say, 'Gosh, I don't know if I'm interested as I once was.'"

Collins looks at customers in a dual sense: your internal customers—employees or associates—and your external customers—the people who pay the freight to keep you in business.

"To me," Collins says forcefully, "when you *squeeze* your internal customer to win an award, you're really making a mockery of the whole thing."

But for the companies that take the Baldrige application guidelines and implement them without competing, Peach says the quality goal remains the biggest motivator.

"In my exposure both to applicants and other companies that are using the practice and guidelines independent of applying, I feel that they have the right perspective, that companies identify this as a pretty good practice of what quality practice should be," expounds Peach. "And they're using it that way. That's healthy; that's good."

Deming says it best: "I never said it would be easy; I only said it would work." And this piece of wisdom can pertain to the implementation and competing processes of both the Baldrige Award and the Deming Prize. But although sometimes not easy to pursue, these awards spark many companies to the awareness and benefits of a quality system. But as more companies win the Baldrige, more critics are discussing which accolade—the Baldrige or the Deming—holds more advantages over the other.

ROUND 5: ADVANTAGES VS. DISADVANTAGES

With a U.S. company capturing the Deming Prize, U.S. businesses are no longer without a choice of which world-class quality award to pursue. Motorola, before it went for the Baldrige Award, contemplated which award would improve Motorola's quality best, according to Stewart Clifford, president of Enterprise Media, a documentary film company that specializes in management topics. In a recent interview with Motorola's quality staff, Clifford asked if Motorola was interested in questing for the Deming Prize.

"I asked them the question about if they were looking at applying and going for the Deming," remembers Clifford. "And they said that they felt frankly that while the Deming Prize had some valuable points for them, the reason why they liked the Baldrige Award better was because of its much more intense focus on the customer."

But Voehl claims this is a misconception and that both approaches focus heavily on the customer. "Florida Power & Light really got a lot of negatives from our counselors that we weren't zeroing in on the external and internal customers enough," recalls Voehl. "We had to demonstrate how our quality improvement process was a means of planning and achieving customer satisfaction through TQC."

Section Seven of the Baldrige Award covers total customer satisfaction, and it's worth more points than any other section. In the Deming criteria, total customer satisfaction may seem lost among the need for applicants to document, document, document and use statistical approaches.

One reason Collins says he would compete for the Baldrige instead of the Deming is the Deming's unbending demand to have everything documented. "If you say something, you have to have a piece of paper that covers it," he jokes. "Having worked for the government for 33 years, I see that as a bureaucratic way of doing things. And the Japanese are extremely bureaucratic."

And in an open letter to employees from James L. Broadhead, FPL's chairman and CEO, printed in *Training* magazine, his employees confirm Collins' beliefs: "At the same time, however, the vast majority of the employees with whom I spoke expressed the belief that the mechanics of the QI [quality improvement] process have been overemphasized. They felt that we place too great an emphasis on indicators, charts, graphs, reports and meetings in which documents are presented and indicators reviewed."[3]

However, Collins says that what he likes about the Deming Prize criteria that's missing in the Baldrige Award criteria is the first two examination items of the Deming Prize: policy organization and its operation.

If you want people to understand what you mean by quality, you have to spell it out, you have to define it as policy, explains Collins. As far as objectives go, he remembers asking a Japanese firm what their objectives were. The president of this company said, "First to provide jobs to our company." "How many American firms would say that?" asks Collins. Organization and understanding its operation is extremely important. He says, "Those two criteria are the bedrock foundation of the Deming Prize that makes it somewhat stronger and of greater value than the Malcolm Baldrige National Quality Award."

Another point that may persuade a U.S. company to compete for one of the two awards is cost. All things considered, U.S. companies going for the Deming Application Prize to Oversea Companies seems more costly than U.S. companies competing for the Baldrige Award. Leach describes Globe's venture as very inexpensive: "It doesn't have to cost an arm and a leg for the Baldrige. You don't have to reinvent the wheel of what you're already doing." Peach worked with a small-category company that spent $6,000 on its Baldrige Award venture, and that included the application fee and retaining a technical writer for $1,000.

But these are small companies with 500 employees or fewer. FPL, on the other hand, with about 15,000 employees, spent $1.5 million on its quest for the Deming Prize, according to Neil DeCarlo of FPL's corporate communications. And there are some Baldrige applicants that have spent hundreds of thousands or even millions of dollars on their quality quest, according to *Fortune* magazine.[4]

But no matter how much the Baldrige applicant pays, whether it be $6,000 or millions, it still receives a feedback report as part of the application cost. In comparison, those companies not making it past the first level of the Deming Prize criteria may pay JUSE for counselors, who will come into the company and do a diagnostic evaluation.

Because FPL was a pioneer in the oversea competition, many of the costs that would have otherwise been associated with this award for an overseas company had been waived by JUSE, according to Voehl. But still, FPL dished out $850,000 of that million-and-a-half for counselor fees, says DeCarlo—an amount Voehl claims would be three or four times more if FPL had to hire a U.S. consulting firm.

One of FPL's reasons to go for the Deming award was because in 1986, when it decided to go for a quality award, the Baldrige Award did not yet exist. In fact, what many people, including some FPL critics, don't know is that the company heavily funded the activities leading to the Baldrige Award.

FPL agreed not to try for the Baldrige Award for five years to deter any conflict of interest, says Voehl. Also, FPL had an excellent benchmarking company in Japan's Kansai Electric, which had already won the Deming Prize.

The Deming Prize puts no cap on the number of winners; the Baldrige allows a maximum of two winners for each of the three categories. Leach contests that by putting a limit on the winners, you make the Baldrige Award a more precious thing to win. Peach agrees. "I think there should be a limit," he says. "You just don't want scores of winners to dilute this."

Voehl disagrees. "We should take the caps off," he argues. "I think we'd do a lot more for the award, for the process if we didn't have a win–lose mentality toward it."

ROUND 6: CONTROVERSY

"The Baldrige is having such an impact," asserts Peach, "that now people will take a look at it and challenge. That will always happen—that's our American way." And at four years old, the Baldrige Award has already received a fair share of controversy. One of the most disturbing criticisms aimed at the Baldrige Award comes from Deming himself. Deming called the Baldrige Award "a terrible thing, a waste of industry" in a recent issue of *Automotive News.* The article states: "Among the reasons Deming denounces the award is its measurement of performance and the effects of training with numerical goals, which he cites as 'horrible things.'

"'It's a lot of nonsense,' he said. 'The guidelines for 1991 (make that) very obvious.'"[5]

Golomski says that Deming is unhappy with two parts of the Baldrige guidelines. One is the concept of numerical goals, which Deming believes can cause aberrations within companies. "I don't take quite as strong a stand as Deming does," Golomski explains. "He makes another statement about goals and that far too often, goals are set in the absence of any way of knowing how you're going to achieve these goals."

Leach does not know what to think of "Deming's non-supportive or active disregard for the Baldrige Award." He finds it ironic that "a company could very much have a Deming-type philosophy or a Deming-oriented kind of company and could do quite well in the Baldrige application. I'm sure that Cadillac [1990 Baldrige Award winner] must have had a number of Deming philosophies in place."

Even if Deming is trying to be the burr under the saddle and spark U.S. companies into a quality quest, Leach doesn't think that Deming's "serving the pursuit of quality in general or himself very well by making public statements like that."

But Voehl agrees with some of Deming's points. "Cadillac got severely criticized by the board of trustees of the Baldrige because Cadillac took the Baldrige Award and General Motors tried to use it as a marketing tool," he says. "And that's not the intention. Those sort of things do not do the Baldrige Award any good because it seems like all you're interested in is public relations."

Cadillac has fallen under scrutiny from many critics for taking home the Baldrige Award.

After returning from consulting in Israel, Collins heard that Cadillac had won the Baldrige Award. "I couldn't believe my eyes," Collins exclaims. "Cadillac has gotten so much bad press over the last decade—transmission problems, difficulty with their diesel engines, their service record—a whole number of things that to me when they said Cadillac won it, I said, 'Impossible. They couldn't win it. Somebody's pulling a cruel joke.'"

Deming is not the only quality guru criticizing the Baldrige Award. Philip Crosby says in *Quality Digest* (February 1991) that customers should nominate the companies that compete for the Baldrige, not the companies themselves.

It is difficult to come by harsh criticism about the Deming Prize since few Americans are familiar with it. However, Collins questions FPL's quest for winning as superseding their quest for quality.

"There's no question in my mind that Florida Power & Light's John Hudiburg was intent on leading Florida Power & Light in a blaze of glory," insists Collins. "And money was absolutely no consideration as far as winning the Deming Prize. I don't know what the final tab on it was, but he bought the prize—there's no question about it."

Collins' comments do not go without backing. A number of articles on FPL's quest contain complaints from disgruntled employees who worked long hours to win the Deming Prize.

"If the goal is to win an award, then the cost of winning the award is not worth the award itself," Voehl admits. "The focus needs to be on the outcomes for the organization." And Voehl feels that FPL's quality outcomes very much outweigh the cost put forth.

ROUND 7: CONSULTANTS

With the two awards, there's a big difference in the use of consultants or counselors, as they're called in Japan. In the case of the Deming Prize, a successful applicant uses counselors trained by JUSE throughout the examination, explains Golomski. "For the Baldrige, you're on your own or you use whomever you wish to help you—if you think it's worth it."

Deming Prize Application Checklist: Items and Their Particulars

---

1. Policy

- Policies pursued for management, quality and quality control
- Methods of establishing policies
- Justifiability and consistency of policies
- Utilization of statistical methods
- Transmission and diffusion of policies
- Review of policies and the results achieved
- Relationship between policies and long- and short-term planning

2. Organization and Its Management

- Explicitness of the scopes of authority and responsibility
- Appropriateness of delegations of authority
- Interdivisional cooperation
- Committees and their activities
- Utilization of staff
- Utilization of quality circle activities
- Quality control diagnosis

3. Education and Dissemination

- Education programs and results
- Quality-and-control consciousness, degrees of understanding of quality control
- Teaching of statistical concepts and methods and the extent of their dissemination
- Grasp of the effectiveness of quality control
- Education of related company (particularly those in the same group, subcontractors, consignees and distributors)
- Quality circle activities
- System of suggesting ways of improvements and its actual conditions

4. Collection, Dissemination and Use of Information on Quality

- Collection of external information
- Transmission of information between divisions
- Speed of information transmission (use of computers)
- Data processing, statistical analysis of information and utilization of the results

5. Analysis

- Selection of key problems and themes
- Propriety of the analytical approach
- Utilization of statistical methods
- Linkage with proper technology
- Quality analysis, process analysis
- Utilization of analytical results
- Assertiveness of improvement suggestions

6. Standardization

- Systematization of standards
- Method of establishing, revising and abolishing standards
- Outcome of the establishment, revision or abolition of standards
- Contents of the standards
- Utilization of the statistical methods
- Accumulation of technology
- Utilization of standards

7. Control

- Systems for the control of quality and such related matters as cost and quantity
- Control items and control points
- Utilization of such statistical control methods as control charts and other statistical concepts
- Contribution to performance of quality circle activity
- Actual conditions of control activities
- State of matters under control

8. Quality Assurance

- Procedure for the development of new products and services (analysis and upgrading of quality, checking of design, reliability and other properties)
- Safety and immunity from product liability
- Process design, process analysis and process control and improvement
- Process capability
- Instrumentation, gauging, testing and inspecting
- Equipment maintenance and control of subcontracting, purchasing and services
- Quality assurance system and its audit
- Utilization of statistical methods
- Evaluation and audit of quality
- Actual state of quality assurance

9. Results

- Measurement of results
- Substantive results in quality, services, delivery, time, cost, profits, safety, environment, etc.
- Intangible results
- Measuring for overcoming defects

10. Planning for the Future

- Grasp of the present state of affairs and the concreteness of the plan
- Measures for overcoming defects
- Plans for further advances
- Linkage with long-term plans

"Considering the tremendous number of brochures I get every day," says Collins, "it appears that everybody and his brother is an expert on the Malcolm Baldrige National Quality Award. And my experience tells me that there *ain't* that many experts on the Malcolm Baldrige National Quality Award."

So, are some consultants or counselors using the Baldrige Award to prey on aspiring companies? Voehl says he sees it happening all over and calls it "absolutely preposterous and absurd and unethical."

Voehl compares it to just like everybody jumping on the TQC bandwagon. "Everybody from a one-man or two-man mom-and-pop consulting company to a 1,000-employee consulting arm of the Big 8 seems to be an expert in TQM," he says. "It's like a dog with a rag: They're shaking it and shaking it, and they won't let it go because they see it can mean money to their bottom line. It's giving the consulting field a terrible black eye. It's giving the people who bring in these consultants the expectations clearly that they are going to win the award. These are false expectations, false hopes and false starts. They shouldn't even be looking at winning the award; they should be looking at implementing a quality system that can ensure customer satisfaction."

But there are good reasons to have consultants help you through the Baldrige quest. Leach points out that if a CEO of a company needs to change his or her approach on something, an employee will probably be intimidated to approach the CEO; instead, a consultant can do this. Also a consultant may carry in an objective view that brings different ideas to the company.

Deming Prize counselors, however, have a reputation to guard. That's why Golomski feels FPL had no chance to "buy the Prize."

"The counselor simply wouldn't agree with them that they [FPL] were ready," Golomski argues. "The counselors help an organization improve itself, but if they don't think the company is ready for the big leagues, they simply won't recommend it."

ROUND 8: MODIFICATIONS

The Baldrige Award criteria are constantly modified to meet changing expectations. This is how it grows stronger, becomes more mature. When awarded the Baldrige Award, recipients must share their knowledge of total quality, but Golomski wants to see better ways of technology transfer.

Collins thinks we will probably have a follow-up award similar to the Japan Quality Control Prize—which is awarded to Deming Prize winners if they have improved their quality standards five years after winning the Deming Prize and pass rigorous examination—but not until the Baldrige Award can be further improved.

Peach feels the Baldrige criteria are at a position where modifications will be in smaller increments. He says cycle time might become important enough to be emphasized more.

The possible modifications of the Deming Prize are hard to predict. However, modifications of the Baldrige Award may be based on the Deming Prize's influence.

ROUND 9: SAVING FACE

Junji Noguchi, executive director of JUSE, was contacted for an interview for this article. When he learned of the subject matter—comparing the two world-class quality awards—he declined to answer. He said, "I am sorry I have to reply that I cannot answer your interviews. That is because the contents were not preferable and that they are not what I was expecting."

Noguchi continued, "Awards or prizes in the country have been established under the most suitable standards and methods considering their own background of industries, societies and cultures. We do not understand the meaning of comparing awards in different countries that have different backgrounds."

Noguchi is displaying some of that ancient wisdom and showing a difference in our cultures that even Americans find difficult to explain. Is this why their award has been going strong for 40 years and why the Baldrige Award is a 4-year-old child growing much too fast thanks to our intrinsic desire to slice it up, examine it and try to put it back together more completely than before? Maybe. But as a result, our U.S. quality award will always remain provocative and exciting and keep the people talking. And this is good.

REFERENCES

1. "YHP Teamwork Takes the Prize," Measure (January–February 1983), 3000 Hanover St., Palo Alto, CA 94304, pg. 6.
2. Measures, pg. 6.
3. James L. Broadhead, "The Post-Deming Diet: Dismantling a Quality Bureaucracy," Training, Lakewood Building, 50 S. Ninth St., Minneapolis, MN 55402, pg. 41.
4. Jeremy Main, "Is the Baldrige Overblown?" Fortune (July 1, 1991), Time & Life Building, Rockefeller Center, New York, NY 10020-1393, pg. 62.
5. Karen Passino, "Deming Calls Baldrige Prize 'Nonsense,'" Automotive News (April 1, 1991), 1400 E. Woodbridge, Detroit, MI 48207.

CHAPTER 3

HOUSE OF QUALITY

The House of Quality metaphor used here describes the basic principles and concepts associated with total quality. The House of Quality represents: (1) a *roof*, or superstructure, consisting of the social, technical, and management systems; (2) the *four pillars* of customer satisfaction, continuous improvement, speaking with facts, and respect for people; (3) the *foundation* of four managerial levels—strategy, process, project, and task management; and (4) the *four cornerstones* of mission, vision, values, and goals and objectives. The remainder of this chapter is devoted to discussing each section of the House of Quality, beginning with its foundation and cornerstones—goals, objectives, and planning.

FOUNDATION AND CORNERSTONES

Here is where the quality process begins. Before a firm implements a quality program, it must set forth a vision, along with appropriate goals, objectives, and plans. These activities are the subject of Chapters 4 and 5. What follows is a brief summary of each set of activities.

Vision, Goals, and Objectives

An organization must map out where it wants to go, communicate and sell that vision internally, get ownership of it at all organizational levels, and then execute the vision. According to Bennis and Nanus, "A vision articulates a view of a realistic, credible, attractive future for the organization, a condition that is better in some important ways than what now exists...With a vision, the leader provides the all-important bridge from the present to the future of the organization."[1] A vision must also be understandable, credible, and uplifting. Great leaders often inspire their followers to higher levels of achievement by showing them how their work contributes to some worthwhile outcome. In 1980, Jack Welch, CEO of General Electric, articulated his vision of GE as follows:

> A decade from now I would like General Electric to be perceived as a unique, high-spirited, entrepreneurial enterprise...a company known around the world for its unmatched excellence. I want GE to be the most profitable highly diversified company on earth, with world quality leadership in every one of its product lines.

Strategy Management

Quality planning needs to be expansive in that it must provide a framework from which organization-wide total quality can be established. Strategy must be developed from both a top-down and bottom-up perspective. The process is initiated by senior management yet developed with company-wide involvement through a variety of consensus, team-building, and brainstorming activities. Ownership of the plan at each level in the organization is important in that it provides focus and a common direction.

Process Management

Operations planning involves harmonizing key processes with the needs and expectations of the organization's customers. Companies are increasingly focusing their attention on managing processes rather than departments, studying ways to improve how tasks pass from department to department. Instead of focusing on how much workers produce, the focus should be on how they produce. This requires collaboration among cross-functional areas such as marketing, sales, production, R&D, and technical service, where process and indicator functions are appropriately assigned. The outcomes are a common process and language for documenting and communicating activities and decisions and for realizing less waste and duplication of effort.

Project Management

Project planning involves the effective planning, analyzing, organizing, implementing, and control of resources and activities to successfully launch quality programs. Teams are utilized here to establish both process and policy-related initiatives. Team activities are linked to operational objectives and improvement targets. Teams also identify key success factors including tracking mechanisms, control systems, designated milestones, and various performance indicators. For example, teams might help identify and develop customer and employee satisfaction measures.

Individual Task Management

Personal quality planning gives workers the means to implement the changes produced through total quality efforts. However, companies must first determine how well their employees understand the company strategy and the extent to which they "buy into" and understand the philosophy of total quality. Key objectives, with quality indicators and personal controls, are established. Outcomes of individual task management are committed, empowered, informed workers who sense a connectedness to the organization.

THE PILLARS OF QUALITY

The roof of the House of Quality is supported by four pillars: customer satisfaction, continuous improvement, managing with facts, and respect for people. Each of these is discussed below.

Customer Satisfaction

Allen F. Jacobson, chairman of the board and CEO of the 3M Corporation, says, "I'm convinced that the winners of the 90s will be companies that make quality and customer service an obsession in every single market [in which] they operate." When a greater emphasis is placed on learning and satisfying customer requirements, satisfaction is more easily attained and achieves a more lasting effect. Managing customer satisfaction is a key aspect of total quality management.

What is customer satisfaction? Satisfaction is an emotional response to the difference between what customers *expect* and what they ultimately *receive*. Customers form an expectation of value and act on it. They then learn whether the offer lived up to the value expectation, which affects their satisfaction and the likelihood of their repurchase. Repeat business is the lifeblood of any business. Peter Drucker once stated "that the purpose of a business is to create and keep a customer."

Customer satisfaction is important to a business in the following ways. A satisfied customer:

- Buys more and stays loyal longer

- Buys additional products as the company introduces and upgrades its products

- Speaks favorably about the company and its products

- Pays less attention to competing brands and advertising and is less price sensitive

- Volunteers product/service ideas to the company

- Costs less to serve than new a customer because transactions are routinized

Having determined the importance of customer satisfaction, how can it be managed? Quality function deployment (QFD) provides managers with a powerful tool for closing the gap between design and marketing so that the design properly represents the customers' wants and needs. QFD was pioneered by Mitsubishi Heavy Industry in 1972 and has been used extensively by a variety of industries. QFD applied in a simple but powerful form can help managers develop and refine measures of internal and external performance that relate directly to customer satisfaction. As a fully integrated technique, QFD is a multiphase procedure by which customer needs are translated into technical requirements. In other words, the *voice of the customer* is carried through product design, to manufacturing process development, to distribution, and, finally, to servicing the product. The voice of the customer is incorporated when the firm solicits input (before design) from current or prospective customers.

QFD fully utilizes a team approach, relying heavily on brainstorming, Pareto analysis, cause-and-effect diagrams, and consensus building. A typical QFD team might consist of representatives from marketing, sales, design engineering, and operations, as well as functional participants from customer organizations. QFD team members discuss and analyze products or services by detailing customer requirements, needs, expectations, and perceptions.

How do companies ensure that the voice of the customer is deployed in design, engineering, manufacturing, distribution, and service processes? A technique called customer-driven engineering (CDE) is a market research and measurement model that attempts to capture these processes (see Figure 3.1). (For additional information, see Abstract 3.1 at the end of this chapter.)

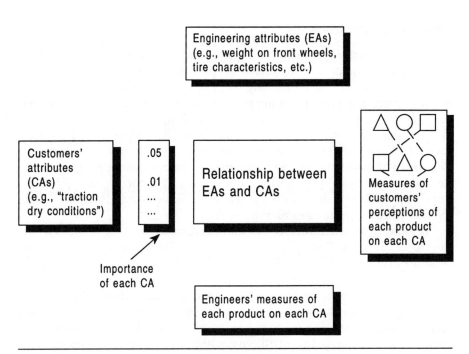

Figure 3.1 Customer-Driven Engineering.

The CDE model attempts to reconcile customer attributes and engineering attributes. The rows in the CDE matrix are customer attributes (CAs), which are defined in the customer's own language. For example, a customer's preferences for the door of an automobile might include being "easy to open" or "stays open on a hill." The columns in the CDE matrix are the engineering attributes (EAs) that represent physical characteristics. The EA should be measurable and directly affect the customer's perceptions. Returning to the example of an automobile, an EA for the car door might be the "foot pounds of energy required to close the door." It should be noted that an EA might affect more than one CA. For example, the foot-pounds of energy used to construct a car door will also affect road noise and leaking when it rains.

In sum, QFD is an effective tool that leads to the following benefits:

- Improved lead time—concept to market

- Flexibility—adapting to changing market needs

- Accurate, reliable measures of product performance

- Improved competitive analysis

Continuous Improvement

Just as customer satisfaction is supported by strategy management, so is continuous improvement supported by process management. Continuous improvement, or *kaizen*, means ongoing improvement that involves everyone in the organization, including both managers and workers. In business, everything changes, including customers and suppliers; therefore, key marketing processes (such as product development, sales, delivery, and support) must change accordingly. The first goal of continuous improvement is to develop processes that are reliable; that is, each time they produce the desired output with a minimum of variation. A second goal of process improvement is to redesign the process to produce output that better suits the customer's current or evolving requirements.

Several tools are useful for planning processes. Deming and Shewhart developed the *Plan, Do, Check, Act*, or PDCA, cycle. The PDCA cycle represents a never-ending cycle of improvement that occurs in all phases of the organization (see Figure 3.2).

The first step, *plan*, involves asking key questions such as what changes are needed, what results are desired, what obstacles need to be overcome, and, perhaps, what information is needed to address these questions. Environmental scanning and competitive analysis can provide direction during this stage by revealing opportunities or strategic "gaps." *Do* is the implementation of a small change or pilot test to provide data for later action. For example, *test marketing* is often utilized by companies introducing new products to get an initial read on the market. *Check* involves measurement and assessment of the change introduced as a result of the *plan* phase. Finally, the *act* step involves asking whether the data confirm the intended plan, whether other variables are influencing the plan, and whether the risks in proceeding are necessary and worthwhile.

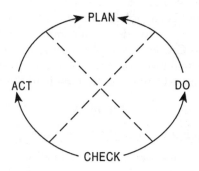

Figure 3.2 Plan, Do, Check, Act.

Another tool that is useful in the continuous improvement process is a flowchart. A flowchart is simply a graphic means of depicting the steps in a process. For example, a flowchart can be developed to show a schematic for any process in an organization. The steps in issuing tickets to an airline traveler are diagrammed in Figure 3.3.

Customers usually expect firms that provide service to understand the full extent of the relationship they have with that provider. The highly fragmented nature of a service activity is composed of a series of discrete activities performed by numerous players. Consequently, customers can easily get lost in the system and feel that nobody knows who they are or what they need. Flowcharting service delivery is a very useful approach to help in understanding how all the pieces fit together. Finally, flowcharting the service process from the customer's perspective enables the service provider to isolate the various "moments of truth" and, hence, look for ways to improve the process.

Speak with Facts

The third pillar of the House of Quality deals with basing decisions on solid research rather than simply on intuition, hunches, or organizational politics. Successful planning of marketing strategies requires information— information about potential target markets and their likely responses to marketing mixes as well as information about competitors.

The job of marketing research is to help managers *understand the voice of the customer*. To help increase the value of market research to managers, the following should be kept in mind:

- Keep key executives in touch with customers.

- Use observation research and intelligence gathering, not just question-naire research. For example, use "listening posts" such as conducting focus groups, listening at trade shows, reading customer complaint let-ters, and using mystery shoppers.

- Practice "backward" marketing research. Start by identifying the key marketing decisions to be reached and work backwards to specify the marketing data and research useful in making those decisions.[2]

Another useful type of research involves carrying out a *customer value analysis*. The purpose of a customer value analysis is to identify the benefits that customers in a target market segment want and how they perceive the relative value of a competitor's offering. In other words, a firm should consider conducting this type of analysis when searching for a competitive advantage. The major steps in customer value analysis include:

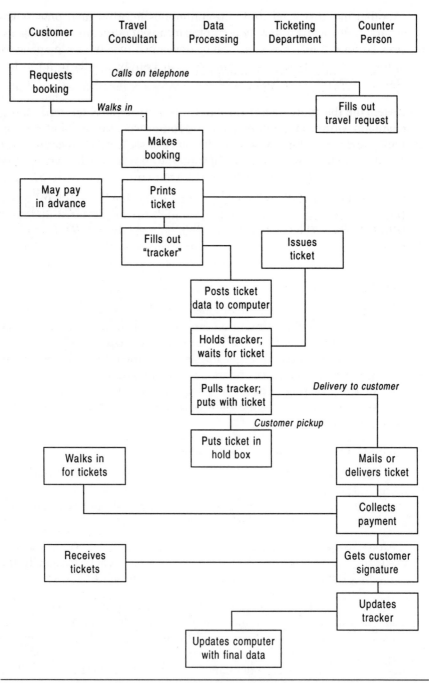

Figure 3.3 Service Flowchart. (Source: Karl Albrecht, *Service Within*, Dow Jones-Irwin, Chicago, 1990.)

1. **Identify the major attributes that customers value.** Ask customers what functions and performance levels they look for in choosing a product and its vendors.

2. **Assess the quantitative importance of the different attributes.** Ask customers to supply both ratings and rankings of the different attributes.

3. **Assess the company's and its competitors' performance on the different customer values against their rated importance.** Ask customers how they view the company and each competitor's performance on each attribute. Ideally, the company's performance should be rated high on those attributes that customers value most.

4. **Examine how customers in a specific segment rate the company's performance against a specific major competitor on an attribute-by-attribute basis.** The key to gaining a competitive advantage is to examine how the company's offer exceeds the competition's offer on the important attributes, whereby the company can charge a premium for its products.

5. **Monitor customer values over time.** Although fairly stable in the short run, customer values shift with changes in technology and desired features. For example, safety has become more salient to the automobile buyer during the 1990s.[3]

Respect For People

The workplace has changed dramatically since the end of World War II. Work at that time consisted of a series of simple, manual tasks performed mostly by unskilled laborers. Companies were organized in a task-oriented, hierarchical structure, fashioned after the military. Authority was top-down, where the boss assigned tasks and then closely monitored those who performed them.

Contrast that with today's workers, who are better educated, are more highly skilled, enjoy working autonomously, and desire involvement in their work. Thus, today's worker wants to be empowered instead of controlled.

Empowerment encompasses a variety of actions that a firm can take to give employees a greater sense of control and participation in the events and decisions that affect their business life. According to a study conducted by KPMG Peat Marwick, the three most common steps in developing effective empowerment are (1) authorizing employees to respond to customer requirements, (2) enhancing employee authority to act when quality standards may be compromised, and (3) decreasing the required levels of approval necessary to make operational decisions. Respect for people can be achieved by following some simple guidelines:

- Create a sense of purpose in the workplace so that people are motivated to do their best.

- Keep people informed and involved, and show them how they are a part of the bigger picture.

- Educate and develop people so that everyone is the best that they can be at what they do.

- Help people communicate well so that they can perform their jobs with peak effectiveness.

- Delegate responsibility and authority downward so that people are not just doing what they are told, but are taking the initiative to try to make things work better.[4]

First, empowerment involves *alignment*. Employees need to understand the vision and mission of the organization. Employees will be more committed when they clearly understand the direction in which the company is moving and their role in it.

Next, empowerment requires *capability*. Employees must possess the skills and knowledge to do their jobs, yet the company must also supply the necessary resources so that employees can perform in a customer-friendly manner.

Finally, empowerment requires *mutual trust*. Trust is a two-way street; employees need to trust management and must also feel that management trusts them. As a leading author on leadership and management explained, "Change occurs in two primary ways: through trust and truth or through dissent and conflict...positive change requires trust, clarity, and participation.[5]

THE ROOF: SYSTEMS AND TOTAL QUALITY

The roof of the quality superstructure is made up of the social system, the technical system, and the management systems. Each of these is discussed below.

The Social System

The social system consists of characteristics such as the organizational culture, interrelationships among individuals and groups (both formal and informal), and the behavior patterns exhibited by members of the organization, including roles and communication. The social system may impact the organization in areas such as motivation, creativity, innovativeness, and teamwork.

Social system activities exert both positive and negative influences, planned or not. Organizational values may differ considerably across various classes of workers. For example, a bank teller may not share the bank president's opinion concerning how the bank's image is perceived by the local community.

A social system must be developed that fosters customer satisfaction, continuous improvement, managing with facts, and a genuine respect for people. This involves change, which is often viewed with suspicion in many companies. The prevailing attitude is why rewrite the rules if you are already winning the game. Yet businesses in the 1990s will succeed or fail on the basis of their ability to anticipate and creatively respond to rapid change.

Truly successful companies change when the cost of remaining the same becomes greater than the benefit of an alternative condition. For example, in 1979, Hewlett-Packard set a company-wide goal of a tenfold improvement in quality within ten years. The goal was met. Hewlett-Packard achieved this remarkable result by driving continuous and rapid improvement, establishing customer-focused organizational units, developing workers with multiple skills, and offering expanded reward and recognition programs.

A fishbone, or cause-and-effect, diagram of the social system characteristics that help build total quality organizations is presented in Figure 3.4. According to the diagram, there are six areas in the social system that need to be managed in order to create a quality culture in an organization: (1) environment, (2) methods, (3) organizational structure, (4) product/service, (5) people, and (6) a TQM mindset. From a product/service perspective, quality can be planned for and improved by obtaining customer input in product/service development. Customer focus groups are an excellent means of including the voice of the customer in product or service planning.

The Technical System

The technical system is concerned with measuring quality and applying various tools to improve it. The technical system deals with the flow of work through the organization, guided by its mission and service to the customer. The core elements of the technical system in most organizations include:

- Decision-making processes
- Job definitions and responsibilities
- Availability and use of information
- Pursuit of standardization
- Number and type of work steps

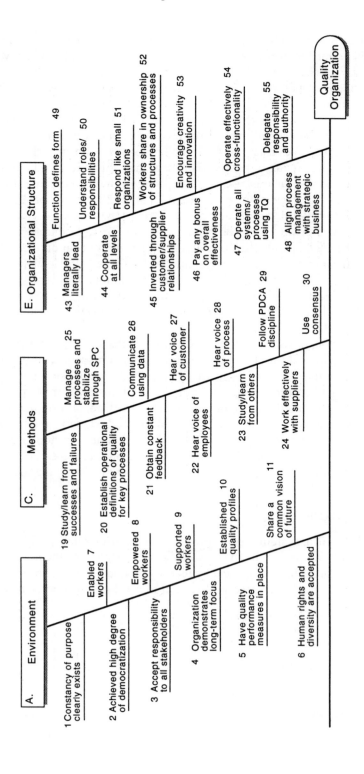

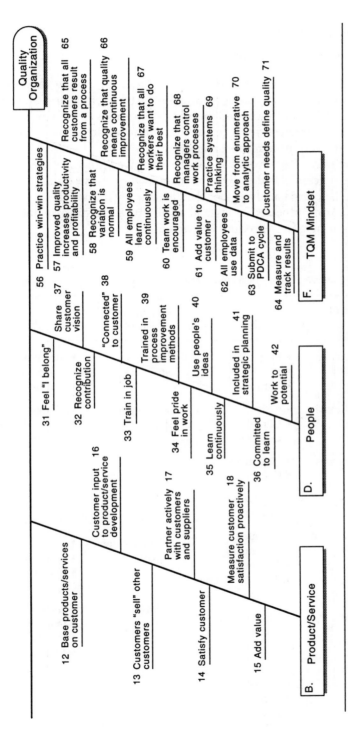

Figure 3.4 Social System Characteristics of a Total Quality Organization (Fishbone Diagram).

- Machine/person interface

- Accumulation of technology

The benefits that accrue from analyzing and improving the technical system include reduced waste, less variation, faster learning, less down time, fewer bottlenecks, and increased employee control over the work process. Yet perhaps the greatest result comes from improved customer satisfaction through faster and more responsive service.

An example of how quality can be improved through the technical system is a process called design for manufacture and assembly (DFMA). DFMA is a structured analysis tool used to simplify design, decrease assembly costs, improve product quality and reliability, and reduce operation time required to bring a new product to market.

Table 3.1 Twelve Angles of Management Quality

Management factor	Subfactor	Management factor	Subfactor
Corporate history	• Past • Present • Future	Business structure	• Business fields • Business mix • Market standing
Corporate climate	• Core • Climate • Culture	Management resources	• Money • Materials • Information • People
Strategic alliances	• Objectives • Coherence	Management design	• System • Organization • Authority • Responsibility
Channels	• Suppliers • Buyers		
Management cycle	• Planning • Organizing • Leading • Implementation • Control	Management functions	• Decision making • Interrelationships • Quality
Environment	• Economic • Societal • Global	Management performance	• Growth • Scale • Stability • Profits • Market share
Management targets	• Inputs • Markets • Technologies • Products		

The Management System

The management system provides a framework for introducing and coordinating policies, procedures, practices, and leadership for the organization. The management system is operationalized at four levels: strategy, process, project, and individual task management. Each of these areas represents the foundation of the quality superstructure and each was discussed earlier in the chapter.

Focusing on the innovation of management may represent the next evolution of managing quality. Total integrated management (TIM) is a method that helps drive this innovation. There are a number of factors, or "angles," that are critical to the success of TIM. The management factors and the subfactors that comprise the twelve angles of management quality are presented in Table 3.1.[6] The management cycle is the most important factor among the twelve management factors because the level of quality present in the management cycle will either elevate or detract from the quality levels of all the other factors.

Before an organization can build the total quality infrastructure described in this chapter, it must assess the key components of its infrastructure. Exercise 3.1, which appears at the end of the chapter, is designed to assist a firm in diagnosing the emphasis which it currently places on the key drivers of total quality.

DISCUSSION QUESTIONS

1. What is customer satisfaction and what is its long-term impact on a business?

2. How can a customer value analysis be used by firms when searching for a competitive advantage?

3. Choose a product or service in a particular industry and devise an action plan for obtaining customer input and feedback. How would data generated by such a plan be used for process improvement?

4. Choose a product or service and list four or five characteristics that you as a customer would expect to be offered. Now rank these characteristics in order of importance.

ENDNOTES

1.   Bennis, W. and Nanus, B. *Leaders*, Harper and Row, New York, 1985, pp. 89–90.

2. Hodock, C. "The Decline and Fall of Marketing Research in Corporate America." *Marketing Research,* June 1991, pp. 12–22; Adressen, A. "Backward Marketing Research." *Harvard Business Review,* May–June 1985, pp. 176–182.
3. Porter, M. *Competitive Advantage,* The Free Press, New York, 1985, p. 225.
4. Lewis, R. and Smith, D. *Total Quality in Higher Education,* St. Lucie Press, Delray Beach, Fla., 1994, pp. 99–100.
5. Bennis, Warren. *Why Leaders Can't Lead,* Jossey-Bass, San Francisco, 1990, p. 27.
6. Yahagi, S. "After Product Quality in Japan: Management Quality." *National Productivity Review,* Autumn 1992, p. 503.

EXERCISE

EXERCISE 3.1
TOTAL QUALITY MANAGEMENT (TQM) INVENTORY*

Gaylord Reagan

Often the process of total quality management (TQM) serves to differentiate successful organizations from unsuccessful ones. After inventing and then discarding the principles of TQM approximately five decades ago, American managers once again are learning *continuous improvement* for the quality of products and services they offer to internal as well as external customers. The basic criteria of TQM are simultaneously very simple and highly complex; however, they can be mastered by committed organizations. A necessary first step in learning about and implementing TQM is to assess the emphasis that an organization places on these eight basic criteria.

THE INSTRUMENT

Theoretical Framework

Total quality management is not a short-term, morale-boosting and efficiency-improvement program. In fact, TQM is not a "program" at all. It can be defined best as a strategic, integrated management philosophy based on the concept of achieving ever-higher levels of customer satisfaction. These higher levels are a result of the emphasis that an organization's senior managers place on using participative management, total employee involvement, and statistical methods to make continual improvements in their organization's processes.

The Total Quality Management (TQM) Inventory is based on the eight criteria identified by the President's Council on Management Improvement, the Office of Personnel Management, the Federal Quality Institute, and the Office of Management and Budget. In turn, specific content of the criteria is based on the following models: Deming's (1982) statistical process control, Juran's (1986) project-by-

---

* Reproduced from *The 1992 Annual: Developing Human Resources*, by J.W. Pfeiffer (Ed.). Copyright ©1992 by Pfeiffer & Co., San Diego, California. Used with permission. This instrument is based on the Federal Quality Institute's *Federal Total Quality Management Handbook 2: Criteria and Scoring Guidelines for the President's Award for Quality and Productivity Improvement*, Office of Personnel Management, Washington, D.C., 1990.

project continuous improvement, Crosby's (1986) zero defects, and Feigenbaum's (1983) total quality control.* Following are the eight TQM criteria:

Criterion 1: Top Management Leadership and Support. This criterion examines upper management's role in building and maintaining a total quality environment. It focuses on the following factors: visible senior management involvement in TQM; existence of written policies and strategies supporting TQM; allocation of human and other resources to TQM activities; plans for removing barriers to TQM implementation; and creation of a value system emphasizing TQM.

Criterion 2: Strategic Planning. This criterion probes the level of emphasis placed on total quality during the organization's planning process. The focus here is on the existence of strategic TQM goals and objectives, the use of hard data in planning for TQM, the involvement of customers and employees in planning for TQM, and the injection of TQM into the organization's budget process.

Criterion 3: Focus on the Customer. This criterion examines the degree to which the organization stresses customer service. It focuses on assessing customer requirements, implementing customer satisfaction feedback mechanisms, handling customer complaints, empowering employees to resolve customer problems, and facilitating the communication processes required to support these activities.

Criterion 4: Employee Training and Recognition. This criterion explores the extent to which the organization develops and rewards behaviors that support total quality. It centers on the existence of a training strategy designed to support TQM, the use of needs assessments to identify areas in which TQM training is needed, the allocation of funds for TQM training, the assessment of the effectiveness of TQM training, and the recognition of employee accomplishments.

Criterion 5: Employee Empowerment and Teamwork. This criterion delves into the breadth and depth of total quality involvement that organizational members are encouraged to demonstrate. Its focus is on increasing employee involvement in TQM activities, implementing feedback systems through which organizations can become aware of employee concerns, increasing employee authority to act independently, identifying ways to increase employee satisfac-

---

* Through mid-1991, four publications on these topics have been published by the Federal Quality Institute; another eight are scheduled to be released at later dates. Following are the titles published through mid-1991: (1) *How to Get Started: Implementing Total Quality Management—Part 1*; (2) *How to Get Started: Appendix—Part 1A*; (3) *Criteria and Scoring Guidelines: The President's Award for Quality and Productivity Improvement*; and (4) *Introduction to Total Quality Management in the Federal Government*.

tion, and using data to evaluate human resource management practices within the organization.

Criterion 6: Quality Measurement and Analysis. This criterion scrutinizes the organization's use of data within a total quality system. The focus here is on using hard data to assess TQM results and on using the results of that assessment to identify changes needed to achieve higher levels of customer satisfaction.

Criterion 7: Quality Assurance. This criterion looks at the organization's use of total quality practices in connection with the products and services provided to customers. It focuses on implementing new methods for achieving greater customer satisfaction, using rigorous scientific methods to certify that the new methods actually achieve their intended purposes, and assessing the outcomes of the new methods.

Criterion 8: Quality and Productivity Improvement Results. This criterion explores the actual results produced by the organization's total quality efforts. Its focus is on identifying specific instances in which the organization's TQM efforts over a long period of time (three to six years) actually resulted in higher levels of customer satisfaction in areas such as timeliness, efficiency, and effectiveness.

Extensive detail on the eight criteria can be found in the Federal Quality Institute's publication *Criteria and Scoring Guidelines for the President's Award for Quality and Productivity Improvement* (Federal Quality Institute, 1990).* As the publication's editors point out (p. vi), "Other management systems may contain certain elements of these criteria, [but] it is the combination of all eight that distinguishes TQM."

Reliability and Validity

The Total Quality Management (TQM) Inventory is designed for use as an action–research tool rather than as a rigorous data-gathering instrument. Applied in this manner, the inventory has demonstrated a high level of face validity when used with audiences ranging from executive managers to nonmanagement personnel.

Administration

The following suggestions will be helpful to the facilitator who administers the instrument:

1. Before respondents complete the inventory, discuss briefly the concept of TQM. It is important that respondents understand that TQM is not another faddish, short-term productivity improvement "program." Instead, TQM is a strategic, culture-based commitment to meeting customer requirements and

* The President's Award is the United States Federal government's version of its private sector's Malcolm Baldrige National Quality Awards and Japan's Deming Prizes.

to continually improving products and services. The foundations on which that commitment is built can be found in the eight criteria forming the core of the instrument. Similar criteria are included in Japan's Deming Prizes and in the United States' Baldrige Award (Walton, 1986).

2. Distribute copies of the TQM Inventory Theory Sheet. Review the descriptions of the eight criteria to ensure that respondents understand the focus of each one. Explanatory remarks should be simple and to the point. The purpose of this step is to clarify the meanings of the criteria, not to encourage respondents to initiate a premature discussion of their organizations' placements on criterion ranking scales.

3. Distribute copies of the instrument and read the instructions aloud as the respondents follow.

4. Instruct the respondents to read each of the six statements listed under each criterion. Each respondent chooses the statement that best describes how he or she perceives the present situation in his or her organization. Choices range from exceptionally strong performance to total absence of performance for each criterion.

5. Request that the respondents wait to score the instrument until everyone has completed it.

Scoring

Each respondent should be given a copy of the TQM Inventory Scoring Sheet. The left column of the scoring sheet lists the eight criteria of total quality management. The right column of the scoring sheet lists point values for each of the six possible responses to each criterion. Respondents simply transfer their answers from the TQM Inventory to the appropriate rows and columns on the scoring sheet. After responses have been circled for all eight criteria, each respondent totals the circled point values to obtain an overall score for the inventory.

Interpretation and Processing

When respondents finish determining their overall scores on the inventory, the facilitator should distribute the TQM Interpretation Sheet. The Interpretation Sheet consists of five score categories ranging from "world-class TQM" to "absolutely no interest in learning about TQM." Each category offers brief guidelines for preparing appropriate TQM goals.

The numbers listed in the Response Categories/Points section of the scoring sheet also represent the approximate weights attached to each individual TQM criterion by the Federal Quality Institute's President's Award. For example, note than an organization's score for "Quality and Productivity Improvement Results" is much more central to successful TQM implementation efforts than its score on a criterion such as "Employee Training and Recognition"—although it is difficult to see how the former could be achieved without the presence of the latter. Respondents may wish to refer back to "A" statements for each criterion as bases for discussing "world-class" TQM activities.

Some groups find it useful to prepare a copy of the scoring sheet on a newsprint flip chart. In this case, the facilitator polls the individual respondents as to the option letter they selected for each criterion. Their differing perceptions then form the basis for discussion. In order to provide respondents with group norms, it may also be useful to compute average scores for each of the eight criteria and for the overall score.

Uses of the Instrument

The TQM Inventory is designed to accomplish the following objectives:

1. To offer the respondents the opportunity to identify and to define eight key criteria of TQM

2. To differentiate the importance of each criterion

3. To provide a framework for respondents to assess an organization's current emphasis on each of the eight criteria

4. To initiate discussions about the adequacy of the organization's level of activity for each of the eight criteria

5. To stimulate planning designed to increase the organization's level of TQM involvement

Therefore, the TQM Inventory can be used to diagnose the organization's readiness for involvement in total quality management. The instrument can focus on perceptions of the overall organization or of individual units or departments within the organization.

REFERENCES

Crosby, P.B. (1986). *Quality Is Free.: The Art of Making Quality Certain*. New York: New American Library.

Deming, W.E. (1982). *Out of the Crisis*. Cambridge, MA: Massachusetts Institute of Technology Center for Advanced Engineering Study.

Federal Quality Institute. (1990). *Federal Total Quality Management Handbook 2: Criteria and Scoring Guidelines for the President's Award for Quality and Productivity Improvement*. Washington, D.C.: Office of Personnel Management.

Feigenbaum, A.V. (1983). *Total Quality Control*. New York: McGraw-Hill.

Juran, J.M. (1989). *Juran on Leadership for Quality: An Executive Handbook*. New York: The Free Press.

Walton, M. (1986). *The Deming Management Method*. New York: Perigree Books.

TOTAL QUALITY MANAGEMENT (TQM) INVENTORY THEORY SHEET

The Total Quality Management (TQM) Inventory is based on eight criteria identified by the President's Council on Management Improvement, the Office of Personnel Management, the Federal Quality Institute, and the Office of Management and Budget. Following are the eight TQM criteria:

Criterion 1: Top Management Leadership and Support

This criterion examines upper management's role in building and maintaining a total quality environment. It focuses on the following factors: visible senior management involvement in TQM; existence of written policies and strategies supporting TQM; allocation of human and other resources to TQM activities; plans for removing barriers to TQM implementation; and creation of a value system emphasizing TQM.

Criterion 2: Strategic Planning

This criterion probes the level of emphasis placed on total quality during the organization's planning process. The focus here is on the existence of strategic TQM goals and objectives, the use of hard data in planning for TQM, the involvement of customers and employees in planning for TQM, and the injection of TQM into the organization's budget process.

Criterion 3: Focus on the Customer

This criterion examines the degree to which the organization stresses customer service. It focuses on assessing customer requirements, implementing customer satisfaction feedback mechanisms, handling customer complaints, empowering employees to resolve customer problems, and facilitating the communication processes required to support these activities.

Criterion 4: Employee Training and Recognition

This criterion explores the extent to which the organization develops and rewards behaviors that support total quality. It centers on the existence of a training strategy designed to support TQM, the use of needs assessments to identify areas in which TQM training is needed, the allocation of funds for TQM training, the assessment of the effectiveness of TQM training, and the recognition of employee accomplishments.

Criterion 5: Employee Empowerment and Teamwork

This criterion delves into the breadth and depth of total quality involvement that organizational members are encouraged to demonstrate. Its focus is on increasing employee involvement in TQM activities, implementing feedback systems through which organizations can become aware of employee concerns, increasing employee authority to act independently, identifying ways to increase employee satisfaction, and using data to evaluate human resource management practices within the organization.

Criterion 6: Quality Measurement and Analysis

This criterion scrutinizes the organization's use of data within a total quality system. The focus here is on using hard data to assess TQM results and on using the results of that assessment to identify changes needed to achieve higher levels of customer satisfaction.

Criterion 7: Quality Assurance

This criterion looks at the organization's use of total quality practices in connection with the products and services provided to customers. It focuses on implementing new methods for achieving greater customer satisfaction, using rigorous scientific methods to certify that the new methods actually achieve their intended purposes, and assessing the outcomes of the new methods.

Criterion 8: Quality and Productivity Improvement Results

This criterion explores the actual results produced by the organization's total quality efforts. Its focus is on identifying specific instances in which the organization's TQM efforts over a long period of time (three to six years) actually resulted in higher levels of customer satisfaction in areas such as timeliness, efficiency, and effectiveness.

TOTAL QUALITY MANAGEMENT (TQM) INVENTORY

Gaylord Reagan

Instructions: For each of the eight total quality management criteria listed below, choose the statement that best describes the present situation in your organization. Write the letter of that statement in the blank to the left of each criterion.

_____ **Criterion 1: Top Management Leadership and Support**

A. Top managers are directly and actively involved in activities that foster quality.

B. Top managers participate in quality leadership activities.

C. Most top managers support activities that foster quality.

D. Many top managers are supportive of and interested in quality improvement.

E. Some top managers are beginning to tentatively support activities that foster quality.

F. No top management support exists for activities involving quality.

_____ **Criterion 2: Strategic Planning**

A. Long-term goals for quality improvement have been established across the organization as part of the overall strategic planning process.

B. Long-term goals for quality improvement have been established across most of the organization.

C. Long-term goals for quality improvement have been established in key parts of the organization.

D. Short-term goals for quality improvement have been established in parts of the organization.

E. The general goals of the organization contain elements of quality improvement.

F. No quality improvement goals have been established anywhere in the organization.

_____ **Criterion 3: Focus on the Customer**

A. A variety of effective and innovative methods are used to obtain customer feedback on all organizational functions.

B. Effective systems are used to obtain feedback from all customers of major functions.

C. Systems are in place to solicit customer feedback on a regular basis.

D. Customer needs are determined through random processes rather than by using systematic methods.

E. Complaints are the major methods used to obtain customer feedback.

F. No customer focus is evident.

_____ **Criterion 4: Employee Training and Recognition**

A. The organization is implementing a systematic employee training and recognition plan that is fully integrated into the overall strategic quality planning process.

B. The organization is assessing what employee training and recognition is needed, and the results of that assessment are being evaluated periodically.

C. An employee training and recognition plan is beginning to be implemented.

D. An employee training and recognition plan is under active development.

E. The organization has plans to increase employee training and recognition.

F. There is no employee training and there are no systems for recognizing employees.

_____ **Criterion 5: Employee Empowerment and Teamwork**

A. Innovative, effective employee empowerment and teamwork approaches are used.

B. Many natural work groups are empowered to constitute quality improvement teams.

C. A majority of managers support employee empowerment and teamwork.

D. Many managers support employee empowerment and teamwork.

E. Some managers support employee empowerment and teamwork.

F. There is no support for employee empowerment and teamwork.

_____ **Criterion 6: Quality Measurement and Analysis**

A. Information about quality and timeliness of all products and services is collected from internal and external customers and from suppliers.

B. Information about quality and timeliness is collected from most internal and external customers and from most suppliers.

C. Information about quality and timeliness is collected from major internal and external customers and from major suppliers.

D. Information about quality and timeliness is collected from some internal and external customers.

E. Information about quality and timeliness is collected from one or two external customers.

F. There is no system for measuring and analyzing quality.

_____ **Criterion 7: Quality Assurance**

A. All products, services, and processes are designed, reviewed, verified, and controlled to meet the needs and expectations of internal and external customers.

B. A majority of products, services, and processes are designed, reviewed, verified, and controlled to meet the needs and expectations of internal and external customers.

C. Key products, services, and processes are designed, reviewed, verified, and controlled to meet the needs and expectations of internal and external customers.

D. A few products and services are designed, reviewed, and controlled to meet the needs of internal and external customers.

E. Products and services are controlled to meet internally developed specifications that may or may not include customer input.

F. There is no quality assurance in this organization.

_____ **Criterion 8: Quality and Productivity Improvement Results**

A. Most significant performance indicators demonstrate exceptional improvement in quality and productivity over the past five years.

B. Most significant performance indicators demonstrate excellent improvement in quality and productivity over the past five years.

C. Most significant performance indicators demonstrate good improvement in quality and productivity.

D. Most significant performance indicators demonstrate improving quality and productivity in several areas.

E. There is evidence of some quality and productivity improvement in one or more areas.

F. There is no evidence of quality and productivity improvement in any areas.

TOTAL QUALITY MANAGEMENT (TQM) INVENTORY SCORING SHEET

To determine your scores on the inventory, complete the following three steps:

1. For each of the *Total Quality Management Criteria* listed in the left column, find the letter under the heading labeled *Response Categories/Points* that corresponds to the one you chose on the questionnaire.

2. Then circle the one- or two-digit *Point* number that corresponds to the letter you chose.

3. Finally, add up the points circled for all eight criteria to determine your *Overall Score*.

Note: The numbers you are about to circle correspond to the relative weights attached to individual Quality/Productivity Criteria in the President's Award.* Therefore, in addition to helping to score your responses, the points also identify the categories that are more significant than others. For example, scores on Criterion 8 (Quality and Productivity Improvement Results) are better indicators of an organization's orientation toward quality and productivity than are its scores on Criterion 4 (Employee Training and Recognition).

Total Quality Management Criteria	Response Categories/ Points					
	A	B	C	D	E	F
1. Top Management Leadership and Support	20	16	12	8	4	0
2. Strategic Planning	15	12	9	6	3	0
3. Focus on the Customer	40	32	24	16	8	0
4. Employee Training and Recognition	15	12	9	6	3	0
5. Employee Empowerment and Teamwork	15	12	9	6	3	0
6. Quality Measurement and Analysis	15	12	9	6	3	0
7. Quality Assurance	30	24	18	12	6	0
8. Quality and Productivity Improvement Results	50	40	30	20	10	0
SCORES FOR CHOICE CATEGORIES:	—	—	—	—	—	—
OVERALL SCORE:	—	(Range: 9–200)				

TOTAL QUALITY MANAGEMENT (TQM) INVENTORY INTERPRETATION SHEET

160–200 points: An overall score in this range indicates a "world-class" organization with a deep, long-term, and active commitment to improving quality and productivity. At this level, goals should focus on the challenge of maintaining gains as well as seeking ways to attain even higher levels of quality and productivity.

120–159 points: An overall score in this range indicates than an organization with a sound, well-organized philosophy of quality and productivity improvement is

* This instrument is based on the Federal Quality Institute's *Federal Total Quality Management Handbook 2: Criteria and Scoring Guidelines for the President's Award for Quality and Productivity Improvement*, Washington, D.C.: Office of Personnel Management, 1990.

beginning to emerge. At this level, goals should focus on fully implementing a sound TQM effort while continuing to build on current levels of excellence.

80–119 points: An overall score in this range indicates an organization that is starting to learn about and plan quality and productivity improvements. At this level, goals should focus on moving from the planning stages to actually implementing a TQM effort in order to gain the necessary hands-on experience.

40–79 points: An overall score in this range indicates an organization that is vaguely aware of quality and productivity improvement but has no plans to learn about or implement such activity. Scores at this level approach the danger point; if long-term organizational viability is sought, progress must be made quickly. Goals should focus on strongly encouraging top managers to learn more about TQM while reexamining their assumptions about possible contributions that the process can make to the health of their organization.

0–39 points: An overall score in this range indicates an organization that currently has neither an awareness of nor an involvement with quality and productivity improvement programs. Unless an organization has an absolute, invulnerable monopoly on extremely valuable products or services, this level represents a de facto decision to go out of business. Goals should focus on an emergency turnaround. Learning about total quality management must occur at an accelerated rate, and plans to bring quality and productivity consciousness to the organization must be implemented immediately.

PROFILE

BOEING

Before Boeing considered the introduction of its new wide-bodied 777-200 aircraft, it asked its airline customers and suppliers to help design the plane from scratch. Areas of common concern and unique differences were identified early in the design process by the participating airlines. Although Boeing had always asked airlines what they wanted in a plane, asking them to join design teams was hotly debated. It was tough enough making decisions within Boeing; adding outsiders could mean the plane would never get off the ground. Airline representatives contributed more than 1000 design changes.

The designing of the new Boeing aircraft was done completely on a computer using CAD technology. Its entire design in three dimensions was drawn on computer screens, and some of the parts were actually crafted from digital information. This "digital sharing" allowed detailed design work on the fuselage, performed by Boeing's Japanese partners, to be viewed almost instantaneously by their counterparts in Washington. This process has resulted in 50 percent fewer changes and errors, while avoiding the costly full-scale mockups used with earlier designed planes.

ABSTRACT

ABSTRACT 3.1
MARKETING'S LEAD ROLE IN TOTAL QUALITY

O'Neal, Charles R. and LaFief, William C.
Industrial Marketing Management, May 1992, pp. 133–143

The marketing concept—to determine precisely the needs of the customer and effectively involve and focus all organizational units to meet those needs—should be the responsibility of the entire organization, say the authors. In this article, they note the cost relationship of the marketing concept and the definition of quality: "conformance to requirements." Traditional companies with a sales-buying concept are too compartmentalized, they say, and thus produce poor customer satisfaction and rejected product. A pair of graphics compare the traditional organizational structure with the structure of companies that have adopted the marketing-total quality concept. To achieve customer satisfaction, the authors say, a cross-functional team from the manufacturer must speak and understand the language of its customer's counterparts as a product is being designed. The authors describe a nine-stage quality function deployment (QFD) system, and they highlight the stages (indicated with an asterisk) in which the marketing function takes a lead role:

1. *State customer requirements.

2. Translate the customer requirements into technical specifications.

3. Develop a relationship matrix which describes the degree to which each technical characteristic influences the customer-desired requirements.

4. Build the "roof matrix"—a correlation matrix that identifies how a change in one product control characteristic affects other characteristics.

5. *Add the market evaluation, which covers customer-expressed importance ratings for the listed requirements.

6. Provide competitive evaluations of product control characteristics.

7. *Develop the key selling points for a new or modified product.

8. *Develop the target values for each of the product control characteristics.

9. *Determine the selection of the product control characteristics that are to be emphasized throughout the remainder of the QFD process. (*©Quality Abstracts*)

CHAPTER 4

MANAGEMENT SYSTEM

In Chapter 3, the components of the House of Quality, including the management system, were discussed. Management is perhaps the key to driving total quality in an organization. In fact, according to Juran and other leaders in total quality, lack of top management involvement is cited most frequently as the reason why total quality efforts fail. According to Deming, the job of management is not supervision but rather leadership. Management must work on sources of improvement, the intent of quality of product and of service, and the translation of the intent into design and actual product.[1] Joseph Jaworski, chairman of the American Leadership Forum, suggests that "quality depends upon a vision of excellence and that a vision becomes reality through excellent, compelling leadership."[2]

What does it take to be an effective manager? According to research by the Management Research Group in Portland, Maine, six behaviors distinguish effective from less effective managers and are important at all management levels. These behaviors hold true across a variety of businesses, including public and private enterprises, and transcend the type of work performed.[3]

- **Communication:** Highly effective managers are clear in defining their expectations for employees.

- **Management focus:** Highly effective managers are comfortable in the management role; they derive joy and satisfaction from performing as managers. They are comfortable dealing with issues of power and conflict and are at ease in assuming managerial accountability.

- **Production:** Highly effective managers not only are clear about what they expect, but also tend to expect high levels of performance.

- **People:** Highly effective managers balance their strong concern for production and performance with empathy and genuine concern for employee growth and development.

- **Control:** Highly effective managers have systems in place that allow them to periodically and consistently review and monitor employee performance. This process takes into consideration previously established expectations and objectives and is done to assist rather than police employees in their efforts to attain good job performance.

- **Feedback:** Highly effective managers provide regular, ongoing, and spontaneous feedback concerning the positive and negative aspects of employee performance. Again, feedback is based upon previously articulated expectations.

Management as we know it today is undergoing a transformation. New competitive challenges and a changing work force call for a new understanding of management. According to Rosabeth Moss Kanter:

> The old bases of managerial authority are eroding, and new tools of leadership are taking their place. Managers whose power derived from hierarchy and who were accustomed to a limited area of personal control are learning to shift their perspectives and widen their horizons. The new managerial work consists of looking outside a defined area of responsibility to sense opportunities and of forming project teams drawn from any relevant sphere to address them. It involves communication and collaboration across functions, across divisions, and across companies...Thus rank, title, or official charter will be less important factors in success at the managerial work than having the knowledge, skills, and sensitivity to mobilize people and motivate them to do their best.[4]

The results of a Korn-Ferry International study of 1500 executives from 20 countries to predict change expected in management characteristics by the year 2000 are summarized in Table 4.1. It is apparent from these results that

Table 4.1 Important Management Characteristics in the Present and Future (Percentage Ranked as Very Important by Respondents)

	Year		
	1988	2000	Change
Readily reassigns/terminates individuals	34	71	37
Frequently communicates with customers	41	78	37
Frequently communicates with employees	59	89	30
Promotes management training and development	58	85	27
Conveys strong vision of the future	75	98	23
Rewards loyalty and length of service	48	44	−4
Personally makes all major decisions	39	21	−18

future managers will be required to communicate more with customers and employees, promote more management training and development, and be able to supply a vision for the future.

The quality management cycle referred to in Chapter 3 represents a powerful instrument for addressing these new challenges while at the same time directing quality behaviors. Managers can promote and guide actions by orchestrating the organizational context in which quality initiatives are introduced. The task of management basically remains the same today: to make people capable of joint performance through common goals, common values, the right organizational structure, and the proper training and development they need to perform and to respond to change.[5] As illustrated in Figure 4.1, the management cycle consists of planning, organizing, leading, implementation, and control. Planning requires marketing managers to gather inputs from various functional areas in a firm to produce a plan that others are willing to implement. Planning will be discussed further in Chapter 6. (For additional information, see Abstract 4.1 at the end of this chapter.)

ORGANIZING

Organizing, the second component of the management cycle, involves the deployment of people in the organization around the value-added processes that benefit the customer. The organizational structure is an apparatus

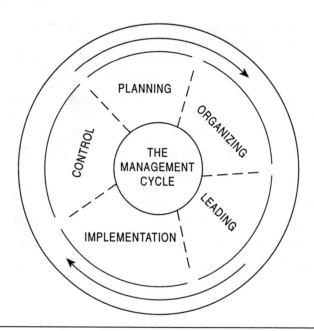

Figure 4.1 Management Cycle.

geared toward supporting, rather than exerting control over, the firm's front-line workers. Because work is organized around processes and the teams that perform them, lines of communication in the organization are necessarily shorter. People communicate with whomever they need to. Control is vested in the people performing the process.

The organization's structure also changes when organizing around core processes. That is, instead of a hierarchical and top-heavy configuration, the firm uses a "flatter," more horizontal structure. Flatter organizations move senior executives closer to customers and to the people performing the company's value-adding work. A horizontal firm largely eliminates both hierarchy and functional boundaries; everyone in the organization works together in multidisciplinary teams that perform core processes such as product development or sales generation. The result is an organization that has fewer layers of management between the president and the staff. Eastman Chemical took an even more radical approach to redesigning its organization by using a circular form to show that everyone is equal in the organization (see Figure 4.2).

If the trend is toward horizontal management, how is such an organization created? The following are a number of steps that a company can take to create a horizontal organization:

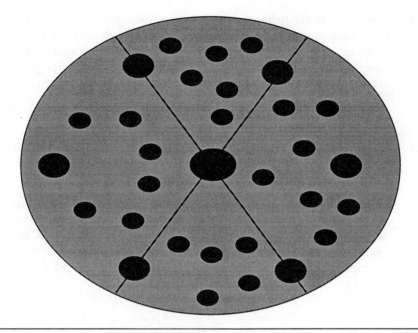

Figure 4.2   Eastman Chemical's "Pizza" Organizational Chart.

1. **Identify strategic objectives:**   Before a company reorganizes, it should analyze the markets and the customers it wants to reach.

2. **Analyze key competitive advantages to fulfill objectives:**   Complete a customer value analysis to determine the benefits that customers in a target market segment want and how they perceive the relative value of a competitor's offer.

3. **Define core processes:**   Link them to the organization's key goals. Instead of creating a structure around functions or departments, build around core processes, such as product procurement or product development.

4. **Organize around core processes:**   Each process should link related tasks to yield an output that is of value to the customer.

5. **Eliminate all activities that fail to add value or contribute to key objectives.**

6. **Cut function and staff departments to a minimum,** while preserving key expertise.

7. **Appoint a manager or team as the "owner" of each core process.**

8. **Create multidisciplinary teams to run each process:** Jobs evolve from narrow and task-oriented to multidimensional. Functional departments lose their reason for being. Make self-managed teams the building blocks of the organization. Give the team a common purpose and hold it accountable for measurable goals.

9. **Set specific performance objectives for each process** (i.e., a 90 percent reduction in cycle time).

10. **Empower employees with authority and information to achieve goals:** Train employees in how to use raw data and how to perform their own analyses and make their own decisions.

11. **Change training, performance appraisal, and compensation to support the new structure:** Pay for performance and promote for ability. Reward systems should reflect team results instead of just individual performance. Workers should be encouraged to develop multiple skills. The focus should be on *education* instead of simply training. Continuing education becomes the norm.

LEADERSHIP

The third element of the management cycle is leadership. Someone once mused that leadership was "repairing the decay faster than it could occur." While that approach may have worked in the past, leading a total quality effort today requires a different set of behaviors. The Leadership Triangle, comprised of people, person, and purpose, is illustrated in Figure 4.3. Each of these elements is discussed below:

*   **People:** According to Dunn and Bradstreet, 85 percent of failure as a manager is due to the inability to work with people. Leaders must be openly sensitive to the concerns of the people they manage. They must give them responsibility and earn their trust. They must recognize and take advantage of diversity in their organizations. They must be open to input from others. Leaders also create genuine opportunities for others in the organization to reach their potential.

*   **Purpose:** Leaders must also have a sense of what the organization can and should become and rally others around that vision. They need to set priorities and clearly communicate them to others. Leaders set quality, not necessarily quantity, goals. (Former President Lyndon B. Johnson once said, "We need people more concerned with *quality* of their goals than quantity of their goals.")

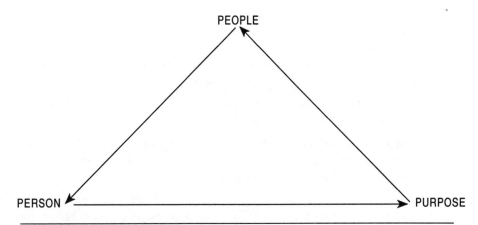

PEOPLE

PERSON

PURPOSE

Figure 4.3 The Leadership Triangle.

- **Person:** Leaders are distinguished by their goals and the extent to which they consistently and ethically pursue them. Leaders possess moral integrity and affirm good values. Leaders understand servanthood—the greatest leaders are those who serve. Leadership is essentially a condition of "indebtedness." Leaders remain vulnerable; they set aside the "not-invented-here" syndrome and do not surround themselves with clones.

In summary, the new breed of leader will need to demonstrate a concern for people, customers, and quality. Leaders will need to understand and effect change. They will also need to recognize that change requires a form of dying and have the courage to let it happen. A list of questions that leaders might expect to hear from subordinates in the organization of the future is provided in Exercise 4.1 at the end of this chapter. (For additional information, see Abstract 4.2 at the end of this chapter.)

IMPLEMENTATION

Once the business has developed plans and an organizational structure to support those plans, it must work toward carrying them out. Well-thought-out plans and an adequate support structure go only so far, as the firm may fail at implementation. Implementation is the "blocking and tackling" of a business. Most quality efforts only get to first base because they are treated as a "program" instead of a sound approach to doing business. As such, many total quality implementation efforts are prematurely short-circuited.

The McKinsey 7-S Framework shown in Figure 4.4 provides the manager with a set of analysis points from which to implement total quality in the

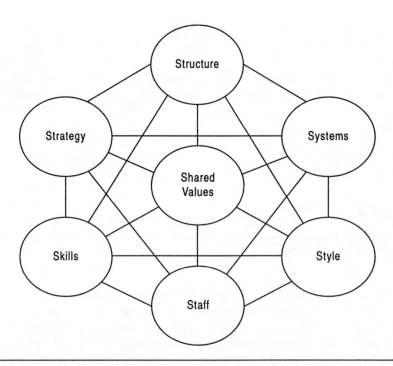

Figure 4.4 7-S Framework. (Source: Tom Peters and Robert J. Waterman, Jr. *In Search of Excellence: Lessons from America's Best-Run Companies.* Copyright ©1982 by Thomas J. Peters and Robert H. Waterman, Jr. Reprinted by permission of HarperCollins Publishers, Inc.)

organization. Implementing quality programs in marketing is first facilitated by developing a **strategy** that is communicated externally to the company's public and internally to its employees. The strategy unifies company operations and lets front-end workers know what management expects. The strategy also spells out who your customers are, what product/service attributes they value, and what your competitive position entails.

The **structure** provides an apparatus to help support those who directly or indirectly serve the customer. Implementing total quality means organizing in a way that makes it easy to service customers and those in the organization who serve the customers. Quality management requires a team culture and a more flexible, less rigid organizational structure. When General Motors introduced the Oldsmobile Aurora, it spread the responsibility among an overlapping network of small teams, each with its own mandate and bosses. The original Aurora product development team consisted of representatives from engineering, planning and marketing, and production.

The **systems** in the 7-S Framework refers to the forms, policies, procedures, physical facilities, computer hardware/software, billing, and rewards that facilitate quality efforts. These systems must support the employees in their endeavor to create and deliver value. They should be customer friendly as well, to support the delivery of customer value rather than serving to frustrate the customers. McKesson Corporation, a large drug wholesaler, gave computers to its retail customers so that they could track product movement and place orders directly into McKesson's computers. The stores benefited through improved inventory control and product profitability, while McKesson gained a more loyal and satisfied "retail partner."

Style, another element in the 7-S Framework, refers to a common thinking and pattern of behavior within the firm. Managers can create a style, as Jack Welch did at General Electric. Welch introduced "constructive conflict," a wide-open debating style where ideas are challenged and expected to be defended. As Welch himself has said, "We tee up a subject and then they take each other on." This process encourages the expression of opposing views and gets all of the facts on the table, which results in more balanced judgments.

Hiring able people, training them, and assigning the right jobs to exercise their talents is the element of **staffing**. When asked about his hiring criteria, Stu Leonard, a successful northeastern grocer, once stated, "I hire nice people. I can teach cash register, I can't teach nice." Studying a large number of service organizations, including Marriott Hotels, caused two researchers to take a similar view. They concluded that "finding the right people not only improves service quality, but is also less costly that constantly replacing cheaper help."[6] Most important is the growing evidence that satisfied employees create better satisfied customers.

Skills is another element of the 7-S Framework. It means equipping employees with the marketing planning, financial analysis, and quality improvement skills that are required to carry out the firm's strategy. In one of his Fourteen Points, "institute training and retraining," Deming recommends that employees be trained in the significance of variation and be taught the rudimentary principles of control charts. Other important skills that organizations concerned with quality will need to train their workers in include: benchmarking, problem solving, teamwork, and interpersonal communications. In his article on "The Changing Role of Marketing in the Corporation," Webster intimates that marketing's role is to help design and negotiate strategic partnerships.[7] Thus, negotiation skills will take on greater importance as marketing serves as the integrator, both internally by bridging technology with market needs and externally by bringing the customer into the company as a participant.

Finally, **shared values** represents the driving purpose and creed which everyone in the company knows and takes ownership in. GE's shared values consist of the following:

- **The rule of #1 or #2:** Any business within GE that cannot become a No. 1 or No. 2 player will not remain a part of GE.

- **Integrity:** Each manager is responsible for his or her organization; unethical behavior is neither condoned nor tolerated.

- **Only satisfied customers can provide job security:** The message here is to succeed in the marketplace or be out of a job.

- **Leaders share knowledge rather than withhold it:** Everyone benefits when they know what the leader knows; nothing is secret.

- **Function collectively as one company and individually as many businesses.**[8]

For additional information, see Abstract 4.3 at the end of this chapter.

CONTROL

The last component of the management cycle is control. Because the marketing environment is in a constant state of flux, a company will need to review and perhaps revise its plans, organizational structure, leadership style, and implementation strategies. Marketing activities need to be continuously monitored and controlled and linked to managerial processes and responsibilities. Many companies collect customer service data but do not link those data back to the processes that are being managed. A diagram of the quality measures collected by the General Business Systems Division of AT&T is provided in Figure 4.5.[9]

Measurement of overall quality begins with defining the core **business processes**. In Figure 4.5, the business processes are product, sales, installation, repair, and billing. The core business processes will vary depending on the type of business. Yet someone in the organization needs to take ownership over the results of these processes. As illustrated in the figure, overall quality is made up of the combined quality of each process. The relative contribution of each process to total quality is also indicated. For example, 30 percent of the variation in total quality is explained by *product*.

Next, **customer needs**, as defined in the customer's words, are linked to each process. In the example in Figure 4.5, customer needs in terms of repair are customers expect no repeat trouble, the problem is fixed fast, and customers are kept informed. These are service attributes which can be monitored in a fairly straightforward manner, such as on a service quality questionnaire. Initial identification of customer needs can best be achieved by using exploratory research approaches, such as focus groups. Again, as with the

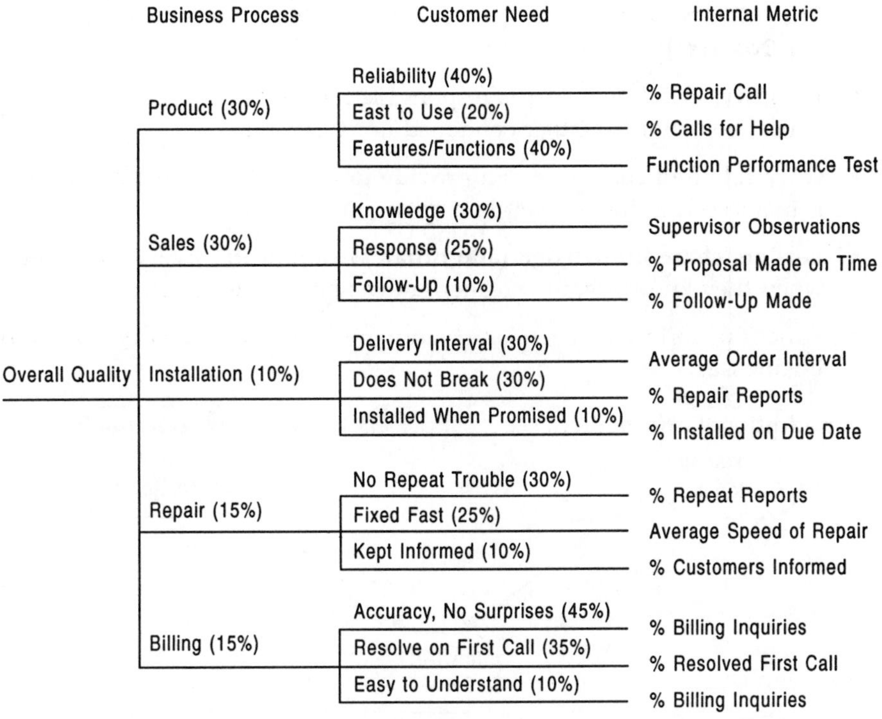

Business Process	Customer Need	Internal Metric
	Reliability (40%)	% Repair Call
Product (30%)	East to Use (20%)	% Calls for Help
	Features/Functions (40%)	Function Performance Test
	Knowledge (30%)	Supervisor Observations
Sales (30%)	Response (25%)	% Proposal Made on Time
	Follow-Up (10%)	% Follow-Up Made
	Delivery Interval (30%)	Average Order Interval
Installation (10%)	Does Not Break (30%)	% Repair Reports
	Installed When Promised (10%)	% Installed on Due Date
	No Repeat Trouble (30%)	% Repeat Reports
Repair (15%)	Fixed Fast (25%)	Average Speed of Repair
	Kept Informed (10%)	% Customers Informed
	Accuracy, No Surprises (45%)	% Billing Inquiries
Billing (15%)	Resolve on First Call (35%)	% Resolved First Call
	Easy to Understand (10%)	% Billing Inquiries

Overall Quality

Figure 4.5 Strategic Marketing Information Used to Focus Business Processes.

business processes, the relative importance of each attribute in terms of customer satisfaction is indicated.

Finally, **internal metrics** are used to link business processes and customer needs. Because customer needs are not generally expressed in managerial terms, relevant and meaningful measures for each customer need to be developed. Improving a business process should ultimately lead to an improved internal metric score.

Business processes, customer needs, and internal metrics are all developed with the goal of total quality in mind. Yet another important outcome is market share and, more specifically, the impact that total quality has on market share.

Intuitively, one would surmise that the relationship between total quality and market share would be positive. Two factors dictate changes in market share: retaining existing customers and attracting new ones. Customers who are satisfied also tend to be more loyal and thus are more likely to be retained as customers. Loyal customers tend to initiate positive word-of-

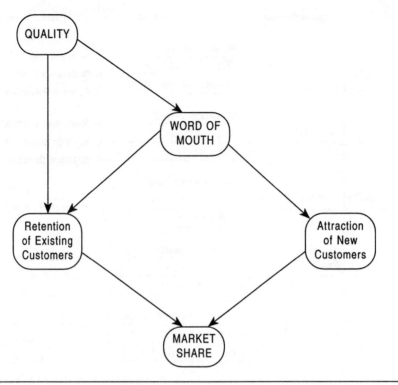

Figure 4.6 How Market Share Results from Quality.

mouth communications, which produces new customers. The importance of keeping existing customers is fairly obvious. In fact, by most accounts, 65 percent of business comes from existing customers. The relationship between quality and market share is conceptually illustrated in Figure 4.6.[10] (For additional information, see Abstract 4.4 at the end of this chapter.)

TRANSFORMING THE ORGANIZATION

The organization of the 21st century will barely resemble the organization as we know it today. The new organizational paradigm will be more flexible and adaptive to the changing business environment, as well as more responsive to the company's stakeholders. The challenge for managers will be to close the gap between where the organization is today and the direction in which it needs to be moving. A framework for completing the kind of organizational transformation needed today is provided in Figure 4.7.

The traditional organization is characterized by a hierarchical structure

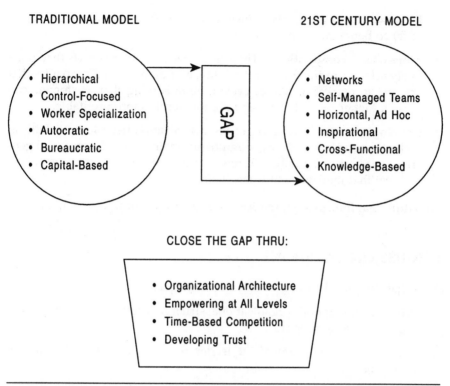

Figure 4.7 Transforming the Organization.

that is control based. That is, decision making is top-down oriented and information is held exclusively my top management. The organization promotes worker specialization and tends to be capital intensive.

The 21st century model offers a radically different view. The organizational structure will resemble ad hoc networks comprised of self-managed teams. Further, these teams will be organized around customer processes rather than strictly by functional area. Managers will lead by inspiring and enabling rather than controlling. The organization of the 21st century will be knowledge based, where superior knowledge of the customer and how this customer knowledge is managed become a competitive advantage. Toffler refers to knowledge as "the most basic of all raw materials."[11]

Finally, completing the transformation from the traditional to the 21st century organization will require the following changes in the way the organization conducts business:

- **Organizational architechture:** Forming teams and strategic alliances that best serve the company's market objectives.

- **Empowering at all levels:** Pushing decision making down the line in order to better serve the customer.

- **Time-based competition:** Time is a manageable resource that positively affects productivity, profitability, and innovation. Companies that are first to market or reduce cycle time in serving their customers can claim a higher market share and are inherently more profitable.

- **Developing trust:** Members of the organization need to have faith in each other and honor their commitments, maintain confidence, and generally support one another. Further, employees need to trust managers and feel that management trusts them.

For additional information, see Abstract 4.5 at the end of this chapter.

DISCUSSION QUESTIONS

1. What does it take to be an effective manager?

2. Why are "horizontal" organizational structures better suited for managing total quality programs?

3. Describe the "new breed" of leader needed to direct total quality programs.

4. How can top management communicate the need for quality throughout the organization?

5. Using the example in Figure 4.5, diagram a business's core processes, along with identifying the customer needs and the internal metrics.

6. Describe what is involved in completing an organizational transformation.

ENDNOTES

1. Deming, E. *Out of the Crisis*, MIT Center for Advanced Engineering Study, Cambridge, Mass., 1986.
2. Whitely, R. "Creating a Customer Focus." *Executive Excellence*, September 1990, p. 9.
3. Jamieson, D. and O'Mara, J. *Managing: Workforce 2000*, Jossey-Bass, San Francisco, 1991.
4. Kanter, Rosabeth Moss. "The New Managerial Work." *Harvard Business Review*, November–December 1989, pp. 85–92.

5. Drucker, Peter. *The New Realities,* Prentice-Hall, Englewood Cliffs, N.J., 1989.
6. Schlesinger, L. and Heskett, J. L. "The Service-Driven Organization." *Harvard Business Review,* September–October 1991, pp. 71–81.
7. Webster, Frederick. "The Changing Role of Marketing in the Corporation." *Journal of Marketing,* October 1992, Vol. 56, p. 11.
8. Tichy, N. and Sherman, S. *Control Your Own Destiny or Someone Else Will,* Doubleday, New York, 1993.
9. Gallagher, R. "Driving Your Business with Customer Satisfaction Measurements," Telecom Corporation of New Zealand, 1992.
10. Korf upleski, R., Rust, R., and Zahorik, A. "Why Improving Quality Doesn't Improve Quality." *California Management Review,* Spring 1983, p. 92.
11. Toffler, A. *Powershift: Knowledge, Wealth, and Violence at the Edge of the 21st Century,* Bantam Books, New York, 1990.

EXERCISES

EXERCISE 4.1
QUESTIONS LEADERS MIGHT HEAR FROM SUBORDINATES

Instructions: The following are a list of questions that you might hear from your employees. By giving thoughtful and honest answers to these questions will you discover your leadership tendencies.

1. What may I expect from you?

2. Can I achieve my own goals from following you?

3. Can I reach my potential by working with you?

4. Can I entrust my future to you?

5. Are you ready to be ruthlessly honest?

6. Do you have the self-confidence and trust to let me do my job?

7. What do you believe?

8. What are the values of this institution?

EXERCISE 4.2
DEMING MANAGEMENT SYSTEM AUDIT

The following series of self-examination questions corresponds to each of the Fourteen Points of the Deming Management Method. Answering these questions will help you diagnose your own quality management system.

POINT 1: Constancy of purpose
a. Has your organization published/disseminated its mission?
b. What processes do you have to determine customer needs?
c. What processes do you have to improve consistency of purpose?

POINT 2: Adopt the new philosophy
a. Is this new philosophy part of your training at all levels?
b. Do you know the loss incurred by not meeting your customers' needs?

POINT 3: Cease dependence on mass inspection
a. Where do you rely on mass inspection?
b. What are you doing to eliminate it?
c. What is an example of continuing improvement in a process that you manage?
d. How do you know that you are improving to meet your customers' needs for now and three years from now?

POINT 4: End the practice of awarding business on basis of price alone
a. Do purchasing, manufacturing, and engineering have common goals?
b. How many single-source suppliers do you have?
c. How many long-term relationships do you have with suppliers?

POINT 5: Improve constantly and forever the system of production and service
a. Can you demonstrate the Deming cycle (Plan, Do, Check, Act) on a process that you manage?
b. Do you encourage your employees to identify ways that the systems within which they work could be improved?

POINT 6: Institute training
a. Is training part of everyone's objectives?
b. How do you know when training is effective?
c. How do you monitor what your employees know about their job?

POINT 7: Institute leadership
a. How much time do you spend managing people rather than outcomes?
b. What are your criteria for giving feedback?
c. What barriers have you removed which inhibit your people from improving?

POINT 8: Drive out fear
a. Do you feel that your boss propagates fear?
b. Do your subordinates fear you? How do you know?
c. What steps are you taking to reduce fear?

POINT 9: Break down barriers between staff areas

a. Are people in your immediate area involved in cross-functional teams with people outside your group to improve common processes?
b. Do you train for teamwork?
c. Are your evaluations and rewards based on teamwork?

POINT 10: Eliminate slogans, exhortations, and targets for the work force

a. What targets do you have and how were they arrived at?
b. What is the process by which you will reach your target?

POINT 11: Eliminate numerical quotas for the work force

a. How do you measure work output for administrative processes?
b. Where are the places your organization uses work standards?

POINT 12: Remove barriers to pride of workmanship

a. Have you surveyed your organization to identify barriers to continuing improvement?
b. What are you doing about removing them?
c. When your employees work in teams, is their role clear enough so that they can take pride in a job well done?

POINT 13: Institute vigorous program of education and self-improvement

a. What training have you attended during the past 12 months?
b. What have you done to personally train your people?
c. What should your people know 10 years from know?
d. What recognition do you provide for people who have applied their new learning to their work?

POINT 14: Put everyone to work on the transformation

a. How often do you discuss the Fourteen Points with your subordinates?
b. What are you doing to learn more about statistical methods? How are you helping your employees to learn basic statistical methods?

PROFILE

THE DEMING MANAGEMENT METHOD

The Deming Management Method contains a prescriptive set of fourteen points that serve to guide appropriate organizational behavior and practice regarding quality management. Deming's Fourteen Points can also help the organization develop and implement "profound knowledge." As principles of transformation, the fourteen points are based on a set of assumptions about how work is accomplished and how the outcomes should be evaluated. A listing and discussion of Deming's Fourteen Points follows (see also Exercise 4.2):

POINT 1   **Create constancy of purpose for improvement of product and service.**   Continuation of business requires a core set of values and a purpose that is stable over time.

POINT 2   **Adopt the new philosophy.**   Western management must learn new responsibilities and take on leadership of change.

POINT 3   **Cease dependence on mass inspection.**   Quality does not come from inspection, but rather from improvements in the process.

POINT 4   **End the practice of awarding business on the basis of price alone.**   Price has no meaning apart from perceived quality. Minimize total costs. Move toward a single supplier for any one item, forming cooperative, long-term relationships with suppliers.

POINT 5   **Improve constantly and forever the system of production and service.**   Build quality into the product in the first place. Systems should be redesigned continually for improved quality. Variation should be minimized.

POINT 6   **Institute training.**   Training should provide managers and workers with the tools that they will need to evaluate processes and improve systems, including training in basic statistical methods.

POINT 7   **Institute leadership.**   Deming maintained that leaders should know the work they supervise. ("There is no substitute for knowledge.") The aim of leadership should be to help workers do their jobs better. Leadership drives the business system toward optimization.

POINT 8   **Drive out fear.**   Deming claimed that workers perform best when they feel secure. Fear breeds hidden agendas, padded numbers, and may cause workers to satisfy a rule or quota at the expense of the company.

POINT 9   **Break down barriers between staff areas.**   Workers in the various functional areas need to work together. Interstaff teams break down territorial barriers and permit greater communication.

POINT 10   **Eliminate slogans, exhortations, and targets for the work force.**   According to Deming, such exhortations only create adversarial relationships. The real cause of low quality and productivity lies in the system.

POINT 11   **Eliminate numerical quotas for the work force.**   Deming believed that overemphasis on extrinsic motivators, such as quotas or other numerical goals, work against quality and productivity improvements. Quotas, according to Deming, do not consider quality.

POINT 12   **Remove barriers to pride of workmanship.**   Remove any bureaucratic hindrances that rob workers' pride of workmanship. Listen and follow up on worker suggestions and requests.

POINT 13   **Institute a vigorous program of education and self-improvement.**   Deming advocated lifelong learning, whether formal or informal.

POINT 14   **Put everyone to work on the transformation.**   If business systems are to be improved, then everyone needs to be involved.

A recent study* reported the concepts underlying the Deming Management Method. Each of these is presented below:

- **Visionary leadership:**   Clarity of vision, long-range orientation, coaching style of management, participative change, employee empowerment, and planning and implementing organizational change.

---

* Anderson, J., Rungtusanatham, M., and Schroeder, R. "A Theory of Quality Management Underlying the Deming Management Method." *Academy of Management Review,* July 1994, Vol. 19 No. 3, p. 480.

- **Internal and external cooperation:**   Firm/supplier partnerships, single-supplier orientation, collaborative organization, teamwork, systems view of organization.

- **Learning:**   Process knowledge, continuous self-improvement.

- **Process management:**   Prevention orientation, reduction of mass inspection, understand variation, eliminate quotas.

- **Continuous improvement:**   Pursue incremental and innovative improvements of processes, products, and services.

- **Employee fulfillment:**   Exhibited by worker satisfaction and pride of workmanship.

- **Customer satisfaction:**   Firm has "customer-driven" focus.

ABSTRACTS

ABSTRACT 4.1
AFTER PRODUCT QUALITY IN JAPAN: MANAGEMENT QUALITY

Yahagi, Seiichiro
National Productivity Review, Autumn 1992, pp. 501–515

This is one of the most important new articles to come out of Japan in 1992, and the implications for the marketing and sales arena are enormous. The author proposes the use of expert systems featuring a 12-factor model organized into 41 "elements" of measuring subfactors. Japanese management has moved beyond product quality, says the author, to an emphasis on total integrated management (TIM)—management concerned about each facet of the company and interrelating them into a concerted, comprehensive corporate management policy of innovation. The author has developed an expert system which measures the 12 factors that determine management quality, divided into 41 subfactors:

- Corporate history: past, present, and future

- Corporate climate: core, climate, and culture

- Strategic alliances: objectives and coherence

- Channels: suppliers and buyers

- Management cycle: vision, strategy, planning, organizing and implementing, controlling

- Environment: economic, societal, and global

- Management targets: inputs, markets, technologies, and products

- Business structure: business fields, business mix, and market standing

- Management resources: money, materials, information, and people

- Management design: system, organization, authority, and responsibility

- Management functions: decision making, interrelationships, and quality

- Management performance: growth, scale, stability, profit, and market share

He sees six factors as critical to the success of a company: management cycle, business structure, management resources, management design, corporate culture, and management performance. These six factors are interrelated in a circulatory system of Management Quality factors which have a cause-and-effect relationship as follows. The management cycle acts as the driver and influencer of the four factors of structure, resources, design, and culture, which in turn affect management performance. If the quality level of the management cycle is low, then the six factors generate a negative or bad feedback loop which finds management passively waiting until poor results of management performance force reactionary feedback into the management flow.* If the quality level of the management cycle is "high," then these six factors generate an excellent feedforward loop in which management perceives the strategies and plans needed for success of each management factor and then proactively formulates and implements them.

The author's consulting organization conducts an annual survey of the management practices of Japanese firms, and in this article he presents the results of the most recent survey, which represented input from about 200 firms. Graphs and charts show comparisons between the worst-scoring and best-scoring companies, and he uses creative graphics to illustrate his analytical technique and to summarize questionnaire responses. From this comparison, he deduces a number of principles: (a) management quality factors must be well-balanced, (b) management cycle is the key to the management quality loop, and (c) the dynamics of TIM must be considered. He then goes on to describe the management cycle, which consists of the following key components: vision, strategy, planning, organizing, implementing, and controlling. The author recommends using an annual questionnaire to first analyze management factors within a company and then develop a multiphase action plan to restructure an organization for TIM. This article by Yahagi is must-reading for anyone who wants to remain on the leading edge of new application-oriented technology.

---

* According to Yahagi, the circulatory aspects of the management quality system are a key to understanding the relationships of this system to others, such as the Malcolm Baldrige National Quality Award. See Chapters 8 and 9 of this book for more detail.

ABSTRACT 4.2
WHAT IS LEADERSHIP?

Smolenyak, Megan and Majumdar, Amit
Journal for Quality and Participation, July–August 1992, pp. 28–32

What leadership type can empower employees to develop their inherent capabilities? The authors answer this question by describing three types of leaders:

- **The champion** is characterized by uncontested authority, usually resulting from a feat or event he or she has masterminded. This kind of leader is tough and determined and thrives in an autocratic, hierarchical world. The champion is normally patronizing toward followers.

- **The visionary** inspires others through a commitment to a vision of monumental proportions. This leader persuades people to follow by tapping their emotions. The visionary's relationship with followers can be described as paternalistic. The danger with this type of leadership is that the loss of the leader can mean the end of the movement.

- **The servant** attains stature through the accomplishments of followers by bringing out the "leader" in each of them. The servant is respected and admired but does not seek self-glorification. This type of leader is approachable and interactive, thriving on open communications. Most of all, the servant is an enabler who helps others develop their inherent capabilities in support of a mutually agreed upon mission. The followers then have a sense of ownership in the mission.

Many companies that practice TQM are already using servant leadership, say the authors, especially with self-managed work teams. When managers make the transition from boss to coach, they are adopting the servant style of leadership. Those who stubbornly resist this style may eventually have to leave for the good of the company. The good news, according to the authors, is that the supply of servant leaders as opposed to other types is very generous. (©*Quality Abstracts*)

ABSTRACT 4.3
MANAGING QUALITY: THE PRIMER FOR MIDDLE MANAGERS

Schuler, Randall S. and Harris, Drew L.
Addison-Wesley, Reading, Mass., 1992, 202 pp.

Most overviews of total quality management are written to convince executives who have the power and resources to effect change in their companies. This book, however, is written for the middle manager, who may be in one of three positions: (a) the company has a well-planned quality improvement process, (b) the company has merely given a mandate to "improve quality" but little direction, or (c) the manager has no company support but still desires to improve quality in his or her department. This thoughtfully written book gives a helpful overview of quality issues, where middle managers fit into the larger picture, a glance at quality improvement tools, the human resource aspect of quality management, and quality interfaces with suppliers as well as customers. In order to tie all the parts together, the authors include two case studies of quality improvement: at Ensoniq Corp., an electronic musical instrument manufacturer, and at the HR department of Swiss Bank Corp. Two useful appendices include an annotated reading list on quality and a glossary of terms used in TQM. Chapter contents include:

1. **Why Look at Quality and the Middle Manager?** The authors identify with middle manager issues and offer a simple plan for quality improvement.

2. **What Is Quality?** They discuss the contributions of Juran and Deming, and then they define quality as "delivering loyalty-producing products and services along all dimensions of quality with a single effort." They discuss quality from a process and systems viewpoint.

3. **Tools for Improving Quality.** Using a narrative describing a quality improvement project, the authors introduce elements of a typical quality improvement process, including tools such as control charts, flowcharts, cause-and-effect diagrams, as well as other diagnostic tools.

4. **Quality Enhancement, the Manager, and the HR Function.** They discuss the transformation of the HR function to the line manager and vice-president for quality and describe alternative HR management philosophies.

5. **Choices in Human Resource Management.** The authors link HR practices with competitive strategy, and they describe HR decisions which must be made in planning, staffing, appraising, compensating, training, and labor–management negotiating.

6. **Quality from External Relationships.** They describe varying relationships between customers and suppliers and the differences between internal and external relationships. (©*Quality Abstracts*)

ABSTRACT 4.4
INSIDE THE BALDRIGE AWARD GUIDELINES—
CATEGORY 1: LEADERSHIP

Sullivan, Rhonda L.
Quality Progress, June 1992, pp. 24–28

This first in a series of articles on the guidelines for the seven categories of the Baldrige Award focuses on leadership. "The 1992 Baldrige Award criteria are built on 10 core values and concepts," says the author. She briefly discusses each: customer-driven quality, leadership, continuous improvement, full participation, fast response, design quality and prevention, long-range outlook, management by fact, partnership development, and public responsibility. "By completing the award application's leadership section," she says, "a company will determine whether its organizational structure will support its objectives." In addition to a copy of the actual Baldrige Award criteria for Category 1, and a table of scoring guidelines, the author offers advice on areas of importance in the leadership category, such as:

- Don't rely solely on management by walking around. Develop a formal structure and strategy to ensure that leaders are accessible.

- Insist on enthusiastic personal involvement from senior executives.

- Stress two-way communication.

- Develop multiple methods for accomplishing an objective to ensure validation. (©*Quality Abstracts*)

ABSTRACT 4.5
BUILDING A TOTAL QUALITY CULTURE

Batten, Joe
Crisp Publications, Menlo Park, Calif., 1992, 88 pp.

"People want to be led, not driven," insists the author. Providing the kind of tough-minded leadership that will produce a total quality culture is the focus of this motivational book (which includes a foreword by Zig Ziglar). Rather than presenting a formula for TQM, the book aims at developing the attitudes which support successful TQM leaders. Chapter titles are:

1. The Path to the Future

2. The New Leaders

3. Making Quality Possibilities Come True

4. Peak Performance at All Levels

5. Winners Can Be Grown

6. Tomorrow's Culture

Some of the themes include tough-minded leadership (the title of one of the author's former books), servant leadership, being a winner, motivating one's subordinates, excellence, and dreams. The author draws on the upbeat quotations from a variety of individuals to bolster his points. The book concludes with a 14-page glossary of terms which serve to spell out Batten's philosophy of leadership. For example, he defines "builder": "The CEO who stands tall is, above all, a builder. Committed to vision, stretch, empowerment, synergy, responsiveness, flexibility—toughness of mind—a builder ensures that all dimensions of each P in the pyramid are intensely focused on creation, growth, and building." (©*Quality Abstracts*)

CHAPTER 5

TOTAL QUALITY IN MARKETING REQUIRES VISION

Where there is no vision, the people perish
Book of Proverbs

Vision is the art of seeing things invisible
Jonathan Swift

Most organizations today, both public and private, communicate a vision statement to both customers and stakeholders. Many of today's successful companies credit their company's vision as a strong foundation in providing direction and competitive differentiation to sustain growth or even survival during the turbulent 1990s.

What powers does a vision possess? What is the message that is communicated to both employees and customers by developing and sharing a company's vision? Let's examine several companies and how they benefitted by creating and communicating their visions.

First of all, it is important not to confuse vision with a mission statement or slogans or mottoes. Examples of vision statements include:

Ford Motor Company	*Quality Is Job 1*
General Motors Corporation	*We sweat the small stuff*
IBM	*Market-Oriented Quality*
Xerox	*Leadership Through Quality*
Walt Disney	*To provide the finest in family entertainment for people of all ages everywhere*
Holiday Inns	*No surprises*

Again, let's define vision and the value it offers a company. Peter Senge, author of *The Fifth Discipline* and MIT professor of management theory, offers the following view:[1]

Vision is the picture we carry around in our heads of what we want to create.

Vision creates a sense of commonality that binds people together for a greater good.

Vision uplifts people's aspirations.

The statements of vision that Senge provides are aimed at individuals and teams; however, they carry a parallel value in corporations, large and small.

Peter Drucker,[2] Harvard professor and management guru, looks at the value of vision from a competitive strategy viewpoint. When a company begins to lose market share or its competitive edge or management senses a loss of direction, it is time to ask some fundamental, probing questions: What is our business? Who is the customer? What will our business be? What should our business be? (For additional information, see Abstract 5.1 at the end of this chapter.)

In May 1994, Richard Chvala, co-author of this book, gave the keynote address at an American Marketing Association conference on "Developing a Marketing Plan." During a question-and-answer period, Mr. Chvala was asked to identify the difference between a vision and a mission statement. The following text is taken from an audiotape of the conference:

...the task of marketers during the 1970s and early 1980s was developing advertising campaigns and assisting sales in moving product. As the late '80s grew more turbulent, and companies downsized their way out of the recession, the more innovative marketers seized the opportunity to involve the whole company toward satisfying the customer. They also saw that the best approach to involving all departments was to get the chairman, president, and/or CEO to do the speaking. These executive communications were both visions and mission statements. For vision, think big. Make it valuable to the whole company and all its stakeholders: employees, customers, shareholders, competitors, and the citizens aware of the company. For a mission statement, keep it focused on what you currently have as a market and what you currently have as a product line.

As an example, "Be the best at what we choose to do" is a fair vision. However, for a mission, "we will build the highest quality slide rules in the world." See what I mean. You can get into trouble being too focused with your vision. Anybody still own or use a slide rule?"[3]

Philip Kotler, professor of marketing at the Kellogg Graduate School of Management at Northwestern University and a world-renowned expert on marketing, provides the following views on vision and mission. Vision must allow a company room to grow into new markets and new technologies. The mission statement should embody a number of characteristics to make it maximally useful. It should focus on certain distinctive values rather than go after everything.[4]

Vision may carry a more personal value. Stephen R. Covey, author of the best-selling book *The Seven Habits of Highly Effective People,* structures the first habit—"be proactive"—around the principles of personal vision. "I will be" becomes the initial step toward mastering your personal values and success in life.[5]

How does vision support TQM? All four of the previously mentioned quality gurus utilize vision as an effective means of communicating the goals of an organization.

- **Deming's first principle:** Create constancy of purpose

- **Baldrige's first category:** Leadership

- **Joseph Juran's first step to quality:** Build awareness of opportunities to improve

- **Frank Voehl's House of Quality:** The four cornerstones of mission, vision, values, and goals and objectives

Often, the leadership of an organization can provide direction, motivation, and pathways toward synergy within the organization by creating a vision. Listed below are six corporate visions and the six companies that created them. Test your visionary skills and try to match the company with its vision (answers are provided at the end of the chapter).

A. "To maximize shareholder value by becoming widely regarded as among the best ___ in the United States by 1995"

B. "To be at the top of our customers' lists of suppliers"

C. "People, Product, Profits"

D. "A man on the moon by the end of the decade"

E. "Ribbons of steel binding the continent together"

F. "The choice of the new generation"

1. The Trans-Continental Railroad

2. Ford Motor Company CEO Red Poling's vision during Ford's most profitable 5 years, 1989–1993

3. Ethyl Corporation, famous for spinning off four separate *Fortune* 500 companies during a ten-year period ending in 1994

4. Pepsi-Cola Companies

5. Signet Bank

6. President John F. Kennedy, sparking the United States to lead the Soviets during the 1960s space race

Note that each vision sets a tone of achievement. In all cases, the visionary, individual leader or management team promoted an improvement for the organization with the vision. The pathway toward this vision is fundamentally grounded in some form of quality improvement process.

What is the vision for your company? If your firm does not have a vision, it is one of a shrinking minority. A recent American Management Association poll found that 84 percent of *Fortune* 500 companies invested the time and expense to develop a vision statement to communicate to their stakeholders. Most vision statements are not the result of one leader in the organization, but rather follow the quality process. They are developed through a series of interventions. This process involves the leadership team, often composed of the company's top management, and represents a strategic goal as well.

President Kennedy's vision of placing a man on the moon by the end of the decade provided the power to fuel NASA to become one of the most powerful government institutions of the 1960s. Similarly, many of the marketing successes of the 1980s and 1990s were the result of a strong, strategic vision, well communicated to all stakeholders.

Lexus, the luxury automobile division of Toyota, entered the U.S. luxury car market in 1988. Lexus's slogan, "the relentless pursuit of perfection," was the strategic base for its vision: to gain a leadership position in the U.S. car market within five years. Initially, Ford's Lincoln car group and GM's Cadillac division were not overly concerned with Toyota's announcement. They were aiming at their European competitors, Mercedes-Benz and BMW. (For additional information, see Abstract 5.2 at the end of this chapter.)

History is the best judge of a vision statement, and the jury is still out on IBM. IBM grew into a global data systems giant after Thomas Watson, Jr. took over the company's leadership from his father. In a now-famous story, Tom Watson suggested that the whole world would only need about six of his firm's computers. His son, Tom Watson, Jr., provided a vision centered around three basic beliefs: pursue excellence, provide the best customer service, and, above all, show employees respect for the individual. These guidelines were the foundation of the growth and endurance that made IBM the top-performing company during the first half of the 1980s. IBM enjoyed 40 percent of the industry's worldwide sales and 70 percent of its profits in the mid-1980s.[6]

As leadership changed, the vision suffered from competitive strategies that sought out niches which "Big Blue" was too slow to defend. The personal computer market, growing faster than successor John Akers estimated, cost IBM its dominance in the market. Now, in the 1990s, Louis V. Gerstner, Jr., once the youngest partner at McKinsey & Company, has the responsibility, as IBM's chief executive, to bring Big Blue back into a leadership position. Mr. Gerstner is struggling with a culture change which involves moving away from the vision that many IBMer's believe made the company successful in the first place. Mr. Gerstner's new principles appeared in *The Wall Street Journal* on May 13, 1994 as a front-page article entitled "Gerstner Is Struggling as He Tries to Change Ingrained IBM Culture."

These principles, also called values, have assisted companies in changing a culture that might detract from today's quality movement. Recall from Chapter 3 how the House of Quality is centered on similar principles. All three quality gurus—Deming, Juran, and Voehl—attribute these value strengths with making a quality process work in an organization. IBM's vision and principles are as follows:

IBM's Vision

Create long-term relationships with customers by providing expert assistance and world-class offerings using the full breadth of IBM skills, products, services and business partners which contribute to the customer's success.[7]

IBM's new principles of conducting business are described in Table 5.1.

A training benchmark study conducted in 1991 by the American Society of Training and Development (ASTD) showed that vision and values were growing at a near equal pace in North American companies (see Figure 5.1). (For additional information, see Abstract 5.3 at the end of this chapter.)

A typical example of a company's vision and values is represented by those developed by Ethyl Corporation's Quality Council, made up of the top management from each of its divisions (chemicals, pharmaceuticals, petro-

Table 5.1 IBM's New Principles

1. The marketplace is the driving force in everything we do
2. At our core, we are a technology company with an overriding commitment to quality
3. Our primary measures of success are customer satisfaction and shareholder value
4. We operate as an entrepreneurial organization with a minimum of bureaucracy and a never-ending focus on productivity
5. We never lose sight of our strategic vision
6. We think and act with a sense of urgency
7. Outstanding, dedicated people make it all happen, particularly when they work together as a team
8. We are sensitive to the needs of all employees and to the communities in which we operate

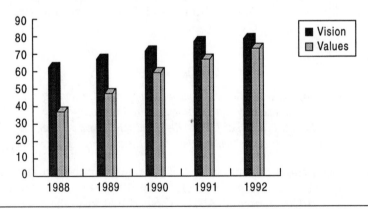

Figure 5.1 ASTD 1992 Study of U.S. Companies Adopting Vision Statements.

leum additives, and life insurance) in 1993. During 1993 and early 1994, Ethyl Corporation "spun off" two divisions, insurance and specialty chemicals. These tax-free spin-offs formed two new *Fortune* 500 companies, First Colony Life and Albemarle Corporation. Both are listed on the New York Stock Exchange and continue to have the founding company's vision and values:

Ethyl's Vision

To be at the top of our customers' lists of suppliers

Ethyl's Seven Values

Respect for People

Unquestionable Integrity

Continually Improving Quality

Our Partners—Customers and Suppliers

Safety and Environmental Responsibility

Good Citizenship

Economic Viability

For additional information, see Abstract 5.4 at the end of this chapter.

Ethyl's Quality Council developed this vision and value system after the company invested years in working to change the culture and strategic direction from a financially controlled production environment toward a market-driven, employee-empowered organization.

It is clear that the 1990s are bringing about change within corporate cultures, in companies both large and small, in an effort to promote the quality process in both the individual and the organization.

For additional information, see Abstract 5.5 at the end of this chapter.

ANSWERS TO QUIZ

A. Signet Bank

B. Ethyl Corporation

C. Ford Motor Company

D. President John F. Kennedy

E. The Trans-Continental Railroad

F. Pepsi-Cola Companies

DISCUSSION QUESTIONS

1. Describe differences between visions and goals.

2. How might TQM assist a company in determining its vision?

3. Develop an organizational chart for a global market introduction of a new product entering a mature market. Be prepared to defend your approach.

4. Describe an effective technique in communicating a company's vision to:

   a. Customers

   b. Employees

   c. Competitors

   d. Public

ENDNOTES

1. See Senge, Peter M. *The Fifth Discipline: The Art and Practice of a Learning Organization*, Doubleday/Currency, New York, 1990.
2. See Drucker, Peter F. *Management: Tasks, Responsibilities and Practices*, Harper & Row, New York, 1982, Chapter 7.
3. Chvala, Richard J. AMA Keynoters on Tour, Richmond, Va., May 4, 1994.
4. Kotler, Philip. *Marketing Management*, 6th ed., Prentice-Hall, Englewood Cliffs, N.J., 1988.
5. Covey, Stephen R. *The Seven Habits of Highly Effective People*, Simon & Schuster, New York, 1989.
6. Hays, Lauarie. "Gerstner Is Struggling as He Tries to Change Ingrained IBM Culture." *Wall Street Journal*, May 13, 1994.
7. Cortada, J. *TQM for Sales and Marketing Management*, McGraw-Hill, New York, 1993, p. 54.

ABSTRACTS

ABSTRACT 5.1
QUALITY IN THE MARKETING PROCESS

Stowell, Daniel M.
Quality Progress, October 1989, pp. 57–62

This was one of the first articles in the field to directly address the relationship and importance of total quality to the marketing and sales cycle, and six years later the message still comes home—loud and clear. Many organizations have committed to the concept of total quality, with quality improvement techniques being applied to almost every area of product development, manufacturing, operations, administration, and customer service, as well as the distribution network. The rub is that marketing is almost never mentioned, except as a source for determining customer requirements.

The author argues the need for a master plan that covers the integration of total quality into marketing and sales functions in order to achieve important benefits such as understanding customer requirements, identifying marketing's products and services, matching requirements to products/ services, and eliminating or improving upon inferior processes. He states that to add new products, we must review very carefully the processes for each new product. This involves, among other things, improving the customer buying process. He finishes with an exhortation to involve all employees in the marketing of quality. "Quality in marketing can have a major impact upon an organization by increasing sales, reducing marketing expenses, improving customer satisfaction, as well as providing a competitive edge." This article is thought-provoking reading, even if it is almost six years old.

ABSTRACT 5.2
DREAM IT. DEFINE IT. DO IT!

Carroll, Robert
Journal for Quality and Participation, July–August 1992, pp. 16–22

Vision was the key motivator at Venture Lighting International, Inc., a nine-year-old manufacturer of metal halide lighting products. The author relates the Venture Lighting story using the four phases of the visioning process as an outline:

1. **Conceiving the initial vision.** The three founders left General Electric and formed a new company with the guiding vision "to be the best metal halide lighting company in the world," and took as their slogan "Lighting a Better World" to demonstrate an interest in broader human needs.

2. **Broadening the vision holder base.** Employees can see and want to *be* visions, says the author. He describes hiring, training, pay scales, and core values. "Visions need to be graphic, appeal to the senses, and be an image in the mind," he says. A sketch, a collage, or role playing sometimes plays a part.

3. **Create the momentum.** He discusses operationalizing the vision through wide-ranging employee discussions, posting the vision statement prominently, and developing a motto: "Dream it. Define it. Do it." He also describes a vision slump and how the company's leadership pulled out of it.

4. **Light the after-burner.** The company used applying for the Baldrige Award as a way of refocusing the company's energies. The company was also flattened to three layers, and people who were not part of the vision were jettisoned. The company uses a sailboat metaphor with three groups of people: those trimming sails and carefully watching the wind, those on the front deck and taking a break in the sun, and those in the water like anchors. While everyone needs a break, says the author, the company could not tolerate anchors.

The article concludes with statistics that show the success of the renewed vision: raw material inventory reduced 86 percent, work-in-process inventory reduced 67 percent, and rework reduced 91.6 percent. (*©Quality Abstracts*)

ABSTRACT 5.3
WHAT'S THE BOTTOM LINE PAYBACK FOR TQM?

Usilaner, Brian and Dulworth, Michael
Journal for Quality and Participation, March 1992, pp. 82–90

While TQM is popular, say the authors, little research has been done to determine whether organizations that implement TQM efforts have improved their performance and competitive position in the marketplace. The authors assess a 1990–91 study by the General Accounting Office (GAO) of the TQM efforts of the 20 companies which have scored highest on the written portion of the Baldrige examination since 1988. The GAO was careful to include only information in the study for which there was an audit trail. Four areas were measured, with the following results:

- **Employee relations indicators:** Employee satisfaction, attendance, turnover, safety/health, and suggestions received

- **Operating indicators:** Reliability, timeliness of delivery, order processing time, errors or defects, product lead time, inventory turnover, cost of quality, and cost savings

- **Customer satisfaction indicators:** Overall satisfaction, customer complaints, and customer retention

- **Financial performance indicators:** Market share, sales per employee, return on assets, and return on sales

Based on the information and data collected, a TQM model was developed which shows the interrelationships among the major elements of a typical TQM strategy. The GAO distilled six particular TQM elements that contribute to improved performance:

1. Focus on meeting customer quality requirements

2. Top management leadership in disseminating TQM values

3. Employees asked and empowered for continuous improvement

4. A flexible and responsive corporate culture

5. A fact-based decision-making system

6. Partnerships with suppliers used to improve product or service quality

The GAO found that it took an average of 2.5 years for the 20 companies studied to realize substantial change in their organizational culture and systems. This article includes a sidebar that lists seven benchmarks of excellence. (©*Quality Abstracts*)

ABSTRACT 5.4
WHAT IS CUSTOMER-DRIVEN MARKETING?

Naumann, Earl and Shannon, Patrick
Business Horizons, November–December 1992, pp. 44–52

While the 50s and 60s were "sales-oriented," and the 70s and 80s were "market-oriented," say the authors, these emphases are now fading as we enter the "customer era." They discuss three states through which a firm must pass to become truly customer-driven:

1. **Bliss**—essentially reactive in terms of customer complaints, lacking a good customer database

2. **Awareness**—more proactive toward customers, with efforts such as extended customer service hours, toll-free calling, and bilingual staff

3. **Commitment**—changing the customer from a target to a partner

Committed firms, the authors say, operate under a philosophy of total customer integration: (1) seeing customers as valuable assets, (2) involving current customers as partners in many decision-making processes, (3) instituting customer panels to meet with various functional areas of the organization, (4) developing complaint analysis and customer satisfaction surveys, and (5) involving suppliers in the decision-making process as well. The reason firms have been so slow in adopting this philosophy, they believe, is blindness toward the true costs of customer dissatisfaction, such as customer service overhead, liability charges, reduced managerial productivity, underestimating the effect of dissatisfaction (only 4 percent of dissatisfied customers complain), and customers lost through the ripple effect of word-of-mouth complaints. Changing to a customer-driven culture, the authors conclude, requires five prerequisites:

- Strong leadership by the CEO

- Conception of the change as a long-term evolution

- Involvement of all organizational levels and areas

- Extensive training and development of the work force

- Continual evaluation, monitoring, and reinforcing   (©*Quality Abstracts*)

ABSTRACT 5.5
BUILDING A VISION COMMUNITY

Ferris, Gregory L.
Journal for Quality and Participation, October–November 1992, pp. 18–20

A new CEO took over at Batesville Casket Co. of Batesville, Indiana, where the previous leadership style had been one of mandates. The CEO asked all employees to view Joel Barker's video "Discovering the Future—The Business of Paradigms" and then discuss it in small groups. As a result of feedback, the CEO dethroned the MBO system which was not soliciting ideas or innovation from employees. What emerged was a vision-driven process, which involved two steps:

1. In an overview presentation, vision was characterized as a means to drive the business plan and as a performance management system. The specifics of the plan were presented to managers through numerous department focus groups, and feedback showed that managers needed training to understand the system.

2. Vision training involved two workshops. (1) The first workshop increased awareness through the CEO's presentation of his vision for the organization, a discussion of issues, and Barker's video "The Power of Vision." Then each employee was asked to begin developing a draft of an individual vision. (2) Four months later, a second session provided structural aids to help employees write their vision statements, and the session concluded with the comment: "Vision without action is merely a dream; action without vision just passes time; vision with action can change the world."

The shift from MBO to vision was difficult for many employees during the first year, says the author. However, after introduction of a vision/risk leadership profile and a vision workbook—both of which the author describes—two years of visioning has brought excellent results: creative ideas, proactivity, frequent reviews for adjustment, and improvement in organizational communication. *(©Quality Abstracts)*

CHAPTER 6

STRATEGY: USING TQM TO COMPETE GLOBALLY

Visions demand a strategy, strategy requires a plan.

Chapters 4 and 5 focused on management and vision, respectively. Neither of these quality leadership attributes will produce results without a plan, known in the business world as a strategy or in written form as a strategic plan. Philip Kotler, world-renowned expert on marketing, examines strategy as the key ingredient in what makes a company excellent. Excellent companies, namely those that climb to the top of their markets and stay there, attribute much of their success to a market-oriented strategic plan.

Strategic planning is the managerial process of developing and maintaining a viable fit between the organization's objectives and resources and its changing market opportunities. The aim of strategic planning is to shape and reshape the company's businesses and products so that they combine to produce satisfactory profits and growth.[1]

How might TQM improve the activities of strategic planning? Let's examine the routine steps in strategic planning and see how a marketer's approach to TQM may provide companies with an edge in the marketplace.

Step	Activity
1	The Executive Summary
2	Current Marketing Situation
3	Opportunities and Issues Analysis
4	Objectives—Marketing and Financial
5	Marketing Strategy
6	Action Programs
7	Controls
8	Contingency Plans

Figure 6.1 The Marketing Plan Strategy Development Steps. (Source: Philip Kotler, *Marketing Management*, 6th ed., Prentice-Hall, Englewood Cliffs, N.J., 1988, p. 33.)

These steps, routinely called a marketing plan, enable a company to communicate its strategy decisions throughout the organization. The eight steps in developing a marketing plan (Figure 6.1) are discussed below, followed by a comprehensive review of such a plan. (For additional information, see Abstract 6.1 at the end of this chapter.)

STEP 1: EXECUTIVE SUMMARY

This step provides a brief review of the strategy and its implications for top management and directors. One way to involve top management in providing direction and support for its strategy would be to demand that managers use TQM in evaluations of the strategic plan. Few, if any, *Fortune* 500 corporate business units and small- to mid-sized businesses check back to earlier strategic plans to analyze the success in strategy implementation or even if the forecasted sales volumes approached reality. Many company strategic planners refer to this as the "hockey stick" approach to planning (see Figure 6.2).

The "hockey stick" approach to planning simply means that sales or profits will drop slightly before returning to and maintaining an upward trend that lasts the life of the plan. Most plans based on strategy are designed for 3 to 5 years in U.S. standards and as long as 10 to 30 years in European

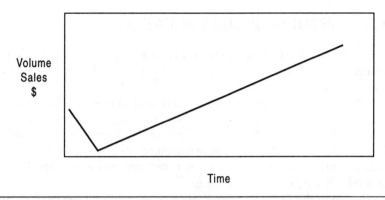

Figure 6.2 Constant Growth Curve: "Hockey Stick" Planning Approach.

standards. The Japanese and Koreans often look outward by developing a 100-year plan.

Using the TQM approach to analyze past performance gives many companies the ability to address their strategies and make changes in order to improve company performance. A histogram, one of the TQM tools, can be used to track past performance. An example of a histogram is provided in Figure 6.3.

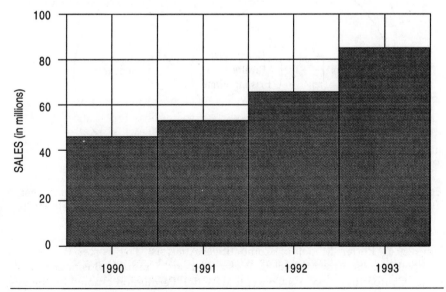

Figure 6.3 Histogram of Past Sales.

STEP 2: CURRENT MARKETING SITUATION

This portion of the strategic plan builds the foundation for gathering data on the marketplace, uncontrollable market forces, and those forces that a company can alter based on its strategy.

The first step in developing this foundation is to examine the impact that world forces have on the market or industry in which a company is competing. Michael Porter, professor at the Harvard Graduate School of Business, developed a model to illustrate the many competing forces that a company or marketer must examine in today's competitive, global marketplace. The Porter model is displayed in Figure 6.4.[2]

As shown in the Porter model, there are five external forces of competition and five internal forces of competition. A brief interpretation of each force follows, as described in an industrial or consumer marketing setting. (For additional information, see Abstract 6.2 at the end of this chapter.)

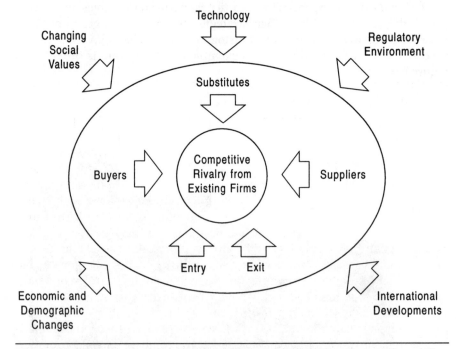

Figure 6.4 Porter Model of Competitive Analysis: The Forces that Affect Competition. (Source: Michael E. Porter. Harvard Graduate Business School. Porter Competitive Analysis Conceptual Model. Permission granted by the author to reprint.)

Changing Social Values

This force may best be described by interpreting the effects of public concern for health on the tobacco industry. At the time of this writing, the Senate and House of Representatives are investigating possible criminal charges against officers of several tobacco firms for their firms' concealment of potentially damaging studies on the health issues surrounding cigarettes.

The push toward nonsmoking began in the late 1960s and early 1970s as the general population was becoming more health conscious. This change in social values escalated in the 1980s, when California passed the first law to require smoking and nonsmoking seating in restaurants and then prohibited smoking altogether in restaurants and public buildings in the early 1990s. By the mid-1990s, most states adopted the California laws. Smoking is now prohibited in airports, on all domestic flights, in public buildings, and in most restaurants. In the United States, the fight against smoking is not over. Public sentiment, led by changing social values, has impacted the tobacco industry in the form of an average reduction in domestic sales of 35 percent since 1975. The only growth regions for the cigarette industry are the Far East and Eastern Europe. Because politicians receive their support from the public, most regulations have been the result of public interest imbedded in changing social values. The tobacco industry claims that over $50 billion, in both sales and defensive strategy measures, has been lost due to society's changing view on tobacco use. This represents quite an impact from a force over which the industry has little, if any, control.

Technology

As a case in point, consider the following scenario. In the early 1970s, the director of marketing of a slide rule manufacturer visited an undergraduate college class. In those days, a great deal of competition was brewing between manufacturers of slide rules and the newly introduced calculator. The director of marketing was emphatic in telling the junior-level class in physical chemistry that his company would continue to make the best slide rules in the world! This statement did not make much of an impression on the students, who were more interested in whether or not their professor would allow them to use the new, highly efficient calculator during a test.

The point is not to hide behind quality and let technology pass you by. Good strategic planning will always keep you aware of technological advances that may impact the market in which you compete. Ethyl Corporation sells over $1 billion a year in fuel additives to diesel, gasoline, and jet fuel refiners. Imagine the effect that the emerging growth of electric car technology will have on the market for fuel additives.

A company can participate in technological advances through research and development; however, one company cannot stop the advances in technology that affect the marketplace.

Regulatory

Probably the best example of the pressure of regulatory forces on a business is Ethyl Corporation, a Virginia-based chemicals firm and at one time the world market leader in sales of lead-based fuel additives. Following a 1974 EPA ruling, auto manufacturers were required to produce cars and light trucks that used unleaded gasoline. Oil companies were mandated to begin phasing out leaded fuel and replace it with unleaded options. Virtually overnight, Ethyl Corporation lost the U.S. market for its best-selling product, a lead-based antiknock additive. Industry analysts projected this loss of market to correspond to approximately $100 to $200 million in annaul profits. Sales of lead additives continued in other world markets, but the U.S. market was limited to aviation fuel. Ethyl was forced to diversify extensively, into such markets as plastics, aluminum windows, pharmaceuticals, and even life insurance, to regain growth during the late 1970s and 1980s. In 1994, Ethyl announced that it would cease production of lead-based products. Although Ethyl had kept its lead-based products alive in other markets for 20 years, it never regained its profitability levels of the 1960s and 1970s. This situation is similar to the story that has unfolded in the tobacco industry in the United States over the last few years.

External competitive forces offer a valuable lesson: whenever changing social values indicate a trend, the regulatory bodies involved will often act upon that trend as the result of political pressure.

International Developments

Increased access to world markets affects virtually every industry. More senior readers may recall their introduction to the Volkswagen Beetle as their first experience with a "foreign" car. Much of today's U.S. economy is affected by the constant battle for market share among global automobile manufacturers. An *American Demographics* magazine report indicates that 38 percent of all goods purchased in the United States are sourced overseas.

The ISO standards and Deming Quality Award originated in England and Japan, respectively. As regions of the world grow more knowledgeable about the benefits of marketing and quality products, understanding the quality process and how it relates to marketing will increase in value. These quality standards issues are addressed in Chapter 9.

The question most frequently asked in today's boardrooms is, "How will we compete in a global marketplace?" Meeting quality demands and certification requirements is the first step.

Economic/Demographic Changes

Tracking trends in the economy is best left to economists; however, the marketer must be cognizant of these trends and how they affect the markets in which he or she participates. A quick glance at the last recession (1990 to 1994) reveals the increased demand for generic goods in consumer industries as well as decreased capital goods spending in the industrial sector. Companies reacted to this downturn by downsizing and then, through competitive analysis, looked to other techniques to give them a competitive edge as a strong global economy returned. Reengineering, supply-chain initiatives, and the related issues of quality process improvement paved the way for "smart" companies to move more quickly in their marketplaces. This knowledge is "trickling down" from the larger, more global corporations to the small, local market companies via consulting firms. Inevitably, marketers will be faced with competing against constantly improving competitors. Successful companies will focus on processes that account for market information and best approaches for dealing with that information.

Demographic changes sometimes require greater understanding and interpretation. Take a close look at the following example. Tredegar Industries, a $600 million manufacturer of plastic sheeting (VisQueen), food bags, and related products, is the major supplier of plastic backing for disposable diapers for Proctor & Gamble. The company's sales have recently increased, despite the competitiveness of the disposable diaper market, simply because the companies that make disposable diapers have discovered that the fastest growing segment of the U.S. market is adults. Attends and Depends, two adult brands, are the fastest growing brands in this niche market. (For additional information, see Abstract 6.3 at the end of this chapter.)

These are examples of how external forces, as described by Harvard Professor Michael Porter,[2] can negatively impact a company. The benefit of applying TQM in marketing is that it provides a pathway for a company to reveal external trends and realize increased profitability.

The following are some examples of how TQM principles can be used to capitalize on the external forces that impact a business:

- Watch for variations in economic trends
- Demographic changes in population
- Effects of technological advancement

Internal Forces of Competition

The next parameter in addressing the market situation of a business is the internal forces of competition. These forces, as described by Porter,[2] can impact a company through its strategic and tactical moves. The following is a brief review of the internal forces.

Substitutes

During the mid-1980s, the global soft drink market was in the grasp of the powerful aluminum can packaging industry. In short, while the entire beverage industry, including beers and juices, was discovering the ease and convenience of the aluminum can as a packaging medium, the packaging industry discovered that the easiest way around a tight market was to raise prices. Most consumers do not realize that, at today's prices, an empty aluminum beverage can (12-ounce size) costs approximately 12 to 14 cents.

When Coca-Cola Company recognized that the price of packaging was creeping into its profits, it searched for a way to send the message to its suppliers of aluminum cans. That message, introduced in 1986, was the plastic can.

Clearly, the impact of a substitute for a product can disrupt a company's strategy or the strategy of its competitors or suppliers at any time. Some substitutes that have impacted their markets are listed in Table 6.1.

Buyers

TQM and its offshoot, supply-chain management, both provide benefits in relating to and understanding the effects that buyers as a force have. One major role of a company's marketing department is to determine the best mix of customers for the company's products or services. A significant portion of that decision rests on the strengths and potential vertical integration capabilities that a buyer may elicit.

According to the 80/20 rule, 20 percent of a company's customers provide 80 percent of its profits. This has a direct relation to volume as well. If one of those customers elects to manufacture the product or service that the company is currently providing, profitability is affected.

Consider the case of Anheuser-Busch, the world's leading brewer. In the late 1970s, it purchased its entire aluminum can needs from a variety of suppliers. Then, while working on Budweiser Light, the company learned how easy it is to manufacture cans. As a result, Metal Container Corporation, once a subsidiary of Anheuser-Busch, became one of the largest can makers in the world. Several previous suppliers to Anheuser-Busch had to regroup

Table 6.1 Product Markets and Their Substitutes

Market	Major product	Substitutes
Transportation	Autos, buses, planes, trains	Airlines, teleconferencing, city clustering
Postal system (written communication)	Mail, FedEx, UPS	Computer cc:mail, facsimile transmissions (faxes), video phones
Natural fuels (gasoline, diesel, coal)	Gasoline—auto fuel Diesel—truck/train fuel	Electric, solar, vacuum tunnel power
Entertainment	Movies, theme parks, recreational activities	Cyberspace, virtual reality
Lubrication	Oils, greases	Synthetics, polyalphaolefin
Soft drinks	Coca-Cola, Pepsi-Cola, Seven-Up, Dr. Pepper, tea, lemonade	Gatorade, Power-Ade, flavored bottled water, Snapple, flavored teas

and, in many cases, merge. As a result, Continental Can, American Can, and National Can became Triangle Industries.

Suppliers

Another internal force of competition results when a supplier stops providing a key service or product/raw material or, by vertically integrating, becomes a competitor. A marketer planning a company's strategy should follow the company's suppliers as closely as he or she follows the company's customers. This is why the team management approach of TQM works so well in marketing. Typically, a marketer relies on the purchasing department to contend with suppliers. In a team relationship, a representative of the purchasing department would be readily available as a participant in the development of the group's marketing strategy. As a result, supplier relationships would be monitored more closely and any competitive moves might be anticipated and possibly countered.

A good example of this force is the car rental industry. The "Big Three" domestic car manufacturers recognized the benefits of using car rentals as a way to market new models as well as a profitable solution to excess inventories during the 1970s and 1980s. Today, all three own large portions of worldwide car rental agencies.

Entry–Exit Barriers

These forces of competition often require intensive study when a company is deciding whether to enter a new field, but can also be used as a protective force when competing in a particular market. In the late 1960s and early 1970s, the craze in the toy market was the "Pet Rock." It consisted of a rock housed in a cardboard package which doubled as a "cage." At the time, it cost $3.95, but is now worth over $50 as a collector's item. Obviously, the only barriers to entering that market were good supplies of large gravel and cardboard and access to toy distribution channels.

Barriers to other markets can be quite forceful. To enter the car manufacturing market, a company would have to set up distribution channels, meet EPA guidelines, and crash test at least five automobiles to study safety features. In order to compete in the chemical manufacturing industry, money and technology are two of the barriers to entry. The average chemical plant today costs over $100 million to design, build, and staff. Any new technology, unless purchased through a licensing agreement, can require years of research in complex facilities staffed by highly compensated chemists and chemical engineers.

Exit barriers correlate directly with entry barriers. Usually, the more it costs to enter a market, the more expensive it is to leave that market.

Actual Competitors

At this point, we have reviewed ten different competitive forces before even beginning to anticipate strategies and tactical moves from the competition. A marketer has little or no control over five of these forces. This is typical of the research that a company must conduct when developing its strategy. Herein lies the value of total quality in that it can provide considerable savings and accelerate competitive response time.

In the House of Quality, described in Chapter 3, the fundamental concepts of total quality were addressed. At the conclusion of this strategic plan review, we will demonstrate how each concept of total quality can improve the effectiveness of planning a company's strategy.

STEP 3: OPPORTUNITIES AND ISSUES ANALYSIS

This step is known as a "wish list" for marketers. Given a particular situation, acceptable and/or courageous paths or strategies to follow are examined. The potential pitfalls or hazards along these paths are also addressed. Each of these opportunities and issues can be assigned a level of priority to indicate the marketer's confidence in that event actually becoming

Table 6.2 Opportunities/Issues for a Global Automobile Firm

Opportunities	Issues
Market new "green car" in Far East (environmentally friendly compact)	Competition is offering a more environmentally friendly subcompact
Devaluation of the dollar makes exporting U.S. autos to Japan more attractive	Increasing profits prompt labor unions to ask for higher wages (potential strike)
Build a new plant in Ireland to serve European market and take advantage of attractive labor rates	Unrest in Ireland makes investment there risky
Ship utility vehicles into Argentina as a result of NAFTA	Regulatory laws in Argentina do not allow for imported utility vehicles, only cars

a reality. A possible list of opportunities and issues that might exist in a marketing strategic plan for a global automobile manufacturer is provided in Table 6.2.

While opportunities and issues may be difficult to prioritize, one of the major objectives of marketing is to determine the best strategy. Total quality management allows the marketer to gauge the strength or size of opportunities and issues.

STEP 4: OBJECTIVES—MARKETING AND FINANCIAL

The purpose of this step is to declare the measurable goals that the marketing unit elects to pursue. Setting goals, and measuring progress toward those goals, often provides a background for analyzing what strategy and/or tactics can best achieve those goals. In marketing terminology, a marketing goal might be a larger percentage of the market, a higher rate of identification after an advertising campaign, or higher margins as the result of differentiation or low-cost strategies over the competition. Financial objectives are measured in monetary units. Common examples are dollars (or currency) of profit, gross sales, etc.

TQM tools such as the control chart, run chart, and Pareto analysis can be used by the marketer to review the progress of a strategy in reaching a goal. Let's examine a model for this purpose.

Baggle Industries manufactures and markets high-impact-resistant rural postal mailboxes. The market for these items is suburban and rural homeowners. The product is channeled through hardware and discount stores, as well as mail-order catalogs that feature practical home accessories.

Table 6.3 Total Quality Tools and Information Needed

Team representative	Concern	TQM tool
Manufacturing	Production rate	Cause-and-effect analysis
Shipping/logistics	Shipping damage	Histogram
Sales	Account coverage vs. number of units sold	Scatter diagram
Purchasing	Lead time for raw materials ordered	Pareto chart
Marketing	Decorator color unit sales vs. standard	Control chart

Baggle's marketing team planned a "differentiation" strategy by offering mailboxes in decorator colors. The goal was 30 percent of the mailbox market (marketing objective) in Maryland, Virginia, Delaware, and the District of Columbia, up from 25 percent last year. This corresponded to a financial objective of an additional $500,000 in sales (1 percent market share equals $100,000 in sales) and $200,000 in operating profit (at 40 percent operating profit, the mailbox industry seems well worth the effort).

Teams are discussed in detail in Chapter 7, but for the sake of this example, let's assume that manufacturing, shipping/logistics, procurement/purchasing, sales, and marketing are members of the Baggle Mailbox team. Although the quality management tools will be of help to everyone involved, certain tools may better support the level of information needed by the different team members. The appropriate total quality tool based on the information need are indicated in Table 6.3 (see also Figures 6.5 to 6.8 later in this chapter).

STEP 5: MARKETING STRATEGY

The initial step in determining a strategy, after the fact-finding steps (Steps 2 to 4) have been completed, is to objectively answer the following fundamental strategic questions:

1. What does the company do well?
2. What does the customer want?
3. What is the competition offering?

If 1 matches 2 better than 3 matches 2, then the company has a competitive advantage. This simple questioning format is adapted from the Executive Marketing Management Program at Duke University's Fuqua Graduate School of Business. This executive program has been ranked as one of the top ten business school programs in the country.

Development and communication of the strategy should include the following areas of a business:

- **Market segmentation:** On what section or "piece of the market pie" will this effort concentrate? (For example, rural users of mailboxes in the state of Delaware)

- **Market position:** How will the company or product differ from the competition? Differentiation or a low-cost producer strategy provides for a company's market position.

- **Marketing strategy:** From the four "P's" of marketing, also known as the marketing mix. The four fundamental elements of the marketing mix, as described by Kotler, are presented in Table 6.4.[2]

Other aspects of product quality, such as service, warranty, and returns, are included under the "P" of product.

Dick Berry, marketing professor at the University of Wisconsin, recently surveyed a sample of marketing managers, customer service managers, product managers, and senior executives to determine which marketing mix variables they considered most important. In addition to the standard four "P's", he added an "S" to represent customer service and two "C's" to represent customer sensitivity and convenience. The four "P's" as well as the three new items are described in Table 6.5, along with a ranking of the managers surveyed.[4] (For additional information, see Abstract 6.4 at the end of this chapter.)

Table 6.4 Marketing Mix Elements

Product	Price	Place	Promotion
Quality	List price	Distribution channels	Advertising
Features	Discounts	Coverage	Personal selling
Options	Allowances	Locations	Sales promotion
Style	Payment period	Inventory	Public relations
Brand name	Credit terms		
Packaging			

Table 6.5 Marketing Mix for the 1990s

Marketing element	Rank
1. Customer sensitivity: employee attitude, customer treatment, and response to customers	1
2. Product: quality, features, and reliability	2
3. Customer convenience: availability to the customer, customer convenience, easy to do business with	3
4. Service: postsale and presale service	4
5. Price: price charged, pricing terms, and pricing offers	5
6. Place: provider accessibility, provider facilities, and availability to customer	6
7. Promotion: advertising, publicity, selling	7

It is interesting to note that customer sensitivity ranked higher than the original marketing mix elements, or four "P's". Marketing in the 1990s will require understanding the dynamics of how employee attitudes influence treatment of the customer.

Also included in forming a strategy, whether for a product or a service or for the consumer or industrial market, are research and development and market research.

Many companies currently include a formal quality program as part of their overall strategy. Most of these companies use their quality program as a part of their advertising or communication to the customer to further differentiate their product or service. Ford Motor Company's "Quality Is Job 1" campaign is credited with communicating the company's quality strategy to both existing and potential customers as well as Ford employees. General Motors' Cadillac Division winning the Baldrige Award is another example of a U.S.-based global automotive giant touting the value of quality to its customers.

STEP 6: ACTION PROGRAMS

Chapter 7 details the value of teams, in terms of both the organization and efficient performance. Many early examples of quality teams were led by marketers and were facilitated by quality management personnel. General Electric, Westinghouse, Ford, and Xerox are examples of *Fortune* 500 firms that developed marketing department lead teams to establish customer satisfaction systems and priorities. Many of these team-based programs, which began in the late 1970s, were prompted by Step 6 of the marketing strategy plan: action programs.

Action programs are best described as the *who, what, where,* and *when* of marketing. After divulging the strategy and objectives desired, this section of the plan is devoted to defining roles and responsibilities among the various departments and teams in order to effectively implement the strategy.

- **Who:** What team members or departments are responsible for which action

- **What:** The action they will carry out

- **When:** A timetable for that action to be implemented

- **How much:** The estimated cost in manpower, equipment, or finances

- **Where:** In what market segment this activity will occur

As an example, let's return to Baggle Industries, the rural mailbox manufacturer. Baggle has decided to introduce a differentiation strategy in the mid-Atlantic U.S. market by marketing impact-resistant polymer mailboxes in decorator colors. The following are typical action items resulting from this strategy:

- R&D will provide manufacturing with a production prototype, at a production cost under $20, by first quarter 1995.

- Manufacturing will tool up to build 75 units per shift at Plant A, with defects under 4 percent and a second-quarter full production start-up.

- Marketing will develop communications and advertising for both direct catalog sales and channel distribution to independent discounters by second quarter 1995.

- Sales will sell 10,000 units, at 40 percent margin, in order to fill distribution channels by third quarter 1995.

The quality approach involving teamwork increased in value as businesses became more complex and required faster speed of service during the 1980s and 1990s.

STEP 7: CONTROLS

This step provides for a system to measure the success of the strategy and its implementation. Basically, any process that will serve as a means for management to evaluate the effectiveness of the strategy is acceptable here.

Some common systems, which parallel quality management tools, include but are not limited to the following:

- **Time/action item control line (Figure 6.5):** A chart detailing the activities required for strategy implementation (action items) categorized on a time line, with success of implementation or delays noted.

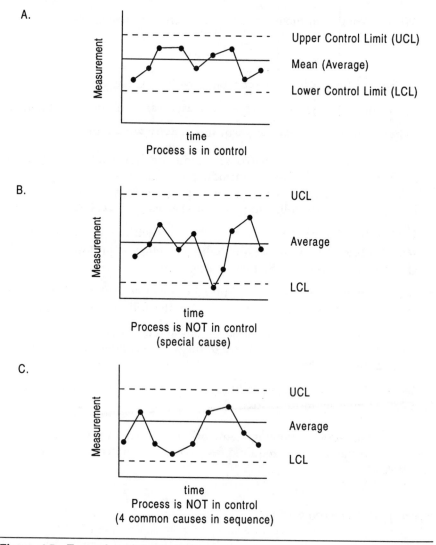

Figure 6.5 Examples of Control Charts.

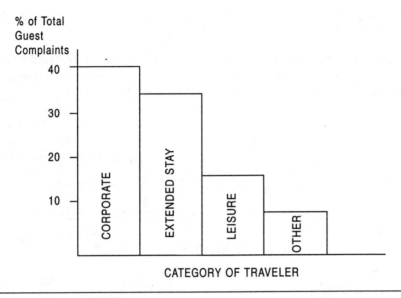

Figure 6.6   Pareto Chart.

- **Pareto chart (Figure 6.6):**   Reasons for not meeting financial or marketing objectives can be surveyed by team members and listed on a Pareto chart.

- **Cause-and–effect-analysis (Figure 6.7):**   List the opportunities that become realities during the course of the plan and what changes they require.

- **Scatter diagram (Figure 6.8):**   Can be utilized by marketing researchers to determine the effectiveness of an ad campaign. Similar to a perceptual map, this chart indicates how customers or focus groups view the value of a product compared to the desired level.

- **Run chart (see Figure 6.3):**   Can be plotted as sales per day/week/ month on a time line chart.

STEP 8: CONTINGENCY PLANS

Step 8 is most commonly referred to as "plan B." This step was formally added to the common marketing strategic plan during the late 1980s, when management began to see the need to have strategists think beyond the "four corners" and provide an alternative plan.

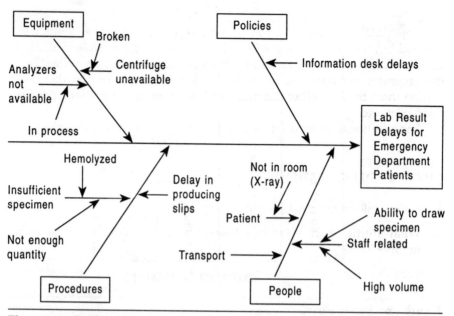

Figure 6.7 Fishbone Diagram. (The fishbone, or cause-and-effect, diagram (sometimes called an Ishikawa diagram, named after the Japanese quality control leader) is drawn during a brainstorming session. The central problem is visualized as the head of the fish, with the skeleton divided into branches showing contributing causes of different parts of the problem.)

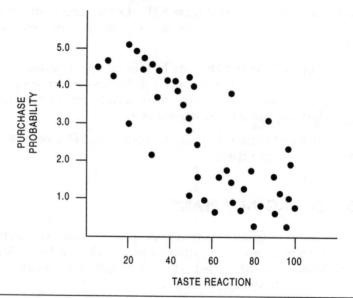

Figure 6.8 Scatter Diagram.

The contingency plan is a mini marketing plan developed to counter any external or internal competitive force that has a strong probability of affecting the accepted strategy. Returning to our example of Baggle Industries, if the decorator mailboxes do not sell, plan B might be to repaint them and market them through other channels, such as mass merchandisers, door-to-door sales, etc.

For additional information, see Abstract 6.5 at the end of this chapter.

DISCUSSION QUESTIONS

1. Define integrated marketing planning.

2. What are the eight steps in a marketing plan? Which of these steps involve TQM?

3. Provide an example of a quality strategy from a *Fortune* 500 company. Describe how this strategy has impacted the company.

4. Identify the five forces of external competition in Michael Porter's model of competitive forces.

5. What make up the five internal forces of competition on that same Porter model?

ENDNOTES

1. Kotler, Philip. *Marketing Management*, 6th ed., Prentice-Hall, Englewood Cliffs, N.J., 1988.
2. See Porter, Michael. *Competitive Strategy*, Harvard Business Press, Cambridge, Mass., 1987.
3. Berry, D. *Marketing News*, December 24, 1990, p. 10.

CASE STUDY

USING TQM STRATEGY IN MARKETING: "THE COLA CAPPER"

During the late 1980s, a large division of a *Fortune* 200 company was growing the market for plastic closures in the beverage industry. Plastic bottle caps, as they are more commonly known, provided great benefits to the beverage industry, both for carbonated and noncarbonated beverages. For those readers unfamiliar with the beverage industry, carbonated beverages (primarily soft drinks) are bottled under pressure to retain the carbonation for the "shelf life" of the beverage.

Most consumers may recall that earlier packages for soft drinks were glass bottles with metal bottle caps, crimped onto the bottle, requiring a bottle opener. Over the years, advancements in production automation and package designs allowed for a metal (aluminum) "twist-off" type of bottle cap. Early examples of this style of cap were difficult to unscrew and sometimes dangerous, and many "grocery store tales" of exploding bottles with the early versions of this cap led to extreme caution with new vendor designs.

One other drawback was the lack of a "tamper-evident" closure. Long before this issue gained critical importance with the nationwide "Tylenol murders," soft-drink bottlers and grocery stores faced a constant problem with competing soft drink "delivery people" and irate customers who twisted off the caps slightly. This "prankster-type" effort released the carbonated pressure and sometimes allowed the beverage to discolor due to degradation. This was an annoying problem for all parties involved; the consumer complained of "flat" soda, the grocery store lost customers, and the bottler lost profits and brand loyalty.

In 1985, Molded Products, a $100 million division of Ethyl Corporation, engineered the first "tamper-evident" plastic closure for use on carbonated beverage bottles. This breakthrough closure was engineered of polyethylene, with a "grip-tread" outer surface to allow a person's fingers to grip a non-skid surface (most bottles, once removed from the refrigerator, become slippery due to condensation from the temperature change). On the inner surface of the closure, below the "screw-on/off" threads, was a "tamper-evident" ring of plastic, which, when the bottle was opened initially, would tear, providing proof to the consumer that the bottle was either still fresh or previously opened.

This type of closure proved to be quite successful, and by the late 1980s, most soft-drink bottlers were adapting their bottling production facilities to accommodate this cap. One such bottler was Mid-Atlantic Coca-Cola, based in Silver Spring, Maryland, with bottling facilities in seven states along the mid-Atlantic region of the United States.

In 1988, according to Archie Frost, then national sales manager for beverage closures for Molded Products, the relationship between Mid-Atlantic Coca-Cola and Molded Products was "more than a basic vendor/buyer relationship, yet nowhere near a partnership." Gaylord Perry, vice-president of operations for Mid-Atlantic Coca-Cola, suggested an even less attractive scenario. "Basically, we (Coca-Cola) view closures as a commodity. We purchase millions each quarter, and due to the competitive nature of the soft-drink industry, we must minimize costs at every opportunity."

The summer of 1988 along the eastern seaboard was typical of mid-south summers—hot, hazy, and humid. July and August temperatures were constantly in the 90s, and the "cola wars" were heating up as well. Then, for at the time an unknown reason, Coke customers were calling the bottler's franchise offices throughout the region, complaining that they could not get the bottles open, or if they did, often with a pair of pliers, the bottle was so shaken up that the soft drink often flowed over the top and onto the floor. Initially, it was a few complaints...then the calls escalated. Mid-Atlantic Coca-Cola customer inquiry personnel estimated the calls at well over 100 per day. Unfortunately, as many marketers realize, only about 20 percent of upset customers bother to contact the offender. Most, due to apathy and the knowledge that oftentimes nothing is done to satisfy the customer, just switch to another brand. In the case of Coca-Cola, that meant Pepsi-Cola, Dr. Pepper, and other global competitors.

With loyal Coke drinkers upset and leaving Coca-Cola, Coke immediately set the blame on Molded Products' tamper-evident closure. The joke around Coke at the time was "Sure, it's tamper-evident. It's tamper-proof, cause you can't get the cap off." With the summer season well underway, it turned out to be rather foul humor. Coca-Cola had no immediate alternative, except to turn to another cap supplier and, in some cases, remove current stock from grocery store shelves.

Molded Products' marketing team was in a crisis situation. The board room, atop the Federal Reserve Building in downtown Richmond, Virginia, became a "war room." If Coke, Molded's number one customer, was canceling orders and "vowing never to return," this would surely damage the reputation and profitability of the company.

What surprised Molded Products the most was the isolation of the problem to Mid-Atlantic Coca-Cola. No other customers were experiencing this situation, or if they were, they were extremely isolated cases. Molded was confident of the uniformity and quality of its closures, due to its adoption of

Deming's quality process in both the production and marketing of this product.

Molded had set up quality improvement teams to handle various issues, both related (production, R&D, logistics, etc.) and external (sales, customer satisfaction, delivery, etc.). At the time, no team was organized to handle an issue of this magnitude.

As the team developed, members included sales, production, customer service, and marketing. Their first visit to the customer was met with apprehension among the team members and outright antagonism by the customer.

According to Archie Frost, "As I recall, we were on the verge of losing our largest account and, potentially, the entire beverage closure business. This would mean approximately 30 percent of the Molded Products revenues (other business units being automotive and household) and potentially the jobs and careers of 50 people."

At the same time, Mid-Atlantic Coca-Cola personnel had the job of explaining to their marketing people why this great idea of a tamper-evident cap, with great graphics appeal, was continuing to lose market share and loyal Coke drinkers daily. Readers may recall that this was in the late 1980s, shortly after Coke introduced "New Coke" and then had to offer "Coca-Cola Classic" to regain loyal customers who were dismayed over the change.

Gaylord Perry said, "First it was 'why did you change Coca-Cola,' and then, during the best season of one of our best years, the customers' cry was, 'We can't get the bottle open.' Most of this was our two-liter and 16-ounce plastic bottle business, which happens to be the family-oriented sales which account for the most loyal and, in our case, most profitable business. Pepsi was laughing all the way to the bank.

"While we were trying to use Deming's approach to openness and 'drive out fear,'" says Archie Frost, "we were plenty scared at the outcome of this venture. While Coke was screaming lawsuit at us, we attempted to intervene with a simple quality process device known as the cause-and-effect chart. Coke looked at us like we were off our rockers."

The approach was simple; however, given the atmosphere of the situation, it was difficult for Molded's quality team to involve the customer personnel to get at the "root cause."

What involved several 14- to 16-hour days, spent both in the customer's operation and at Molded's test labs, ended with a startling conclusion.

As Archie Frost explains, "Through the use of statistical control charting, we found that the customer was actually having machinery difficulties which caused two of their major assembly lines to 'screw the cap on too tight.' However, without a proper system to record this data, and bottling lines running in excess of 2000 bottles per minute, it was almost impossible to ask the bottler to accept the fact that they were at fault."

The solution had to be foolproof, and Molded had to develop a relationship with the Coke plant's people to help them see the benefits of a total quality system or process to keep this from happening again.

Molded's approach was simple, yet difficult to implement. Molded needed to teach Mid-Atlantic the value of adopting Deming's quality process and then have Coke communicate this value throughout the bottling industry to help Molded regain its image as a quality supplier.

Customers are never wrong, and yet if they are "not exactly correct," it is the duty of the supplier to provide more value to the customer than a competitor, after the fact, in a situation like this.

"The bottling industry is a close-knit family," says Gaylord Perry. "If anyone learns that a supplier is 'less than satisfactory,' often within a short time that supplier will lose the beverage industry as a customer. Yet if a supplier demonstrates value above and beyond a regular level of service, that supplier's net value within the industry increases manyfold."

Such was the case of Molded Products. Although no longer owned by Ethyl Corporation, Molded became a portion of a "spin-off" from Ethyl, part of Tredegar Industries, and then was sold to Crown Cork and Seal, one of the premier beverage packaging giants.

That group and Mid-Atlantic Coca-Cola now continue to enjoy a great relationship, and both Coke and the closure group maintain that their relationship is far beyond that of a commodity supplier.

ABSTRACTS

ABSTRACT 6.1
THE IMPACT OF JUST-IN-TIME INVENTORY SYSTEMS ON SMALL BUSINESSES

Sadhwani, A.T. and Sarhan, M.
Journal of Accountancy, January 1987, pp. 118–132

Although written in 1987, this article by Sadhwani and Sarhan is just as timely today for sales and marketing as in the day it was written. The key notion is that Just-in-Time (JIT) inventory management systems, used to reduce inventories and improve quality and productivity, are being adopted more frequently by large manufacturing corporations, thus presenting new challenges for the sales efforts of small businesses as well. JIT, a "pull" system (assembly line triggers withdrawal of parts from preceding work centers), has two aspects that are heavily emphasized by manufacturers: Just-in-Time sales-to-purchasing processes and Just-in-Time delivery and transportation. JIT sales-to-purchasing, which relies heavily on a dependable supplier network, calls for manufacturers to purchase from fewer suppliers, using small lot sizes and statistical quality control techniques.

In addition to using fewer suppliers and signing larger contracts (with suppliers), JIT manufacturers are working with smaller lot sizes, thereby reducing unnecessary inventories and freeing storage areas to reduce cost and improve quality. Statistical quality control is a powerful problem-solving tool that pinpoints variations and their causes and eliminates after-the-fact inspection—an expensive, wasteful procedure that rarely detects the causes of poor quality. More recently, JIT manufacturers have encouraged their suppliers to form "focused factory" arrangements which enable the supplier to focus on a limited number of products and become a specialized maker to a major manufacturer. This usually leads to suppliers relocating closer to their respective manufacturer, one of the tenets of JIT delivery and transportation. In addition to the elimination of centralized loading docks and staging areas, another benefit is information sharing and microcomputer use, exposing small businesses to computerized information systems.

The implications of JIT for small businesses are profound and include better customer relationships and stable sales demand forecast. Not all the benefits come easy, though. For example, sales and marketing professionals must institute statistical process control and understand freight economics, but the benefits of long-term contracts, smooth production, improved quality, and reduced scrap and rework greatly enhance the success of small businesses. Good graphs are provided but no references.

ABSTRACT 6.2
MARKET-LED QUALITY

Morgan, Neil A. and Piercy, Nigel F.
Industrial Marketing Management, May 1992, pp. 111–118

With industry's emphasis on quality likely to be lasting, it is important that marketing functions understand how to gain "ownership" of quality, contend the authors. After explaining the highlights of the quality movement, the authors outline a "Holistic Approach to Quality" which recognizes (1) that customer quality perceptions are the product of the difference between initial customer expectations and their perceptions of the outcomes achieved in buying a product or service; (2) that customers evaluate at least two dimensions of quality—technical, quality, and functional quality; and (3) that customer perceptions of the technical and functional quality of the products and services they purchase can be affected by their image of the supplier organizations. Therefore, the authors suggest two broad areas where marketing is important to the strategic management of quality:

- **The management of customer expectations:** "Managing quality involves the active management of customer expectations," say the authors, "to prevent 2 common problems with existing quality strategies—over-promising and over-engineering." Marketers play a potentially fundamental role by providing formal and informal marketing communications that provide customers with bases for translating their needs, requirements, and past experiences into expectations of the product or service and the supplier organization.

- **The management of customer perceptions:** The authors see supplier image as important to how customers perceive product or service quality. Marketers not only project the corporate image, they also conduct marketing research, track customer satisfaction over the life of the product or service, and provide "confidence messages, rationalization of the purchase choice, implicit cues through pricing, packaging, warranties, and so on."

According to the authors, potential benefits for the marketing function by taking a greater role in the management of quality include: (1) an alternative mechanism for achieving a market orientation within the organization and (2) a way of extending the life cycle of integrated marketing functions. (©*Quality Abstracts*)

ABSTRACT 6.3
TENDING THE SALES RELATIONSHIP

Callahan, Madelyn R.
Training & Development, December 1992, pp. 31–36

Cultivating long-term customers requires a delicate balance between consulting and selling, says the author. This article presents results of research on customer satisfaction from a report entitled *Profiles in Customer Loyalty*, published by Learning International of Stamford, Connecticut. The report shows that salespeople can build the potential for long-term customer relationships if they share useful business information with customers, even when it does not further their sales efforts. A sidebar to the article lists customer expectations of the sales relationship, including:

- **Business expertise and image:** The salesperson needs to understand general business and economic trends, have good personal appearance and personality, understand the decision-making process within his customer's company, and know the competition.

- **Dedication to the customer:** A salesperson must (a) be honest, (b) help solve problems to meet emergency needs, (c) be reachable when needed, (d) take a long-term perspective in doing business, (e) get the backing needed from his company, and (f) suggest creative solutions to business problems.

- **Account sensitivity and guidance:** A salesperson ought to (a) coordinate all aspects of a product or service to provide a total package, (b) offer guidance throughout the sales process, (c) instill confidence, (d) be sensitive to a customer's pricing needs, (e) respond to customer concerns, (f) keep promises, and (g) bring in others from his company to meet customer needs.

Customers would like to view the sales representative as a virtual member of their own company's team rather than as a peddler, says the author. The biggest pitfall for companies that desire to market through consultative selling, she concludes, is an emphasis on making quarterly goals instead of taking a long-term view. (©*Quality Abstracts*)

ABSTRACT 6.4
IS STRATEGY STRATEGIC? IMPACT OF TOTAL QUALITY MANAGEMENT ON STRATEGY

Schonberger, Richard J.
Academy of Management Executive, November 1992, pp. 80–87

While doing research in 1982, the author was struck with the fact that executives in superior Japanese companies seemed to do little of what is thought of as strategic planning. Instead, they spent more time overseeing organizational dedication to the basics of competitive advantage: high quality and short cycle time. He lists 19 principles of TQM, the first of which is "Get to know the next and final customer." Many of these principles are aimed at (1) driving out costly overhead, (2) speeding up the design and production process, (3) improving flexibility of human and physical resources, and (4) eliminating uncertainties caused by rework and shaky suppliers—many of the knotty strategic decisions facing senior management. "Today," he says, "a minority opinion is that high-level managers should *not* engage in numerical goal-setting," perhaps because of Deming's emphasis on the elimination of numerical productivity and work standards goals. On the other hand, he observes, numerical targets for sales, profit, and so forth *are* necessary for budgeting and financial management. "A tenet of TQM is that 'you only improve what you measure,'" he acknowledges. "But aggregate numbers planned and measured high in the organization have little relevance to the work of most people in the organization." He sees self-imposed or team-imposed goals as more acceptable. There is no need, he says, to concoct a number in the improvement goal ("managerial tinkering"). Instead, he believes the focus should be on the *rate* of improvement. "Given their extensive inculcation of TQM practices," he asks, "do fine companies like Motorola and Hewlett-Packard *need* high-level numerical goals? Perhaps not," he answers. He believes top managers' time should be spent in "frequent, active involvement in implementation of TQM-based policy, with successes and problems made visible on wall charts." Time spent visiting internal customers he sees as more valuable than time "in conference rooms over computer sheets and flip-charts." Instead of a "by the numbers" approach to strategic planning, he says, "it's time to alter the mental image. The leader becomes strategically influential less by making decisions and more by seeing that good decisions are made." (©*Quality Abstracts*)

ABSTRACT 6.5
ALIGNING VALUES WITH VISION: ENHANCING THE
TOTAL QUALITY PROCESS

Witmer, Neil T. and Sherwood, Stephen
Continuous Journey, October–November 1992, pp. 30–35

Values, say the authors, are deep-seated pervasive standards that influence all aspects of our behavior—our personal bottom line. Values are especially critical in times of change, when normal policies and habits no longer apply. After discussing how personal values are formed and changed, the authors turn to the importance of corporate values. They present a hierarchy-of-values graphic which shows a *vision of desired values* at the top of a pyramid, below which are *shared corporate values*, then *group values* of various groups in the corporation, followed by *personal operating values and behavior.* "Ultimately," the authors contend, "shared corporate values can unify the efforts of disparate groups and the behavior of employees." After discussing a three-step methodology for assessing values, the authors offer suggestions on how to align company values. Then they identify four types of employees which emerge in a TQM process: (a) those who already possess the desired values and behave accordingly (20 percent), (b) those who easily learn desired values as part of the TQM process (40 percent), (c) those who successfully shift their values with considerable effort and hands-on leadership (20 percent), and (d) those who cannot change their values (20 percent). The last group "will probably have to be outplaced or moved to a more appropriate assignment before they cause costly damage," say the authors. Finally, they discuss some specific strategies to maximize value shifts in a TQM effort:

- Top leaders must keep their fingers on the pulse of the changing norms and culture, identify informal leaders and "gatekeepers" to create a "critical mass" of change, and "walk the talk."

- The company vision, mission, and values must be kept visible through constant communication and storytelling by key leaders.

- Goals and objectives must be clearly specified and understood by all employees.

- Customers must have an open channel of communication and feedback to the organization.

- A well-designed management process should be used to give recalcitrant managers an honest look at their versatility, maturity, confidence, self-awareness, and attitudes.

- People's competencies should be matched to their jobs and career expectations.

- A continuous improvement strategy should continue to develop and reexamine desired values, corporate values, and personal operating values, while the CEO meets regularly to seek input and discuss problems. (©*Quality Abstracts*)

WORKING

CHAPTER 7

WORKING
IN TEAMS

If you want one year of prosperity, grow grain.
If you want 10 years of prosperity, grow trees.
If you want 100 years of prosperity, grow people.

(Old Chinese Proverb)

Today, more and more organizations are looking to work teams, fundamentally changing the way personnel are deployed and how they are managed. In fact, self-directed work teams are an integral part of many total quality programs. According to UCLA management professor David Lublin, about one in five U.S. companies operate self-managed teams, up from one in twenty a decade ago.[1] According to some estimates, 40 to 50 percent of the U.S. work force may work in some kind of empowered team by the end of the decade. In a firm committed to continuously improving its performance, teams are to people what processes are to tasks. In this chapter, we will look at what teams are, why their use is increasing, goals of teams, how teams are organized, the different types of teams, and, finally, the requirements for the successful implementation of self-directed teams.

WHAT ARE SELF-DIRECTED TEAMS?

Self-directed teams (SDTs) are made up of an intact group of employees who are given complete responsibility and authority to perform one or two broad categories of activities. Typically, teams are responsible for an entire work process that delivers a product or service to an internal or external customer. SDTs are not assembled strictly for a special purpose such as a new product launch, but rather work together on an ongoing, day-to-day basis. Teams range in size from as few as 5 or 6 people to as many as 18; however, experience seems to suggest that between 5 to 12 is optimal. Other distinguishing characteristics of SDTs include:

- They are empowered to share various management and leadership functions.
- They plan, control, and improve their own work process.
- They set their own goals and inspect their own work.
- They create their own schedules and review their performance as a group.
- They prepare their own budgets and coordinate their work with other departments.
- They order materials, keep inventories, and often deal directly with suppliers.
- They are often responsible for conducting their own training.
- They hire their own replacements and assume responsibility for disciplining their own members.
- They take responsibility for the quality of their products or services.[2]

WHY TEAMS?

SDTs are more than just a passing fad. Companies are using them because they work. A report in *Business Week* claims that teams can increase productivity by 30 percent or more and can also substantially improve quality.[3] Many companies have experienced a great deal of success using SDTs. Federal Express cut service errors by 13 percent.[4] Carrier, a division of United Technologies Corporation, reduced unit turnaround time in its new Georgia facility from two weeks to two days. Near and Weckler conducted a study in which they compared SDTs with traditional structures on a number of organizational and job characteristics. They found that SDT members scored significantly higher than their traditional counterparts on the following factors: innovation, information sharing, employee involvement,

Table 7.1 Primary Reasons Cited for Moving Toward Self–Directed Teams

Cited as primary reason	Respondents (percent)
Quality	38
Productivity	22
Reduced operating costs	17
Job satisfaction	12
Restructuring	5
Other	6

Source: Wellins, R., Wilson, J., Katz., A., Laughlin, P., and Day, C. *Self-Directed Teams: A Study of Current Practice. A Survey Report*, Development Dimensions International, Associaton for Quality and Participation, and *Industry Week*, Pittsburgh, 1990.

and task/job significance.[5] In another study, researchers examined work design across 70 organizations and found that SDTs correlated with financial and behavioral outcomes such as increased organizational effectiveness, heightened productivity, and reduced defects.[6]

SDTs are also being supported by top management. The primary reasons for moving toward teams are listed in Table 7.1.[7] As revealed in Table 7.1, quality and productivity are the two reasons cited most often by senior line managers for moving toward SDTs. Other reasons given by companies using teams include:

- Labor costs drop
- Morale rises
- Signs of alienation ease
- Faster response to technological change
- Better response to new worker values

For additional information, see Abstract 7.1 at the end of this chapter.

KEY FACTORS IN ESTABLISHING TEAMS

Although there is no cookbook approach to establishing teams, there are some "common denominators" that will yield more satisfactory results. Each of these is elaborated in the discussion that follows.

Information Sharing

Management should share all information that is not considered personal. The individual employee and the team, as opposed to management, should determine which information is important. If employees are expected to pursue organizational goals and make decisions about their own work, then a key requirement is to provide them with sufficient information and feedback to optimize their behavior and interactions. Failing to share information within the organization creates confusion, mistrust, and inconsistency in performance, especially as it concerns customer service. Poorly informed or misinformed employees may perform their jobs inadequately, thus affecting the customer service encounter. Further, sharing information with employees serves as a basis to engage in proactive problem solving.

Individual Motivation

In traditional organizations, management is expected to provide motivation and discipline to individual employees. SDTs, on the other hand, create a climate where motivation and discipline come mainly from within the employee and from fellow employees. Motivation and peer pressure emanate primarily through group conversations.

Empowerment

An organization empowers its people when it allows employees to take more responsibility and make use of what they know. Quinn and Spreltzer[8] describe empowerment as a cycle that begins with learning and growth and ends with innovative outcomes. Their Cycle of Empowerment is illustrated is Figure 7.1

Empowerment is facilitated by several factors:

- Organizational values/leadership actions
- Human resource systems (including rewards and training)
- Organizational structural job design[9]

Organizational values and leadership actions make it possible to invest teams and employees on those teams with authority and decision-making power. Empowerment is further enabled by providing training. Organizations need to realize that empowering workers requires world-class training. Also, there needs to be recognition for performing effectively as a team and a team member. Finally, empowerment can only be maximized to the extent that employees can team up directly with whomever they need to get the job

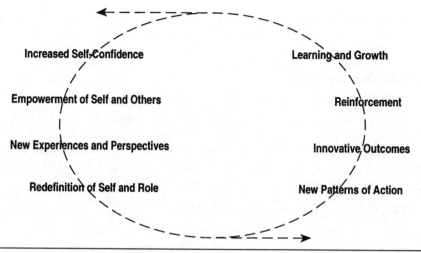

Figure 7.1 Cycle of Empowerment.

done, without worrying about going through the chain of command. Thus, the organizational structure must be adapted to facilitate empowerment.

Clarity in Team Goals

A team works best when everyone understands its purpose and goals. Team goals will be supported to the extent that they are appreciated as being important and worthy of achieving. Also, teams that receive a clear vision from management are better able to determine their goals more easily. The team also needs to be clear about larger project goals and about the purpose of individual steps, meeting, discussion, and decisions. In his book *Zap*, Byham operationalizes goals as part of a three-step approach:

1. **Establish key result areas:** The direction you want to go (e.g., improve output, reduce cycle time, etc.)

2. **Prepare a measurement:** A way to know whether you are moving in the right direction (e.g., a unit of measurement such as time or quantity)

3. **Define a goal:** Something that tells you whether you have achieved a desired level of performance in some key result area[10]

Clearly Defined Roles

Teams operate most efficiently if all members understand their duties and know who is responsible for what tasks. These roles should be periodically reviewed to determine whether they are still consistent with team goals. The team should decide how roles will be assigned and, if necessary, changed.

Use of Quality Tools

Deming believed that education is simple and knowledge of how to use powerful statistical techniques should be required of employees. A variety of tools exist to help identify the significant performance inhibitors. For example, cause-and-effect diagrams (see Figure 6.7) help clarify relationships between business components. Pareto charts (see Figure 6.6) and histograms (see Figure 6.3) demonstrate frequency of occurrence. Run charts and scatter diagrams (see Figure 6.8) show trends in process performance. Control charts (see Figure 6.5) help to distinguish between common process variation and special causes that need immediate attention. Finally, flowcharts (Figure 7.2) are useful in depicting process flows, such as order fulfillment.

Values-Centered

Teams are effective to the extent that every job is viewed as valuable; sincerity, honesty, integrity, and trust are practiced; and each person on the team is respected. How values serve as the centerpiece for successful team development is illustrated in Figure 7.3.

TYPES OF TEAMS

Teams differ according to structure and purpose. Drucker uses sports teams as a metaphor to describe the different types of teams.[11] For example, the first type of team is like a baseball team, where everyone plays a position on the team and each player's performance can be measured individually. This represents one of the strengths of this type of team. Also, members of a baseball team can be trained and developed to the fullest extent of their individual strengths. Every position on a baseball team—engineering, marketing, production—does its job in its own way. Yet a baseball team is inherently inflexible. It works well when the tasks are sequential and repetitive. Thus, this type of team usually operates within a highly defined and repeatable process. Henry Ford's assembly line is an example of a baseball team.

A second type of team is like a football team, where the players have fixed positions yet play as a team. A hospital emergency room that treats a patient at 3 a.m. who is recovering from shock is an example of a football team. Drucker also cites the Japanese auto maker design teams as an example of football teams.

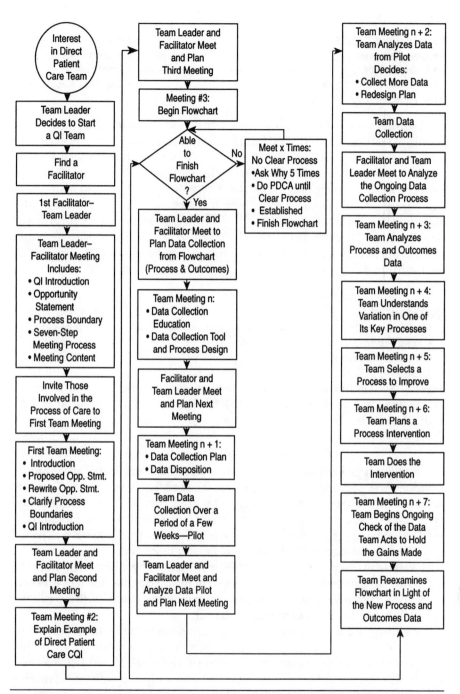

Figure 7.2 Flowchart of Direct Patient Care Team Deployment. (The direct patient care team deployment uses a generic management structure to team development as a framework for analyzing improvement strategies.)

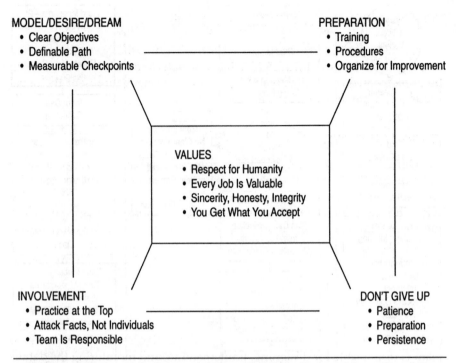

MODEL/DESIRE/DREAM
- Clear Objectives
- Definable Path
- Measurable Checkpoints

PREPARATION
- Training
- Procedures
- Organize for Improvement

VALUES
- Respect for Humanity
- Every Job Is Valuable
- Sincerity, Honesty, Integrity
- You Get What You Accept

INVOLVEMENT
- Practice at the Top
- Attack Facts, Not Individuals
- Team Is Responsible

DON'T GIVE UP
- Patience
- Preparation
- Persistence

Figure 7.3 Attributes for Successful Team Building. (Source: Manz, C. and Sims, H. *Business without Bosses.* Copyright 1993. Reprinted by permission of John Wiley & Sons.)

A third type of team is like a tennis doubles team. Here, according to Drucker, the players have primary rather than fixed positions. They are supposed to "cover" their teammates by adjusting to their strengths and weaknesses. Team members may be asked to perform several functions as well, often being asked to fill in for one another. The team roles are adjusted according to the demands of the game. Performance is determined more by how well team members coordinate their roles than by individual effort. An account management team is an example of how a doubles team operates in marketing. Team member roles may change as the needs of the customer change or with shifts in competitive actions.

Although all three of these types of teams are teams in the truest sense, they differ in the behaviors that they require and in what they do best. Drucker makes a strong case for not attempting to make hybrids from these teams, as each type of team is designed to play only one way and changing from one kind of team to another is difficult. (For additional information, see Abstract 7.2 at the end of this chapter.)

IMPLEMENTING SELF-DIRECTED TEAMS

Once the decision is made to establish SDTs and the type of team to be employed is selected, a further challenge is to determine how these teams can be implemented most effectively. The following stages represent the usual sequence in implementing teams.

Stage 1: Forming

During this initial phase, a steering committee is usually formed to serve as an umbrella for the entire team design process. This committee generally consists of upper and middle management, facilitators, individuals who will serve the teams as leaders and coaches, and a sample of prospective team members. The steering committee clarifies the organization's vision, develops a chart that spells out the purpose and importance of teams, provides a link to the needs of the larger organization, and provides general support for implementation

A design team is also formed. This team might include members of the steering committee but would also include a broader representation of supervisors, team members, human resource specialists, and functional experts, such as individuals from engineering or information resources. The design team is responsible for designing, implementing, and monitoring the details of the SDTs. The design team would likely address such issues as how teams are structured, what tasks teams will be responsible for, what outcomes or results of team efforts will be measured, how teams will get the information they need to manage their business, what training teams might need, and the type of reward systems used.

Some further considerations during the forming stage include:

- Teams should be formed around customers.

- Team members should be trained to perform multiple skills and tasks; each team should have the ability to service virtually all requests made by clients.

- The role of the supervisor should change to that of a team facilitator who works with the team to establish goals and objectives, serves as a liaison with other teams and outside groups, manages projects, and facilitates team building and conflict resolution.

For additional information, see Abstract 7.3 at the end of this chapter.

Stage 2: Team Implementation

During this phase, several issues need to be addressed, including:

- Over what period of time the team structure is going to be rolled out
- What systems must be modified to support teams
- What the training needs are and how they can best be met
- What the barriers to introducing change are and how they will be overcome
- How progress will be measured[12]

Stage 3: Rollout

The rolling out of teams can be handled in several ways. One way is to create a pilot project consisting of a single SDT. A second approach is to use a phased-in conversion process, where teams are gradually introduced and design teams learn as they go along. Finally, the company can follow the total immersion approach, where teams are introduced company-wide and all systems change at once.

Stage 4: Monitoring the Progress

Most implementation efforts will require changes along the way. Rapidly changing technologies, market demands, and organizational maturity force constant re-evaluation. Evaluating teams' efforts can be accomplished through internal audits of team members via questionnaires or interviews. Team performance should also be evaluated against the goals established by the teams. The design team should meet regularly to review the progress of the teams.

SUMMARY

It appears that a revolution is in progress in the workplace. SDTs are helping many organizations to successfully meet their competitive challenges. Teams succeed when they are made semi-autonomous and given authority, training, and freedom to act and are held accountable for their results. Companies have introduced SDTs in order to improve quality, raise productivity, reduce costs, and increase worker satisfaction. The challenge in utilizing teams is clearly in the changing role of supervisors and middle managers, where ambiguity and the perceived loss of control can make the transition more difficult. (For additional information, see Abstract 7.4 at the end of this chapter.)

DISCUSSION QUESTIONS

1. What role does "empowerment" play in establishing self-directed teams?
2. How might membership in a small group lead to improved motivation and hence improved quality?
3. What are the key factors in successful team building?
4. Teams are just another management fad. Discuss.

ENDNOTES

1. Lublin, J. "Trying to Increase Worker Productivity, More Employers Alter Management Style." *Wall Street Journal*, February 3, 1992.
2. Wellins, R., Byham, W., and Wilson, J. *Empowered Teams*, Jossey-Bass, San Francisco, 1991, p. 5.
3. Herr, J. "The Payoff from Teamwork." *Business Week*, July 10, 1989, p. 52.
4. Dumaine, B. "Who Needs a Boss?" *Fortune*, May 7, 1990, p. 55.
5. Near, R. and Weckler, D. "Organizational and Job Characteristics Related to Self-Managing Teams," paper presented at International Conference on Self-Managed Teams, Denton, Tex., September 1990.
6. Macy, B., Norton, J., Bliese, P., and Izumi, H. "The Bottom-Line Impact of New Design: North America from 1961–1990," paper presented at International Conference on Self-Managed Teams, Denton, Tex., September 1990.
7. Wellins, R., Wilson, J., Katz, A., Laughlin, P., and Day, C. *Self-Directed Teams: A Study of Current Practice. A Survey Report*, Development Dimensions International, Association for Quality and Participation, and *Industry Week*, Pittsburgh, 1990.
8. Quinn, R. and Spreltzer, G. M. "The Empowerment Process." *Academy of Management ODC Newsletter*, Summer 1991, pp. 1–4.
9. Wellins, R., Byham, W., and Wilson, J. *Empowered Teams*, Jossey-Bass, San Francisco, 1991, p. 23.
10. Byham, W. *Zap*, Harmony Books, New York, 1988, p. 111.
11. Drucker, P. "There's More than One Kind of Team." *Wall Street Journal*, February 11, 1992, p. 13.
12. Welins, R., Byham, W., and Wilson, J. *Empowered Teams*, Jossey-Bass, San Francisco, 1991, p. 115.

PROFILE

SALES-LED CUSTOMER TEAMS

Following industry trends in total quality management, Ethyl Corporation, a *Fortune* 500 petroleum additives company headquartered in Richmond, Virginia, has initiated sales-led work teams. These teams, composed of internal personnel, meet at regular intervals to discuss initiatives aimed at improving customer satisfaction. The following is an example of how these teams are organized.

The major thrust of Ethyl's customer-focused teams is to create pathways to improve service and communication with the customer. Using the team approach, with leadership coming from the sales contact, allows the team members to quickly learn customer needs and concerns and provides empowerment to act on those needs. Chuck Stevens, Ethyl's sales management coordinator, facilitates the teams' efforts and uses the team activities to construct and implement process efficiencies within the company. "We instituted sales-led work teams in 1992. As a result of the information generated through the teams' communication process, we developed systems to speed up product lead times, order/delivery/payment methods, and most importantly to our customers, a process to involve R&D in developing new specifications for current and future products. The sales-led work teams have given a morale boost to the people inside the company as well. In many cases, these teams have traveled to meet with customers and learn more of how their efforts reach the final customer, the public customer who fills up at the pump."

Although the salesperson is responsible for providing guidance to the team in terms of customer needs, all teams members actually participate in leading the team at different times. The team efforts have enabled the several departments represented to learn about the responsibilities of other positions. This in itself has fostered improvements in "respect for people," which is one of Ethyl's primary company values.

Ethyl's customers have also responded favorably to the effect that empowerment has had on Ethyl's employees. Customer satisfaction surveys have demonstrated a significant increase in favorable responses as a result of employing quality teams.

CASE

FlyingFox: A MANAGER'S TALE

The tale of this adventurous group begins as Team FlyingFox encounters trouble and finds a solution from an unexpected source.

"Ron, we've got a problem and I don't think Team FlyingFox can solve it. We need some direction from you before we waste much more time going around in circles." I'd never heard Carlos sound so upset.

"Tell me about it." I tried to keep my voice from betraying my anxiety.

"We just can't produce FlyingFox within the costs we're talking about and the time deadline and still meet all the criteria of recyclability and aesthetics that the steering committee refers to as Product Delight."

"Is it because of the housing material problem?"

"Yeah. Wesley and Nick were here until late last night with a couple of the R&D guys and some of my people, and we went round and round and ended up nowhere."

"What are the issues?"

"They're what they've been from the beginning, Ron." There was exasperation, annoyance, and fatigue in Carlos's voice. "The plastic we normally would use for a product like this doesn't have the cosmetic properties we need. The material with the best cosmetic doesn't have the structural strength we're after. And the only composite material that provides both isn't recyclable, and it's too hard to work with anyway. We've tried mixing and altering, changing cycle times, doing all kinds of tricks. Nothing works."

"What are the alternatives?"

"We could go one of two ways, I think. First, we could simply tell the steering committee that we can't deliver the recyclability."

"Or?"

"The other possibility is to get the outside design group to back off on some of their cosmetic requirements. I'm beginning to think this partnership approach with an outside group isn't such a good idea. Those people are too demanding. I know we're after quality, I know we're looking for innovation and breakthrough. But these guys don't like to compromise."

"Where do you stand right now?" I asked.

"I can't commit any more time and resources to making prototype after prototype and running test after test chasing this Holy Grail the steering committee calls Product Delight. I'm at the end of my rope. Something has to give."

This was not just peevishness. Carlos was frustrated and feeling abused.

"Let me think about this, and I'll talk to the others. I'll get back to you."

"Sure, but Ron, we've got very little time to build a prototype that will convince the steering committee. The people on that committee really know their stuff, and we can't put anything over on them. Plus, I'm not going to put my reputation on the line by walking in there with some half-assed model that looks like a junior high school kid made it in shop."

"I understand, and I won't put you in that position. I'll get back to you."

Before I had a chance to think about Carlos, I got the second call, this one from Dr. Zanoski, chief of R&D.

"Ron." The voice was neutral, completely without affect.

"Good morning, Doctor."

"I'm sorry, but I cannot allow my staffer, Nick Yu, to work on your project any longer."

"Doctor, as we discussed before, Nick wants to be a team member..."

"Yes," said Zanoski, "but as I told you before, if I saw any disintegration of his performance I would have to step in."

"And have you seen such evidence?"

"That is why I am calling you. I was in early this morning, checking on an experiment, before I met with a visitor. Nick was supposed to have logged some data for me before going home last night, but when I came in, I discovered that he had not done so. Nick told me he would leave it one my desk, but it wasn't there, so I went to see if he had left it in his area instead. I found Nick asleep on the floor of his office. He obviously had not been home last night. When I woke him up, he said he had been unable to log the data because he was at a FlyingFox team meeting until well after midnight."

"That's unfortunate." I said.

"It is more than unfortunate. It has jeopardized the validity of an important experiment, and it is unprofessional behavior besides. This is what I feared would happen from the beginning, and now I simply must pull him off your project."

"Why don't we talk with Nick together."

"There is nothing to talk about."

"I'm sure you can appreciate that Nick plays a crucial role on this team project. He would be difficult to replace at this point."

"I understand that, but you understood the risks from the beginning. Now, I must go. My visitor has arrived."

Zanoski hung up. I called Nick's office, but was transferred into voice mail. I slammed down the phone. It rang immediately.

"Hi, Ron, it's Nick. I'm in the conference room with Keith. Can you come down?"

"I'll be right there." Andrea, my assistant, was just arriving, so I grabbed her and we walked down together. I told her about the developments of the morning so far.

"What are we going to do?" she asked.

"I don't know." That was the one thing I was sure of.

PROBLEMS AND THEN SOME

In the conference room, Nick and Keith were surrounded by drawings and documents. They looked rumpled and harried, tired and stressed.

"I just wanted to warn you..." began Nick.

"I've already heard from both Carlos and Zanoski."

"Why Zanoski?" Nick seemed confused.

"He said you failed to record some data because you were working on FlyingFox last night, and he wants you off the project."

"But I got another guy in the department to do it."

"Does Zanoski know that?"

"I handed the data to him this morning."

"He didn't tell me that."

"Did he say he didn't get that data?"

"No. He just said the experiment was jeopardized."

"It wasn't."

The phone buzzed.

"Ron, what's going on out there?" It was Hartmut, the head of the outside design firm.

"What do you mean?"

"I was in a conference call this morning with Wesley and Carlos. They're telling me that I am being inflexible and that they cannot create what we have developed together. Why wasn't Nick in on that call? Why weren't you? What is going on?"

"I didn't know they had called you, Hartmut. All I know is that Carlos is concerned about meeting all the specs and is particularly worried about the housing material issue. He's saying that you are refusing to compromise on changes."

"Do you know why he's saying that?" Hartmut sounded genuinely angry and disturbed. "Wesley and his people have been making changes to the drawings, changes that affect appearance and user functionality, without discussing them with us. We agreed that they would make only those changes that would affect internal structure or manufacturing tooling. But they have made two important changes that significantly affect the appearance of FlyingFox—for the worse—and make it less easy to use. This we cannot tolerate. They must be discussed with us. It's a mockery of the work we have done!"

"Okay, Hartmut. Let me investigate at this end and we'll be back in touch."

I hung up, and looked to Andrea. "We need a team meeting right away. Would you see if we can get everybody in here on Monday? Hartmut, too."

"Yes, Boss, anything you say, Boss," she said.

Hartmut flew in early Monday morning. The team members all came in also. Cub drove down from a lakeside cabin he visited with his family every weekend. Keith, already in town, stayed over the weekend at Andrea's. Kate, at my urging, postponed a planned trip until later in the day. Nick decided to sneak out of R&D without Zanoski noticing. Wesley brought along two associates. Steadfast Phyllis was there from purchasing.

I looked around at the assembled faces and realized that in the days before this team project, I would not have been bringing these issues before a group like this. I wouldn't have had a group like this one to help at all. Instead, I would have been wrestling with the problems myself or delegating them to (that is to say, dumping them on) someone—and trying to find a way to appease every faction without alienating any other.

Here, as a team, we were focusing on the result, a successful product, rather than trying to affix blame or avoid it. I grabbed a marker and riffled to a clean page on the flip chart.

"Issue number one: Nick's involvement. Dr. Zanoski feels that Nick is too pressed to contribute to other projects. I'm wondering," I said, looking at Wesley and Keith, "if we can reduce Nick's involvement in the project and still keep him involved." Nick and I had agreed to open this issue up for general discussion.

Everyone started to talk at once. I held up my hand. "And, just so we have an agenda, issue number two is the housing material. Carlos is telling me that he thinks we can't meet all the specs for material characteristics that the steering committee requires and that we have to make a serious program change of some kind."

A SOLUTION APPEARS

Three hours of conversation followed. By 11:30 we had explored a hundred solutions and chosen none. Then, during a lull in the tumult, Phyllis tentatively raised her hand.

"Phyllis," I said, nodding at her. "What's on your mind?"

"Has anyone heard of FungiFlex?" she asked mildly.

Blank stares all around. Was this an irrelevancy? I summoned up my active listening skills.

"No, Phyllis. What is FungiFlex?"

"It's a plastic material. I think it could solve both our problems."

The stares turned to curiosity and disbelief.

"How so?"

"Well," Phyllis smoothed her skirt, "I was in a meeting with my boss in purchasing. We were just getting started when Dr. Zanoski came in. He didn't have an appointment, but he insisted on talking with my boss right then and there."

Everyone became more attentive when Phyllis mentioned Zanoski.

"Or course, he ignored me because, you know, who am I but a purchasing agent? And a woman."

Uneasy laughter.

"Well," Phyllis folded her hands and plunked them in her lap. "He wanted to know if we had a source for purchasing liquid crystals."

Nick looked perplexed. "Why wouldn't he buy them through our regular source?"

"He said the reason was that he needed to buy much larger quantities than usual and wanted to get some competitive bids."

This still seemed like a digression, but she had our complete attention.

"My boss asked him about specifications, and Dr. Zanoski gave her a sheet of specs. Then my boss asked what the crystals were for."

Phyllis paused, dramatically.

"Dr. Zanoski said it's for a new plastic material we've been experimenting with. My boss said, 'Oh, really. I haven't heard about it. What is it?' Then Zanoski looked at me again, probably to make sure I really was a nobody," continued Phyllis, "and I guess he decided I was. 'We've been working on it about four year now,' he said. 'It's a thermoplastic composite, reinforced with liquid crystals. It's called FungiFlex.' 'Oh,' said my boss, 'what's the advantage of that?'"

Phyllis paused once again, squeezing the story for every ounce of value.

"Zanoski said, 'It's very strong. Very workable. And has a good surface finish.'" Phyllis's voice dropped to the lowest possible yet still audible volume. "And this is the best part," she said. "He said that FungiFlex can be reused up to five times. You could get 50 years of use out of this material. That would really take care of our need to ensure recyclability."

Phyllis let the impact of this story sink in. Whether FungiFlex was the answer to our problem or not, I realized we had been overlooking one of our most valuable corporate resources, Dr. Zanoski himself, precisely because we were involved in a turf dispute of the type that cross-functional teams were supposed to discourage. I had never brought up the material issue with him, never even thought of doing so.

Could it be possible, I wondered, that Zanoski was being uncooperative not out of spite or obstinance, but because he wanted to be consulted? Could it be possible that he was feeling slighted, even hurt?

I turned to Nick. "Did you ever discuss the material issue with Zanoski?"

"Are you kidding? I've never discussed FlyingFox with him. I was afraid to bring it up at all."

"So," continued Phyllis, reveling in her moment, "I thought, why not make FlyingFox out of FungiFlex? We'd have the material we need. Zanoski probably would be happy too, and he might be more willing to let Nick stay involved."

We all looked at Phyllis as if she were our savior. I thought, if cross-functional eavesdropping is a hidden benefit of teamwork, then we had better take advantage of it.

Even now, when some acute problem faces us and none of the traditional solutions are working, someone will say, "What we need here is a FungiFlex." It is Team FlyingFox shorthand for a solution that is right before our eyes, that solves more than one problem and does so in a way we never would have expected.

ABSTRACTS

ABSTRACT 7.1
STUDY SHOWS STRONG EVIDENCE THAT
PARTICIPATIVE MANAGEMENT PAYS OFF

Lawler, Edward E. III et al.
Total Quality Newsletter, September 1992, pp. 1–4

In this excerpt from a new book, *Employee Involvement and Total Quality Management: Practices and Results in Fortune 1000 Companies,* the authors present comparisons of surveys sent to *Fortune* 1000 companies in 1987 and 1990, with 51 percent and 32 percent response rates, respectively. The article includes several bar graphs and charts which compare 1987 and 1990 data. There seems little difference between the surveys in reasons for implementing employee involvement (EI) programs: improving quality and productivity are still at the top (about 70 percent each), followed by improving employee motivating and improving employee morale (about 55 percent each). "Most employees, in a 3-year period, did not receive training in interpersonal skills or in the kinds of technical/analytical skills necessary for an employee involvement or total quality program to work effectively," say the authors, the data showing little change from 1987. Only 9 percent of the organizations recently trained more than 60 percent of their employees in TQM and statistical analysis, and only 2 percent have trained 60 percent in understanding financial reports and business results. All but 10 percent of the corporations have some employees covered by individual incentives, but they usually cover less than 40 percent of the work force. Overall, the success ratings for the pay-for-performance reward systems associated with EI programs are extremely positive. Highest ratings were for profit-sharing and employee stock ownership programs, but 43 percent of respondents were undecided with respect to the success of gainsharing. Work group or team incentives indicated 51 percent undecided, but few reported failure. While support by top management retained its lead as a condition facilitating EI (50 percent), support by middle management dropped from 39 percent to 26 percent over 3 years, reflecting the ambivalence middle managers have toward EI when they see how the programs will force behavior changes and reduce their numbers. The greatest improvement in internal processes is reported in participatory management, technology implementation, trust management, decision making, and organizational processes and procedures. Quality, service, and productivity are reported improved as a result of EI efforts in about two-thirds of companies. The relationship between TQM and EI follows no clear pattern, with slightly more than one-third of companies managing EI and TQM as one integrated program, a third managing them as separate but coordinated programs, and the other third managing them separately. Still, respondents tended to view EI as part of quality (76 percent), rather than quality as part of EI. (©*Quality Abstracts*)

ABSTRACT 7.2
THE QUALITY TEAM CONCEPT IN TOTAL QUALITY CONTROL

Ryan, John M.
ASQC Quality Press, Milwaukee, 1992, 272 pp.

"This book's intent," explains the author, "is to provide the reader with a comprehensive look at how various techniques, methods, and strategies fit together to restructure an organization's culture by building and implementing an overall team approach to total quality control/just-in-time (TQC/ JIT)." The author focuses on a JIT approach to process improvement as a subset of TQC. In the first chapter, he relates JIT to TQC and discusses basic JIT terms and concepts, illustrating them with a variety of graphs. The second chapter explains how a company can organize the three types of teams required to implement and support a TQC/JIT system:

- **Top-level team (TLT):** He explains how to select participants from the upper levels of management, and then he outlines and explains the specific responsibilities of this team to write and manage a plan for system implementation and maintenance.

- **Corrective actions teams (CATs):** After the TLT identifies company-wide problems, it assigns CATs to solve the problems. This chapter outlines the basic guidelines by which a CAT runs.

- **Functional improvement teams (FITs):** These teams are formed in every department to identify and correct problems which are more or less confined to their own operations. The author gives a list of guidelines for running FIT meetings, along with the responsibilities of the leader.

The next chapter gives a detailed description of how to implement a FIT. The principles, he explains, are nearly identical to those that govern the implementation of CATs. The author introduces flowcharting and the types of graphs through which to communicate information. This section also includes a number of forms and examples of implementation in various companies. The next chapter describes specialized CATs for solving specific problems, such as the pilot line, vendor relationships, value engineering, design for manufacturability, parts commonality, preventive maintenance, foolproofing, process layout and line balancing, lot size reduction, organizing and cleaning the workplace, *kanban*, line stop, SPC, visual signals (ANDON), training (certification), setup time reduction, automation review, and cycle time control. Chapter 5 deals with the principles of cost savings. A final chapter summarizes the commitment needed by top management to make the system work. This book provides practical, detailed help with team implementation. Though most of the examples are from a manufacturing setting, the author assures the reader that the principles also apply to non-manufacturing functions as well.   (©*Quality Abstracts*)

ABSTRACT 7.3
TEAMS AND TQM: WHY TEAMS FAIL

Wiseman, Dan
Continuous Journey, December 1992–January 1993, pp. 6–8

Why do teams fail? The author discusses seven reasons, giving each "syndrome" a cute name, such as "The Oakland not Aukland Syndrome" for teams that lack direction, like the legendary airline passenger who would end up in New Zealand instead of California. The most common reasons that teams fail are:

1. **Lack of a specific direction:**   The author suggests that the team create the charter or mission statement with help of the supervisor or leader.

2. **Isolation from customers:**   Teams should be able to identify their customers and involve them somehow in the decision-making process.

3. **Lack of patience:**   Teams should be nurtured, but not scrutinized so often that they are in a state of constant change.

4. **Sabotage by supervisors:**   Supervisors, threatened by loss of power, need to be involved in defining new high-value activities they can perform.

5. **Failure to understand interdependence:**   Team processes or services must be understood in relation to the needs of the whole organization and charted, examined, and constantly improved. Decisions on boundary changes should be implemented only after careful study of the entire organization.

6. **Communication breakdowns:** The facilitator can observe, give the team feedback, and provide protection, while the team learns to discipline itself to follow a code of conduct.

7. **Obsolete compensation systems:** Compensation systems need to be altered to reward accomplishment of team goals rather than individual goals. (©*Quality Abstracts*)

ABSTRACT 7.4
DESIGNING PAY SYSTEMS FOR TEAMS

Lawler, Edward E. and Cohen, Susan G.
ACA Journal, Autumn 1992, pp. 6–19

While reward for individual achievement has been widely used in traditional organizations, it tends to work against team performance. In this article, the authors first consider the characteristics of three types of teams, and then they discuss which kinds of incentive compensation motivate high team performance and which do not. Six factors are influenced by pay systems, they say: (1) attraction and retention, (2) motivation, (3) skill development, (4) culture, (5) reinforcement and definition of structure, and (6) cost. Then they analyze how these factors should be considered for motivating each type of team:

- **Parallel teams** that supplement the regular organizational structure and perform problem-solving and improvement-oriented tasks (e.g., quality improvement teams) are used by 85 percent of *Fortune* 1000 companies. Job-based pay seems to work best for parallel teams, with individual merit pay for job performance, team recognition or cash for suggestions, and possibly gainsharing.

- **Project teams** involve a diverse group of knowledge workers brought together to conduct projects for a defined but extended period of time. Skill-based pay seems most appropriate for project teams, with profit-sharing or gainsharing for the entire unit. Individual pay is possible if assessed by the team itself. Team pay for performance may be appropriate at the end of the project.

- **Work teams** are self-contained, identifiable work units that control the processes involved in transforming inputs into measurable outputs, and they are used by 47 percent of *Fortune* 500 companies. Skill-based base pay is appropriate here, too, say the authors. They recommend profit-sharing or gainsharing as the major approaches to unit pay for performance. If team members are quite independent of one another, individual achievement could possibly be compensated if it is team-assessed. However, interdependent teams may more easily be rewarded on a team basis.

The authors stress the importance of team participation in designing and sometimes administering a sharing plan, as well as the importance of openness about rewards for performance. (©*Quality Abstracts*)

ARTICLE

HISTORY OF INDUSTRIAL TEAMS*

Peter Mears and Frank Voehl

Early studies of industrial work groups, such as the Hawthorne studies of Dr. Elton Mayo,[1] suggest that the group provided the workers with only marginal motivation to be more productive. Indeed, evidence suggests that working in the old ways has little impact on individual productivity. If the group is to be a truly effective force in motivating the individual worker, group members must be given "responsible autonomy" to make decisions about important aspects of the group's work assignments. On the other hand, sometimes management becomes very concerned about and resistant to relaxing traditional controls over the primary work groups.

This is due to a fear of production slowdown, coupled with the risk of increased overall cost to the organization despite the productivity of individual team efforts. Team coordination became a major problem for management teams during the latter part of the 1960s and 1970s, before the age of the TQM contributors.[2] Pre-TQM research workers such as Maier, Likert, and McGregor realized that their techniques had to be linked to the organizational framework. Likert used what he called "overlapping group families" and "linking pin" functions to tie the participation of teams to all levels within the organization. Similarly, Maier's new direction for organizations envisioned participation in problem-solving conferences at all levels through overlapping membership on all types of teams (vertical, diagonal, and horizontal). This was a precursor to the TQM notion of cross-functional teamwork.

Starting in the 1960s, the concept of T-group (T stands for training) was introduced in the United States by Edgar Schein and Kurt Lewin, while in Japan the Quality Circle movement was initiated by Professor Kauro Ishikawa. Schein introduced the general "Theory of Influence," which held that superficial skills and knowledge are relatively easy to change in bits and pieces, whereas attitudes must be changed in large chunks or not at all. Because

* Reprinted from *Team Building: A Structured Learning Approach*, by Peter Mears and Frank Voehl, St. Lucie Press, Delray Beach, Fla., 1994, pp. 15–18.

attitudes tend to hang together in large interlocking systems, changing only one attitude tends to create cognitive dissonance. A team member may therefore try to restore consistency to his or her attitudes more easily by rejecting the new paradigm than by rejecting or replacing all the old ones.

Kurt Lewin initiated an era of rigorous laboratory studies into the dynamics of how groups function. The most impressive aspects of his studies focused on the Harwood Manufacturing Company, with its teams of machinists involved in democratic methods and group decision making.

While the Harwood results were not effectively duplicated through other research experiments, the die was cast. In 1947, Lewin helped found the Bethel National Training Lab, which eventually led to the T-group movement of the 1950s and 1960s. During the 1950s, new training programs were developed by those looking for new roles for the behavioral sciences as the emphasis continued to shift from individual change to group development. Such established and emerging experts as Maslow, Argyis, Bennis, Bradford, Gibb, and Benne were joined in ranks by the Employee Relations Department of Esso, under the leadership of Robert Blake and Jan Mouton, as well as H.A. Sheppard from the Southwest Human Relations Lab of the University of Texas.[3]

Meanwhile, behavioral researchers Bion, Jaques, Trist, Rice, and others in the United Kingdom performed studies under the guidance of the Tavistock Institute of Human Relations in London, centering around the Glacier Metal research project which began in 1948 and ran in some fashion for ten years. Their research focused on the emotional life of the team and various levels of cooperation which, Bion taught, always functioned at two levels: the conscious level towards its work task and the unconscious level towards satisfaction of powerful emotional drives. Bion believed that the team acted as if it had certain basic assumptions about its aims, which he termed dependence, fight–flight, and pairing. These were the source of emotional drives far different from their task objectives. They are derived from a very primitive level and need to be addressed and successfully discussed and defined in order for the group to be productive and effective. This eventually led to the concept of Autonomous Work Groups, which provided a mechanism to deal with the problems of worker motivation, participation, and power equalization and provided a new role for the team/work group far different from that advocated by Mayo, Lewin, and Likert.[4]

The success of the Tavistock experiments highlighted the failure of research workers and management in general to make basic changes in organizational structure and in the nature and organization of the work, in order to provide greater autonomy and worker self-control. Teams provided an answer to this problem by offering a method of improving autonomy and control over work activities and, if the project is challenging, enhanced task/job content coupled with basic management skills as well. This eventually led to the work of the TQM contributors during the 1960s and beyond, and the teams process was a key component of their teachings and success.

ENDNOTES

1. Early studies by Elton Mayo are contained in *The Human Problems of Industrial Civilization* (New York: Macmillan, 1933), *The Social Problems of an Industrial Civilization* (Cambridge, Mass.: Harvard University Press, 1946), and *The Political Problems of an Industrial Civilization* (Cambridge, Mass.: Harvard University Press, 1947).
2. Notes from *A New Role for the Work Group*, by Maxine Bucklow (Chicago: University of Chicago Press, 1973); also selections from the features of a successful group by Clovis Shepard, published as *Small Groups: Some Sociological Perspectives* (San Francisco: Chandler Publishing, 1964).
3. Suggested readings: W. G. Bennis, "A New Role for the Behavioral Sciences: Effecting Organizational Change," *Administrative Science Quarterly*, Vol. 8, pp. 125–165, 1963; L. P. Bradford, J. R. Gibb, and K. P. Benne, *T-Group Theory and the Laboratory Method* (New York: John Wiley), 1964; C. Argyis, *Interpersonal Competence and Organizational Effectiveness* (New York: Dorsey Press), 1962 and *Personality and Organization* (New York: Harper and Row), 1957; R. R. Blake and J. S. Mouton, "The Developing Revolution in Management Practices," *American Society of Training Directors Journal*, Vol. 16, pp. 29–52, 1962 and *Group Dynamics Key to Decision Making* (Houston: Gulf Publishing), 1961; H. R. Shepard and R. R. Blake, "Changing Behavior Through Cognitive Maps," *Human Organization*, Vol. 21, pp. 88–96, 1962.
4. R. R. Blank, J. S. Mouton, L. L. Barnes, and L. E. Greiner, "Breakthrough in Organization Development," *Harvard Business Review*, Vol. 42, pp. 133–155, 1964; R. R. Blake and J. S. Mouton, *The Managerial Grid* (Houston: Gulf Publishing), 1964.

CHAPTER 8

IMPLEMENTING TOTAL QUALITY IN MARKETING

A journey of a thousand miles must begin with a single step

The Way of Lao Tzu

INTRODUCTION

Marketing has struggled with implementing total quality in part because the behaviors and organizational roles of marketers are often at odds with the total quality philosophy. Quality management requires teamwork—taking a cross-functional approach—yet this is contrary to marketing's desire to "quarterback" the effort. Marketers prefer to call the plays, even though other functions such as production and logistics often affect customer satisfaction.

Neither is marketing accustomed to continuous measurement, which makes continuous improvement difficult to achieve. When carried out, marketing measurements are often qualitative rather than quantitative in nature.

Marketing can make a stronger commitment to total quality by focusing on the processes that comprise the marketing cycle: selling, purchasing, service, product development, distribution, pricing, and so on. How the marketing cycle relates to business processes and process indicators is illus-

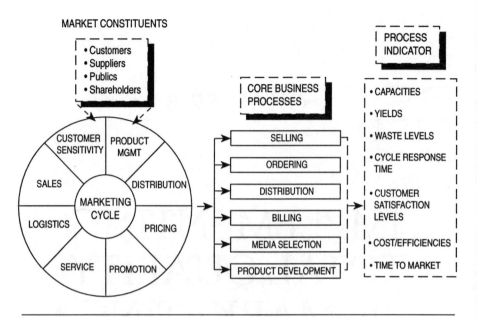

Figure 8.1 The Marketing Cycle and Process Model.

trated in Figure 8.1. Note that the various market constituents such as customers, suppliers, and publics determine how and to what extent the marketing cycle elements are performed. The core processes occur as a result of performing selected marketing cycle functions. For example, the product development process is performed as part of the product management function of the marketing cycle. The process indicators represent the "metrics" for measuring the core processes. It should also be pointed out that a synergy exists within the marketing cycle elements. That is, process breakdown in one area, such as logistics, affects other areas, such as distribution. Finally, total quality practices can be applied to any number of the core processes performed within the marketing cycle, as indicated in Table 8.1. (For additional information, see Abstract 8.1 at the end of this chapter.)

In this chapter, we will examine the steps in process improvement, discuss reengineering and how it differs from continuous improvement, describe the tools used to gauge process improvement, look at how to implement total quality procedures in the product development process, and present the common denominators for successful implementation of total quality in marketing.

Let's take a look at one of these core processes, the product development process, and how total quality tools can be used to help improve the process. A critical path analysis for new product development is illustrated in Figure 8.2.

Table 8.1 Marketing Cycle Functions and Total Quality Tools

Marketing cycle function	Core business process	Metric	Total quality tools
Distribution	Delivery	% on-time deliveries	Pareto chart (histogram)
Promotion	Media selection	Cost per thousand or cost per thousand involved	Control chart
Logistics	Order fulfillment Billing	Transaction time Billing accuracy	Pareto chart Fishbone diagram
Sales	Prospecting Follow-up and complaints handled	Lead conversions Diagnose reasons why problems occur	Pareto chart Fishbone diagram
Product management	Product development process	Time to market Product success rates	Flow diagram (path analysis) Pareto chart

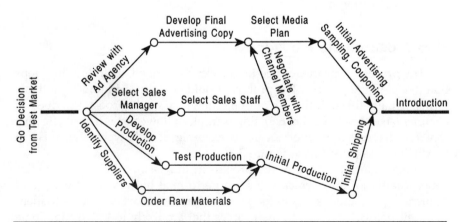

Figure 8.2 Critical Path Analysis of Product Development. (Source: Urban, G. and Hauser, J. *Design and Marketing of New Products*, 2nd ed. Reprinted by permission from Prentice-Hall, Englewood Cliffs, N.J., 1993.)

STEPS IN PROCESS IMPROVEMENT

Process improvement really involves problem solving. The following steps serve as a blueprint for pursuing process improvement.

Step 1: Define the Problem

Some questions that should be asked here might include who are my customers, what do they need, what are their expectations, and does my product or service meet or exceed their expectations.

Research conducted by Zeithaml, Parasuraman, and Berry revealed five generic service quality expectations cited as important by bank, credit-card, repair and maintenance, and long-distance telephone customers. These five service attributes are ranked below in order of their perceived importance:

- **Reliability:** Ability to perform the promised service dependably and accurately

- **Responsiveness:** Willingness to help customers and provide prompt service

- **Assurance:** Knowledge and courtesy of employees and their ability to convey trust and confidence

- **Empathy:** Caring, individualized attention the firm provides its customers

- **Tangibles:** Appearance of physical equipment, facilities, personnel, and communication materials[1]

Step 2: Understand the Process

The process or processes need to be clearly defined, including the steps that make up the process. The process should be defined in understandable terms, usually through the use of one of the total quality tools described in Chapter 6 (see Figures 6.5 to 6.8). For example, a flowchart is a very effective tool for diagramming processes. An example of a flowchart exercise in marketing was provided in Figure 3.3.

Blueprinting the steps of the process in this fashion helps to visualize conceptually not only which steps are performed but also the timing and sequencing of relationships in the process. The flowchart also helps to identify "fail points," or steps in the process that are likely to go wrong. Some other benefits of flowcharting a process include:

- Focuses on the customer and his or her expectations and experiences

- Shows how the technical procedures relate to administrative and relationship-building activities of product or service delivery

- Identifies those activities that can be proceduralized as well as those which must be individualized and given special attention

- Identifies gaps in the market that need to be addressed

- Shows staff members how their own activities relate to one another[2]

MBNA Corporation, the fourth largest credit-card issuer in the United States, keeps its customers twice as long as the industry average by focusing on 14 items that the company believes to be break point issues to its customers, including answering every phone call within two rings and processing every request for an increased credit line within an hour.

Step 3: Measure the Process

According to Tenner and DeToro, there are three ways to measure performance: **process measures**, which define activities, variables, and operation of the work process itself; **output measures**, which define specific characteristics, features, values, and attributes of each product or service; and **outcome measures**, which measure the impact of the process on the customer and what the customer does with the product or service (customer satisfaction measures are often used here to evaluate outcome measures).[3] The process indicators that appear in Figure 8.1 include examples of all three types of measures. Some of the total quality tools illustrated in Chapter 6, such as Pareto charts (see Figure 6.6), scatter diagrams (see Figure 6.8), and control charts (see Figure 6.5), can provide an understanding of why a system is performing the way it is. For example, Pareto analysis is based on the notion that 80 percent of the problems are attributed to 20 percent of the causes. Control charts are also effective for detecting special causes of variation and help differentiate between special and common causes of variation in a process.

Step 4: Simplify or Improve the Process

Based on the data collected from Step 3, decisions should be made to eliminate redundancies, rework, and waste. Corrective actions should be taken at this point to improve the process. There are five ways to improve a business process:

- Eliminate tasks altogether if it has been determined that they are unnecessary

- Simplify the work by eliminating all nonproductive elements of a task
- Combine tasks
- Change the sequence to improve speed
- Perform activities simultaneously

Savin Corporation, a large copier company, conducted a careful study and found that callbacks were related to deficiencies in the training process (callbacks occur when technicians are sent out on service calls). Pareto diagrams were prepared to depict those service engineers responsible for the largest number of callbacks. It was determined that training just five engineers would reduce callbacks by 19 percent. In most cases, the people who perform the specific processes that are under study are the ones most capable of determining how to improve or simplify the process.

Step 5: Evaluate and Monitor Process Improvement

Once a process improvement has been implemented, an effort should be made to measure and evaluate the effectiveness of the change. Comparing before and after indicators would be useful here, as would comparing results with the target performance. Also, some effort should be made to celebrate and reward those who participated in the process improvement activity.

Having discussed the process improvement process, we will now examine how reengineering differs from continuous improvement. (For additional information, see Abstract 8.2 at the end of this chapter.)

REENGINEERING VS. CONTINUOUS IMPROVEMENT

Before talking about the differences and similarities between reengineering and continuous improvement, each term must be defined. Continuous improvement, or *kaizen*, is both a commitment to quality and a process to improve quality continuously through incremental steps. Continuous improvement is ongoing and involves everyone in the organization, including both managers and workers. The goal of continuous improvement is to develop processes that are reliable (i.e., with a minimum of variation) and are well suited to current and future needs of customers.

Reengineering (or process innovation), on the other hand, means abandoning the old way of doing things and starting over. It involves going back to the beginning and inventing a better way of doing work. It is a complete rethinking of the broad-based ways in which an organization develops and delivers its products. Reengineering programs strive for radical, sometimes order-of-magnitude improvements in the cost, time, or quality of a process, instead of merely redesigning work flows and procedures. Also, according to Hammer and Champy, authors of *Reengineering the Corporation*, reengineering is about business reinvention—not business improvement, business enhancement, or business modification.[4]

Reengineering and continuous improvement share many similarities. First, both of these approaches involve *processes* as the primary unit of analysis as well as rigorous measurement of process performance. Both approaches also require organizational and behavioral change in order to be successful.

Reengineering and continuous improvement also differ on several counts. Continuous improvement programs rarely take advantage of improvements offered via information technology—a hallmark of reengineering. Further, successful reengineering programs have the backing and involvement of top management, which many continuous improvement programs lack. Additional differences between these two approaches are highlighted in Table 8.2.[5]

Kodak used reengineering in response to a competitive challenge from arch-rival Fuji. Fuji had just introduced a "disposable" 35mm single-use camera in 1987 for which Kodak had no competitive offering. Because Fuji was first to market with the product, Kodak had to move quickly to preempt Fuji's total domination of this market. Kodak's traditional product development process would have required nearly 70 weeks to produce a rival product. Its old product development process was slowed down due to frequent handoffs during the process. For example, the manufacturing engineers didn't even begin their work until 28 weeks after the product designers had started. Kodak reengineered its product development process by using an approach called concurrent engineering. By employing CAD/CAM technology, Kodak built a product design database that permitted manufacturing engineers to begin their tooling design just ten weeks into the development process. Use of concurrent engineering cut the new camera's development time nearly in half. Also, tooling and manufacturing costs were reduced by 25 percent using the reengineered process.

Kodak and other companies that have reengineered their business processes have found that there are several key success factors:

- Organize around value-added processes instead of tasks. A person's job should be designed around an outcome rather than a single task.

- Have those who use the output of the process perform the task.

- Link parallel activities instead of integrating their results: Forge links with and between functions and coordinate them while their activities are in process rather than after they have been completed.

Table 8.2 Features of Reengineering vs. Continuous Improvement (*Kaizen*)

	Kaizen	Reengineering
1. Effect	Long term and long lasting but undramatic	Short term but dramatic
2. Place	Small steps	Big steps
3. Time frame	Continuous and incremental	Intermittent and non-incremental
4. Change	Gradual and constant	Abrupt and volatile
5. Involvement	Everybody	Select a few "champions"
6. Approach	Collectivism, group efforts, systems approach	Individualism, individual ideas and efforts
7. Mode	Maintenance and improvement	Scrap and rebuild
8. Spark	Conventional know-how and state-of-the-art	Technological breakthroughs, new inventions
9. Practical requirements	Requires little investment but great effort to maintain	Requires large investment but little effort to maintain
10. Effort orientation	People	Technology
11. Evaluation criteria	Process and efforts for better results	Results for profits
12. Advantage	Works well in slow-growth economy	Better suited to fast-growth economy

- Put the decision point where the work is performed, and build controls into the process.
- Capture information once and at the source.

PROCESS IMPROVEMENT TOOLS

Process measurement tools, such as Pareto charts, scatter diagrams, cause-and-effect (fishbone) diagrams, control charts, etc., were discussed earlier. In this section, we will examine yet another process measurement tool: **benchmarking**.

According to Camp, benchmarking is the process of consistently researching new ideas for methods, practices, and processes and either adopting those practices or adapting the good features and implementing them to obtain the best of the best.[6] When done persistently for each company process, management can determine where improvements are possible and realistic expectations for how much improvement is possible. Benchmarking does not set hard goals for how much progress is possible, but it does provide a source of ideas for improvement that goes beyond internal experience. The bottom line is that benchmarking facilitates the search for the practices that will lead to superior industry performance.

In addition to uncovering industry best practices, benchmarking offers other advantages as well. For example, benchmarking may help identify technological breakthroughs that might otherwise have gone unrecognized. Xerox gained knowledge of L.L. Bean's warehousing and materials handling operations technology through benchmarking. Benchmarking enables the company to more adequately meet customer requirements. Benchmarking also helps firms determine true measures of productivity. Finally, benchmarking helps firms attain a competitive position.

Which companies are worthy of being benchmarked? Of course, that depends on the particular area in marketing. A list of companies that excel in applying quality practices in selected marketing areas, and thus represent ideal candidates for benchmarking, is provided in Table 8.3.

Table 8.3 Exemplar Companies in Selected Marketing Areas

Marketing areas to be benchmarked	Companies
Sales management	Xerox, GE Lighting Services, Ball Container
Sales–service support	Maytag, IBM
Direct marketing	L.L. Bean
Industrial marketing	DuPont
Services marketing	AT&T, Ritz-Carlton
New product development	Motorola, Rubbermaid
Advertising	Procter and Gamble, Coca-Cola
Sales promotion	Blockbuster Entertainment, Disney
Distribution	Federal Express
Supplier relationships	Wal-Mart, Kraft General Foods
Retailing	Gap, Nordstrom's

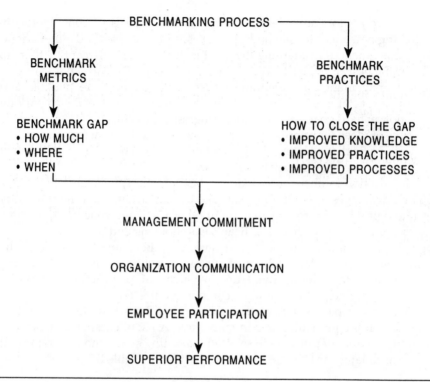

Figure 8.3 Generic Benchmarking Process.

How is benchmarking conducted? In *Benchmarking: The Search for Industry Best Practices that Lead to Superior Performance,* Camp describes a generic benchmarking process, which looks at business processes such as order fulfillment across a range of different industries. Camp's generic benchmarking process is illustrated in Figure 8.3.

It should be noted that the generic benchmarking process is divided into two parts: benchmark metrics and benchmark practices. Metrics represents the practices in quantified form. Practices are the methods used to perform some process. Benchmarking should begin by investigating industry practices. Once industry practices are understood, they can then be quantified to show their numeric effect. Benchmarking must also be understood by the organization in order to obtain the commitment necessary to take action. Management commits to benchmarking by communicating its importance to employees and securing their participation, which leads to the ultimate goal of benchmarking: superior performance.

Perhaps the most difficult part of benchmarking is identifying what is to be benchmarked. The key to determining what is to be benchmarked is to identify the product of the business process. For example, the marketing cycle function of logistics consists of several strategic "deliverables," such as the level of customer satisfaction expected, the inventory level to be maintained, and the desired cost level to be achieved. These deliverables serve as a starting point for benchmarking, where each would need to be broken down into specific activities to be benchmarked. Customer satisfaction may be benchmarked by investigating the factors that are responsible for customer satisfaction.

Finally, there are several common denominators in using the benchmarking process. First, a company needs to thoroughly know its operations and assess the strengths and weaknesses of its internal processes. Second, a company should know the industry leaders or competitors. Only by knowing its competitors can a company differentiate its own capabilities in the market. Third, learn from the industry leaders and emulate their strengths. Ford benchmarked the leading producers of mid-size cars (Honda, Toyota, and others) to develop the Taurus, which is now the best-selling car in the United States. Fourth, benchmarking should be used as a proactive tool by looking not just at competitors, but at what customers value and how other practices meet those needs. Finally, benchmarking needs to be continuous and institutionalized as part of the company culture.

We will now turn our attention to how total quality can be applied to selected marketing cycle processes. A discussion on applying total quality principles to the product development process follows.

TOTAL QUALITY AND PRODUCT DEVELOPMENT

Procter and Gamble's launch of Ultrathin diapers in the mid-1980s was supposed to give it a three- to five-year lead on Kimberly-Clark, but Kimberly-Clark caught up with P&G within months. AT&T used to take two years to design a phone; now it takes one year. The point is that speed is critical to the product development cycle. Time is more than just a scarce resource in product development—it is a competitive advantage. According to a McKinsey and Company study, products that go to market six months late but within budget earn 33 percent less than expected. Products that go to market on time but 50 percent over budget earn only 4 percent less than expected. If speed is critical to the product development process, how can this process be improved? The following discussion focuses on how product development time can be shortened.

The product development process consists of several stages, including opportunity identification, design and testing, commercialization, and product life cycle management and restaging (see Figure 8.4).

The first stage in the process involves opportunity identification. Ideas

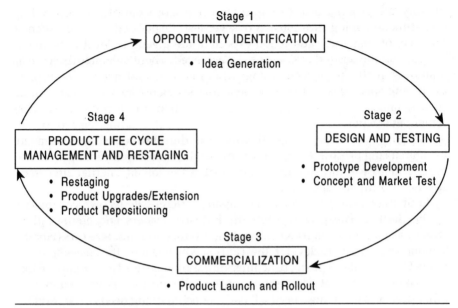

Figure 8.4 New Product/Service Development Process.

are generated from a variety of sources including customers, employees, suppliers, R&D, and the competition. A study conducted by G.P. Putnam's and Son found that most ideas for new consumer products come from analyzing the competition. The next most frequently reported source of new product ideas comes from company sources other than R&D, ostensibly company employees. The study also reported that most ideas for new industrial products come from employees.

The next stage, design and testing, involves developing a concept of the new product or service and testing it with a small number of potential users. After a concept test is completed, a prototype is developed and introduced in either an actual or simulated market test. Here, all variables of the marketing mix are tested, including distribution, promotion, pricing, and target marketing identification. During the market test, positioning, or how the product is going to be perceived, is also determined. Motorola uses a "design for quality" approach in introducing new products, where quality is designed in at the beginning of the process (see profile at the end of this chapter).

Once the product has been tested, it is ready to be introduced. In stage 3, commercialization, a product or service launch is begun in all markets simultaneously or on a market-by-market basis (also called a rollout). It is during this stage that the firm must monitor and manage the marketing strategy. For example, fine tuning of selected strategy elements such as price, promotion, distribution, or even target market selection may be necessary to ensure the long-term viability of the new offering.

Even after the product or service has been successfully launched, changes may need to take place to rejuvenate the product or service. Thus, stage 4, product life cycle management and restaging, often involves repositioning the product or service, restaging or reintroducing the product or service with value-added or service-added features, or simply upgrading the product or service to appeal to a changing market. Listerine mouthwash was restaged by adding a peppermint flavor to its original antiseptic-tasting version. General Mills repositioned Cheerios as a healthy breakfast alternative, emphasizing its high "oat-bran" content.

A closer inspection of the product/service development process reveals that process improvement can occur at any of the four stages. For example, when Oldsmobile introduced the Aurora, it formed cross-functional teams early in the design and testing stage in order to reduce costly glitches later on. Chrysler used a similar approach, called concurrent engineering, before introducing the new Neon in a record-setting 42 months. Ford shortened its new car design and production cycle by turning to trusted suppliers to handle some of the design work. For example, Dana Corporation now delivers sub-assemblies of an entire power train system, including axles, drive shafts, and transfer cases, for the Ford Tempo and Topaz.

Testing can also be shortened by substituting simulated test marketing for traditional in-test marketing. In simulated test marketing, researchers recruit consumers at a grocery store or shopping mall to show them samples of a new product or just the concept itself. A few weeks later, researchers contact these consumers for their reaction to the product and the likelihood of their purchasing the product in the future. Projections are then made from these simulated test responses. This process takes 3 months, as opposed to traditional test marketing which can range from 12 to 18 months.

Process improvement can also occur at the idea generation stage. When MCI began development of its new telecommunications services, it enlisted customers as its designers. Through in-depth interviews, customers told MCI that they wanted a carrier that would represent their interests after the sales order was signed. They wanted proof and they wanted to know they had made the right decision. In fact, customers even steered MCI to the eventual brand name chosen for this service: Proof Positive. Customer insights compressed MCI's service development cycle from months or sometimes years to weeks or even days.

Anheuser-Busch has focused primarily on stage 4 by introducing product enhancements or extensions of existing products. For example, its flagship brand, Budweiser, has experienced several line extensions during the past several years, including Bud Light and Bud Dry and, most recently, Bud

Ice Draft. Anheuser-Busch has also extended its basic Budweiser product line by adding different packages, such as the 22-oz. can and the 24-can case.

We have seen how total quality principles can be applied to processes and the product development process in particular. In the next section, the key factors in successfully implementing total quality in marketing are highlighted. (For additional information, see Abstract 8.3 at the end of this chapter.)

KEYS TO SUCCESSFUL TOTAL QUALITY IMPLEMENTATION IN MARKETING

Marketing processes can be improved or reengineered by applying many of the total quality principles previously discussed. The following is a checklist of tactics for effecting successful total quality implementation in marketing.

- **Design products in cooperation with customers.** Incorporating the "voice of the customer" earlier in the product development process will compress the development process from months or years to weeks by avoiding surprises at the end of the process.

- **Focus the improvement program outward, on market "break points."** The only way to see things as the customer sees them is to define those episodes where the customer comes in contact with the organization and focus on the most critical ones. Also, visualize the complete sequence and "moments of truth" a customer experiences in getting his or her need met. Remember, the customer sees service in terms of a total experience instead of an isolated set of activities. (To gain a better understanding of moments of truth as well the service cycle, complete Exercise 8.1 at the end of this chapter.)

- **Get the slack out of the system.** This can be accomplished by removing unnecessary and bureaucratic procedures. Examine past projects to see if each step was needed and how it could be expedited or possibly even eliminated.

- **Use technology to shorten the steps.** For example, new technologies in computer-aided design (CAD) and computed-aided manufacturing (CAM) can help shorten cycle time by speeding up the exchange of design information among engineers, production, and marketing.

- **Form alliances with customers and key suppliers.** Make the customer a partner when it comes to designing products or services. Invite customers to planning meetings and provide an opportunity for them to become familiar with the operation. Involving customers early in the product development process reduces costly rework later and the risk of alienating those same customers. The same applies to suppliers. Forming partnerships with suppliers can reduce the time to market by bringing more resources to bear on the project and by tapping into the unique skills of suppliers.

- **Develop proper measurements.** Use metrics that are specific in nature, such as 95 percent on-time delivery, 6-month time to market, or number of leads generated. For example, Hewlett-Packard uses the following metrics to measure progress in cycle time performance of new products: break-even time, time to market, break-even after release, and return factor.

- **Reward total quality efforts in marketing.** Employees should be rewarded on the basis of their behaviors (commitment, effort) rather than strictly on the basis of outcomes, such as sales quotas. Using a bonus to reward a salesperson for meeting or exceeding a quota while giving a nominal award such as a pin or plaque to the person who fixes a product or process sends a clear message about the importance of quality.

The goal of successfully implementing total quality practices in marketing is not simply to trigger another purchase, but rather to create a satisfied and loyal customer. The longer a customer stays with a firm, the greater the value of that customer. Taco Bell estimates the lifetime value of a retained customer is $11,000. Furthermore, recent studies have reported that it costs five times more to acquire a new customer than it costs to service an existing one.[7] In services businesses, annual profits can sometimes be doubled simply by keeping 5 percent of the customers who might otherwise take their business elsewhere. (For additional information, see Abstract 8.4 at the end of this chapter.)

SUMMARY

Speed has become the new mantra in marketing, whether it involves new product development or faster response time for an internal or external service. Philip Kotler, the well-known marketing author, calls this "turbo-marketing." When the product development function is modeled and measured with process improvement, the result is new products that move to market faster and contain fewer defects. As indicated in the profile of Motorola at the end of this chapter, a company's salespeople also benefit when quality principles are applied to product development, as they are able to focus on selling benefits already identified by the customer.

DISCUSSION QUESTIONS

1. What is a process? How are processes related to the marketing cycle?

2. How does reengineering differ from continuous improvement?

3. How can benchmarking become an intervention technique for organizational change?

4. How has new product design benefitted from total quality practices?

5. Select a business process that you are familiar with. What are the key inputs and outputs of that process? How would you go about benchmarking that process?

ENDNOTES

1. Zeithaml, V., Parasuraman, A., and Berry, L. *Delivering Service Quality*, The Free Press, New York, 1990, pp. 26–28.
2. Congram, C. "Focuses on the Customer." in *The Handbook of Services Marketing*, The American Management Association, New York, 1991, pp. 479–490.
3. Tenner, A. and DeToro, I. *Total Quality Management*, Addison-Wesley, Reading, Mass., 1992, p. 44.
4. Hammer, M. and Champy, J. *Reengineering the Corporation*, Harper-Business, New York, 1993, p. 33.
5. Imai, Masaaki. *The Key to Japan's Competitive Success*, Kaizen Institute, Ltd., Tokyo, 1986.
6. Camp, Robert. *Benchmarking: The Search for Industry Best Practices that Lead to Superior Performance*, ASQC Quality Press, Milwaukee, 1989.
7. Forum Consulting Group, Boston; Customer Service Institute, Silver Springs, Md.

EXERCISES

EXERCISE 8.1
CUSTOMER BLUEPRINTING

Blueprinting (or flowcharting) is a tool that helps the marketer see the "big picture" of some marketing process from end to end. Albrecht refers this as the *service cycle*. One of the reasons for breakdowns in customer service is that no one is accountable for the complete sequence of events in performing a service. A blueprint helps identify "moments of truth" within this process as well. A moment of truth is defined as any opportunity or episode within a service process whereby the customer develops an impression (positive or negative) of the company.

How well do you understand your service cycle and the moments of truth that potentially occur throughout the cycle? Take a few minutes to complete the following exercise.

1. Draw a diagram of your particular service cycle.

2. Divide the cycle into the smallest possible increments or episodes that make sense conceptually.

3. Identify the moments of truth going on throughout the cycle or any episode where a customer has contact with the company whereby an impression would be formed.

4. Now identify "black holes," where moments of truth are poorly handled or the potential exists for customer needs to go unserviced.

EXERCISE 8.2
QUALITY AUDIT

The following audit allows you to gauge your organization's commitment to achieving breakthrough service. For each of the following statements, rate your organization on the service dimensions listed on a scale of 1 to 5. Circle 5 if the statement describes your organizational perfectly or 1 if the statement does not describe your company.

LEADERSHIP

Leadership in your organization is committed to delivering total satisfaction for customers and employees.	5	4	3	2	1
Leadership advocates umbrella initiatives such as continuous quality improvement and total customer service for customers and employees.	5	4	3	2	1
A mission statement has been developed, reflecting the importance of customers, suppliers, employees, and owners.	5	4	3	2	1

BUSINESS DEFINITION

The business is defined in terms of satisfaction delivered or utility provided to customers and not simply in terms of products.	5	4	3	2	1
Customer groups are clearly defined and their needs identified according to desired results.	5	4	3	2	1

STRATEGY DEVELOPMENT

Strategies are developed to create superior customer value.	5	4	3	2	1
Strategy development is both top-down and bottom-up. Employees have input into strategy development.	5	4	3	2	1
The company understands its customers as well as its customers' entire value chain, that is, its customers' customers.	5	4	3	2	1

INTELLIGENCE GATHERING

Company collects data from its customers.	5	4	3	2	1
Company disseminates data collected from its customers to those in the organization whose jobs are affected by those data.	5	4	3	2	1

Company responds to the data, e.g., by developing plans from those data and then executing such plans.	5	4	3	2	1
Company collects data from its competitors on a regular basis.	5	4	3	2	1

ORGANIZATIONAL STRUCTURE

Jobs are organized around the value-added processes that most benefit the customer.	5	4	3	2	1
Interfunctional teams are formed and are responsible for processes and customers; their performance may be evaluated as a team.	5	4	3	2	1

HUMAN RESOURCE MANAGEMENT

The company conducts internal audits in order to determine employee satisfaction.	5	4	3	2	1
The company is committed to supporting the efforts of the front-line employees in order to better serve the customer.	5	4	3	2	1

MEASURING AND REWARDING PERFORMANCE

Employees are paid for their performance in delivering results for both customers and owners.	5	4	3	2	1
Incentives are used that emphasize customer and employee satisfaction/loyalty.	5	4	3	2	1

PROFILES

MOTOROLA

As Motorola continues to press toward its goal of Six Sigma, or fewer than four defects per million, a profound change in its understanding of the relationship between marketing and quality has occurred. As a result, Motorola views its approach to marketing research, product development and design, and its advertising and corporate communications much differently.

Motorola began with two major quality targets in mind: defect prevention and reduced cycle time. Initially Motorola's total quality efforts were "internal" in nature, looking at things such as defects on printed circuit boards manufactured in the factory. Now, Motorola is establishing quality criteria directly from what its customers value. Its definition of a defect today is "if the customer doesn't like it, it's a defect."

Next, Motorola took aim at reducing cycle time. First, the product development and design engineers made sure that the internal specs match the customer specs when introducing new products. A "design-for-quality" approach has contributed significantly to linking quality with marketing at Motorola. Design for quality is a process that Motorola has applied to services as well. For example, a "dropped" call is a defect for a cellular phone customer.

The result of design for quality is a product design process that puts more emphasis on efforts to produce systems that are robust or very continuous. Products are also developed faster because the process provides an explicit way up front to figure out what the customer wants. Finally, this process has helped Motorola's field salespeople to focus on selling benefits identified by the customer, that is, what the product accomplishes from the buyer's standpoint.

THE MANY FACES OF EMPOWERMENT (THE SALESPERSON)

Empowerment gives employees a greater sense of control and participation in the events and decisions that affect their jobs. Empowering also involves authorizing employees to respond more quickly to customer requirements. Empowerment can be applied to selling in a variety of ways.

First, empowerment can be applied to the sales organization by allowing salespersons to manage their territories as a business. The salesperson becomes, in effect, a *business manager*. In order for this to occur, the salesperson needs to be given the freedom to establish marketing programs, advertising, and sales strategies. In other words, empowerment operates at the sales level when the salespeople are adequately equipped with the authority, information, and resources to make sound business decisions on behalf of their company.

Second, the salesperson should be empowered because of his or her close proximity to the customer. This can only happen to the extent that the salesperson is given timely information and provided the proper tools with which to work. For example, many companies are equipping salespeople with laptop computers in order to access inventory and pricing data. Salespeople can be more responsive to their customers by having access to real-time data from which they can make decisions.

The goal here is to help the salesperson sell "smarter." Companies should be investing in the only remaining sustainable source of competitive advantage: superior knowledge. The logical place to start is with the salesperson. Salespeople need to be armed with superior knowledge about their customers, their customers' customers, and their competitors. Companies can empower their salespeople to the extent that they have convenient and instant access to the company's marketing information system.

CASE

RUBBERMAID

Rubbermaid is a multinational company that manufactures and markets a wide array of houseware, recreational, commercial, agricultural, and institutional products. It also sells office furniture and accessories, indoor and outdoor casual furniture, and Little Tikes traditional preschool and juvenile products. The company continues to be one of the most successful and admired American companies. In fact, it made *Fortune* magazine's list of one of America's ten most admired corporations for three consecutive years during the early 1990s. In 1993, it won the coveted number one spot in *Fortune's Survey of America's Most Admired Companies*. Rubbermaid has succeeded in a market made up of "humdrum" products. The company is now in its 42nd year of record sales and 56th year of profitable performance. Its stock has also richly rewarded its shareholders. Anyone investing $10,000 in Rubbermaid in 1980 would have realized $180,000 in 1990!

BACKGROUND

In 1920, five local businessmen formed the Wooster Rubber Company in a rented building in Wooster, Ohio to manufacture the Sunshine brand toy balloon. The company was then purchased by Horatio Ebert and Errett Grable in the mid-1920s.

During the early 1930s, while shopping at a department store, Grable noticed a line of houseware products that had been developed by James Caldwell. Caldwell's product line, which he named Rubbermaid, included rubber dustpans, drain board mats, soap dishes, and sink stoppers. Grable contacted Caldwell and the two men agreed to join their businesses. In 1943, Wooster Rubber began producing Rubbermaid brand products.

During the 1950s, Wooster Rubber produced its first plastic product, a dishpan, along with a line of commercial goods aimed at hotels, restaurants, and institutions. The company went public in 1955 and two years later changed its name to Rubbermaid.

It was during the decade of the 1980s when Rubbermaid experienced phenomenal growth, during which sales more than quadrupled from just over $300 million to over $1.5 billion. Rubbermaid also went on an acquisition binge, acquiring Cont-Tact (decorative coverings) in 1981, Little Tikes (plastic toys) in 1984, Gott leisure and recreational products in 1985, SECO floor products in 1986, Microcomputer Accessories in 1986, and Viking Brush (cleaning supplies) in 1987. Rubbermaid then entered into a joint venture with the French company Allibert in 1989 to produce resin furniture and the following year established a joint venture with the Curver Group of the Dutch chemical company DSM to market housewares in Europe, Africa, and the Middle East.

Growth through acquisition continued in the 1990s with Rubbermaid's purchase of EWU A.G., a Swiss floor-care supplies company. It also acquired Eldon Industries, a producer of office accessories, and formed a joint venture with the Hungarian Group CIPSA, the number one housewares company in Mexico. In 1992, Rubbermaid purchased Iron Mountain Rorge, a manufacturer of playground equipment.

PERFORMANCE

During the 1980s, Rubbermaid routinely posted double-digit numbers in sales growth. For the year ending 1993, Rubbermaid recorded $211 million in profit on sales of nearly $2 billion. Currently, over 80 percent of Rubbermaid's revenues are earned in the United States; by the year 2000, it is projected that foreign revenues will constitute 25 percent of Rubbermaid's overall sales.

Rubbermaid's total market capitalization in 1993 was $4.8 billion, delivering a return on shareholder equity of 18.7 percent. Its price–earning ratio in 1993 was 23. Rubbermaid has also grown through the years with a surprisingly low level of debt. Its long-term debt as a percentage of total shareholder equity in 1992 was only 3 percent as compared to an average of 61.4 percent for all U.S. manufacturers.

ENVIRONMENT

Rubbermaid has responded to the changing public attitudes regarding the environment by using recyclable plastic whenever possible and designing its containers for easy recycling. It recently introduced a "litterless" lunchbox which can carry food and drink without the need for throw-away sandwich wrappings, paper bags, or juice containers. Rubbermaid annually conducts surveys of the needs and preferences of consumers and recycling coordinators before designing new products. It also sends out recycling kits to retailers and recycling-related educational materials to public schools and uses product labels to inform consumers about the environmental benefits of using recycled goods.

TECHNOLOGY

Rubbermaid continuously invests in state-of-the-art equipment in order to remain a high-quality, low-cost producer. Rubbermaid uses a very chemically advanced mixture of polyethylene as well as a very intricate injection molding process for its plastic products. Between 1980 and 1991, Rubbermaid invested over $600 million to expand manufacturing and distribution facilities, modernize equipment, and install process control systems, automatic packaging systems, upgraded tooling for new products, and increased capacity for producing new products. In 1992, Rubbermaid invested over $132 million to purchase molds for new products, expand production capacity, add new equipment, and keep facilities efficient and productive. Rubbermaid has relentlessly pursued quality. Stanley Gault, former CEO for Rubbermaid, visited several retail stores weekly to see how Rubbermaid products were displayed and to inspect the quality of workmanship. Gault once remarked, "No one surpasses our quality…we use more and better resin…we don't buy cheap resin…and we use a thicker gauge."

STRATEGY

Before retiring in 1991, Rubbermaid's CEO Stanley Gault outlined six basic strategies for "leap" growth: (1) develop new products (with 30 percent of the company's revenues to come from products introduced in the previous five years), (2) enter new markets every 18 to 24 months, (3) acquire new companies, (4) diversify through joint ventures with outside partners, (5) establish stronger bonds with its suppliers, and (6) create specialized goods for its customers.

Creating high-quality, functional plastic products for housewares, the office, and the industrial and farm markets represents a great deal of Rubbermaid's success. Part of Rubbermaid's success is to continually improve the design of existing products, for example revising the design of its ice trays to make it easier to remove the cubes. Yet Rubbermaid's genius lies in its ability to satisfy customer needs precisely and to make the small changes they demand, as well as its ability to imbue otherwise ordinary kitchen and household products with fashion. Rubbermaid has recently diversified by producing storage for clothing, videocassettes, and computer disks. Rubbermaid makes nearly half a million different items, boasts a 90 percent success rate on new products, and obtains at least 30 percent of its sales each year from products less than five years old.

Rubbermaid's new product strategy begins with the customer and thus is market-driven rather than technology-driven. Rubbermaid relies extensively on marketing research to assess customer needs and to identify new product opportunities. Part of Rubbermaid's marketing intelligence also includes studying its competition. Yet rather than benchmark its competitors, it benchmarks against the standards set by its customers. It runs focus groups to test color and style preferences and confirms those preferences by conducting surveys in shopping malls. Rubbermaid also obtains a great deal of feedback from customer complaints. Each complaint that is received either from commend cards or its toll-free number is documented by marketing and is widely distributed, even to the company's executives. Rubbermaid makes good on every customer complaint as well, replacing its products without charge to the customer. The company also runs a day-care program where researchers can observe children having problems with toys and test their own new toys. This input from the customer is then used to modify existing products or develop totally new products.

New products are launched at Rubbermaid with record speed, sometimes within 20 weeks of the birth of the idea. New product cross-functional teams manage the entire process from spotting a need to commercialization. These product development teams, which have considerable autonomy and authority to carry out their objectives, are also rewarded based on achieving those objectives. Traditional test marketing is bypassed because of Rubbermaid's careful homework with customers to develop the right product and its wish to avoid exposing its new products to competitors.

In terms of pricing, Rubbermaid's prices tend to be higher than those of its competitors, due to its higher quality content and stellar reputation. Rubbermaid products command a 5 to 10 percent premium over competitors due to the high-grade plastic that it uses in the manufacture of its products.

Rubbermaid's products are marketed primarily through mass merchandisers and home center stores such as Home Depot. Rubbermaid teams up with its trade partners, such a K-Mart and Wal-Mart, to jointly develop displays, merchandising plans, promotions, and logistics. Rubbermaid provides generous allowances to retailers to help support price promotions and co-op advertising in local markets. Finally, Rubbermaid has shown its trade partners how to increase sales of Rubbermaid products by showing them its "Best Practices Room" in Wooster, Ohio. Retailers who visit this center can see how Rubbermaid products can be most effectively merchandised.

Rubbermaid's field sales force is organized around categories instead of products. Rubbermaid believes that this channel specialization allows for more intensive management involvement with its trade customers. It seems to be paying off, as Rubbermaid has increased its penetration of its served retail market from 60,000 outlets in 1980 to over 100,000 outlets in 1993.

In terms of promotion, Rubbermaid supports its products with national television and radio ads. It also supports its products at the local retail level with trade allowances and co-op advertising. Rubbermaid recently partnered with its retailers in a project called "Earth View," sponsoring programs geared to retail management that reinforced its longstanding commitment to both recycling and utilizing recycled materials in its own products.

INTERNATIONAL OPERATIONS

Presently, 12 percent of Rubbermaid's sales come from its foreign operations. The goal of management is to increase foreign revenues from international operations to 30 percent. Rubbermaid plans to achieve this goal by establishing a strong brand image and developing extensive distribution networks in its international markets. Moreover, foreign assets represented 13 percent of the company's total assets in 1993. Rubbermaid appears to be moving away from a strictly export-based strategy to one of direct foreign investment. For example, Rubbermaid entered into a joint venture in 1989 with the French company Allibert to produce resin furniture. Rubbermaid also formed a strategic alliance with Sommer-Alliber of France to manufacture and distribute resin casual furniture in the French market. It also established a joint venture with Curver Group of the Dutch chemical company DSM to market housewares in Europe, Africa, and the Middle East. Its acquisitions continued in the 1990s with the purchase of EWU A.G., a Swiss floor-care supplies company. In 1992, Rubbermaid acquired CIPSA of Mexico, a leading plastics and housewares company. In 1994, Rubbermaid formed a joint venture with Richell of Japan in which it currently holds a 40 percent equity interest. Rubbermaid formed another joint venture with Royal Plastics Group, Ltd. of Canada for the manufacture and marketing of modular plastic components and kits to build storage sheds for consumer, commercial, and industrial markets. Finally, in late 1994, Rubbermaid acquired Ausplay, an Australian maker of playground equipment.

ABSTRACTS

ABSTRACT 8.1
THE NEW SOCIETY OF ORGANIZATIONS

Drucker, Peter F.
Harvard Business Review, Vol. 70 Issue 5, September/October 1992,
pp. 95–104

Peter Drucker opens this article with gusto in the opening sentence of the first paragraphs: "Every few hundred years throughout Western history, a sharp transformation has occurred. In a matter of decades, society altogether rearranges itself—its world view, its basic values, its social and political structures, its arts, its key institutions." Our age is such a period of transformation, which began with the G.I. Bill of Rights, giving to each American soldier returning from World War II money to attend a university, something that Drucker feels would have made no sense at the end of World War I. This signaled the shift to a knowledge society, in which land, labor, and capital become secondary and knowledge became *the* product. For Drucker's managers, the dynamics of knowledge imposes one clear imperative—every organization has to build the management of change into its very structure, starting with the marketing function. Every organization must learn to exploit its knowledge to develop the next generation of applications from its own successes, and it must learn to innovate.

If the organization is to perform, it must be organized as a team. For more than 600 years, no society has had as many competing centers of power as the one in which we now live. Change is the only constant in an organization's life. Drucker is always the master storyteller, with his tales of Japanese business development (the soccer team), the Prussian army vs. Henry Ford's assembly line (models of teams), PTAs at suburban schools (perfunctory management), university freedom (the autonomous centers of power), who will take care of the common good (unresolved problems of the pluralistic society), and the failure of socialism/communism (leading to cohesive power of knowledge-based organizations). This is Drucker's thirtieth article for *Harvard Business Review* and undoubtedly one of his best.

ABSTRACT 8.2
TQM: A STEP-BY-STEP GUIDE TO IMPLEMENTATION

Weaver, Charles N.
Quality Press, Milwaukee, 1991, 235 pp.

While it doesn't make sense implementing TQM like making "instant pudding," this book does offer a useful step-by-step approach. The author introduces a combination of TQM and a management information system called the "methodology for generating efficiency and effectiveness measures," and he proceeds to use the acronym TQM/MGEEM throughout the book to identify this system. He suggests beginning a comprehensive education based on Deming's and Juran's philosophies to help change the corporate culture a few months prior to introducing TQM MGEEM. The book begins with a description of the quality problem in America. Then successive chapters describe in considerable detail the steps which need to be taken to implement TQM/MGEEM, down to the content of the leaders' talks and the group processes to be used. Briefly, the TQM/MGEEM program revolves around Blue Teams and Gold Teams for each organization within a company.

- The Blue Team for a department is composed of a facilitator, the manager, immediate superiors and immediate subordinates, and representative customers and suppliers. The team uses nominal group techniques to review the department's mission statement, and then it breaks the mission into measurable parts called "key result areas" (KRAs).

- The Gold Teams, formed from the manager's subordinates and key workers, are led by facilitators to develop indicators to measure the KRAs. These teams also build a feedback chart for each indicator to be used for periodic feedback on the KRAs' progress.

- Members of each department participate in monthly feedback meetings, where they (1) review progress on their charts, (2) share ideas on how to improve the process by which work is accomplished, and (3) discuss how to eliminate unnecessary bureaucracy. Suppliers and customers can attend these meetings to provide input on their expectations and ideas for improvement. (©*Quality Abstracts*)

ABSTRACT 8.3
QUALITY IN AMERICA: HOW TO IMPLEMENT
A COMPETITIVE QUALITY PROGRAM

Hunt, V. Daniel
Business One Irwin, Homewood, Ill., 1992, 308 pp.

Quality in America is a readable volume that demystifies the quality movement and presents a clear plan to implement TQM in an organization. The author begins with an assessment of the global marketplace and the importance of TQM to a firm's remaining competitive. Next, he describes the fundamental concepts and vocabulary of quality. Chapter 3 is a helpful characterization of four of quality's pioneers: Deming, Juran, Robert Costello, and Philip Crosby. Then the author compares the emphases of the school of thought attributed to each of these people. "There is no one best way," says the author, but from that point on he describes and promotes his own synthesis of quality principles under the name *Quality First*™. A chart shows the relationship of Crosby's 14 steps, Deming's 14 points, and Juran's 7 points to *Quality First's* 8 tasks, which are summarized under these major categories:

People-oriented tasks:
1. Build top management
2. Build teamwork
3. Improve quality awareness
4. Expand training

Technically-oriented tasks:
5. Measure quality
6. Heighten cost of quality recognition
7. Take corrective action
8. Commit to a continuous improvement process

Chapter 4 describes the Malcolm Baldrige National Quality Award and recommends applying for it. This is followed by a chapter giving a thumbnail sketch of Baldrige Award winners: Federal Express, Globe Metallurgical, Motorola, Wallace Co., Westinghouse, and Xerox Business Products and Systems. Then the author provides a specific outline for implementing quality in an organization. Chapter 6 includes a complete self-assessment questionnaire and scoring evaluation system. After introducing his *Quality First* concepts and principles, the author outlines a 17-step implementation plan. The first 10 steps are planning, followed by 7 implementation steps. Chapter 10 consists of a brief survey of quality tools (e.g., bar chart, fishbone diagram, control chart, Pareto chart, etc.) and techniques (action plan, benchmarking, cost of quality, SPC, etc.). A final chapter reviews the steps and urges the reader to "act now." Three appendices provide basic resources: an executive reading list, a glossary of quality terms, and a list of information sources. This is a helpful "first book" to introduce the quality movement to corporate executives. (©*Quality Abstracts*)

ABSTRACT 8.4
MEASURING THE TOTAL QUALITY OF THE SALES FUNCTION

Welch, Cas and Geissler, Pete
National Productivity Review, Autumn 1992, pp. 517–531

While many managers remain focused on product quality, say the authors, as much as 80 percent of the costs of poor quality can be attributed directly to "soft" functions, such as sales. From analysis of data on a manufacturing company, they observe that a 1 percent reduction in failure cost yields a 4 percent increase in operating margin, since erroneous or incomplete information initiated by salespeople and sent to order-entry clerks can cascade into manufacturing. The authors contend that:

- Salespersons tend to not fully understand the effects of error in their communications to others.

- Salespersons—operating in a relative vacuum—tend to forget that, through accurate and timely information, they add considerable value to the product or service that they are selling.

- With salespersons on the fringes of the business process, managers tend to forget that salespersons are their best source of information about customers.

The authors move to a list of symptoms which indicate the need for TQM in the sales process: the error chase, the overstuffed process, the customer schmooze, misleading data/reports that make managers look good even while the business is performing badly, and narrow views of the business process. The authors point out that conventional performance measurements of sales have an *inward* focus—on the productivity of the salesperson. Instead, they suggest four *outward* measures: the timeliness, relevance, and accuracy of information and the attitudes of employees. The authors conclude with a case study that illustrates the value of including salespersons on cross-functional teams designed to cut order delivery time. (©*Quality Abstracts*)

CHAPTER 9

ADOPTING QUALITY STANDARDS

In the foregoing discussion of quality and its applications in marketing, a dominant theme emerges. Quality is first and foremost about *change*, specifically organizational change. In Chapter 8 reengineering and continuous improvement were discussed as philosophies for change. How to identify and improve processes as a means of effecting change were also discussed at length. The question then becomes to what extent the change is helpful. In other words, *standards* of performance are needed as a target. It is necessary to establish objective benchmarks in these areas in order to determine whether a company is "hitting the mark." In this chapter, the various types of assessment surveys to audit quality endeavors, including the Malcolm Baldrige assessment, Deming Prize audit, and the ISO 9000 audit, are discussed.

BALDRIGE AWARD CRITERIA

By the 1980s, it was clear that an emphasis on quality was no longer optional for American companies doing business in an ever-growing world market. As a result, the Malcolm Baldrige National Quality Award was established by Congress in 1987 to promote quality awareness, to recognize quality achievements of U.S. companies, and to publicize successful quality

233

strategies. The Malcolm Baldrige Quality Award, first presented in 1988, was named for Malcolm Baldrige, who served as Secretary of Commerce from 1981 until his tragic death in a rodeo accident in 1987.

The award is not for specific products or services. Two awards may be given annually in each of the three following categories: manufacturing, service, and small business. The Malcolm Baldrige National Quality Award is managed by the U.S. Department of Commerce Technology Administration and administered by the American Society for Quality Control. The 1994 award criteria publication offers the following principles which encompass the award:

- Awareness of quality as an increasingly important element in competitiveness
- Understanding of the requirements for quality excellence
- Sharing of information on successful quality strategies and the benefits derived from implementation of these strategies

Each year, at several major cities around the United States, the Award Foundation sponsors the Annual Quest for Excellence Conference. This program offers interested companies and individuals a chance to hear presentations and discussions by previous award winners. CEOs and other key individuals in award-winning companies provide insights into their firms' quality strategies and organizational changes.

The Department of Commerce and the American Society for Quality Control state that awards may be given each year, but it is under their authority whether or not an award will be granted for each category each year. Of the estimated more than 2000 entrants since the award's inception in 1988, only 19 companies have been awarded the coveted prize. The Baldrige Award winners since 1988 are highlighted in Table 9.1.

As indicated in Table 9.2, the Malcolm Baldrige National Quality Award follows the major criteria listed below in the examination process. Figure 9.1 is a flowchart which conceptualizes the Baldrige criteria and shows the relationships among the various criteria.

1. Leadership
2. Information and analysis
3. Strategic quality planning
4. Human resource development and planning
5. Management of process quality
6. Quality and operational results
7. Customer focus and satisfaction

Table 9.1 Malcolm Baldrige Award Winners

1988	Motorola, Inc.
	Commercial Nuclear Fuel Division of Westinghouse Electric Corporation
	Globe Metallurgical, Inc.
1989	Milliken & Company
	Xerox Corporation Business Products & Systems
1990	Cadillac Motor Car Division—General Motors
	IBM Rochester
	Federal Express Corporation
	Wallace Company, Inc.
1991	Solectron Corporation
	Zytec Corporation
	Marlow Industries
1992	AT&T Network Systems Group
	Texas Instruments, Inc. Defense Systems and Electronics
	AT&T Universal Card Services
	The Ritz-Carlton Hotel Company
	Granite Rock Company
1993	Eastman Chemical Company
	Ames Rubber Company
1994	AT&T
	GTE Directories
	Wainwright Industries

Descriptions and point values for each category are indicated in Table 9.2.

In analyzing the Malcolm Baldrige Award criteria from a marketer's perspective, most, if not all, of the criteria reveal a company's ability to reach and satisfy customers. The American Marketing Association launched a successful program in 1991, entitled the International Congress on Customer Satisfaction. During the Fourth Congress, conducted in May 1994, several speakers cited the correlation of quality management and adherence to the Baldrige Award criteria as a process toward improving the marketing systems and processes of a company. Since the beginning of the AMA's International Congress on Customer Satisfaction, 9 marketers from the 19 Baldrige Award winners have been featured as keynote speakers during the event. (For additional information, see Abstract 9.1 at the end of this chapter.)

Many of the Baldrige Award speakers have accented the importance of the measurement of progress as outlined in the award criteria. These mea-

Table 9.2 1995 Baldrige Award Examination Items and Point Values

Examination categories/items	Point values
1.0 LEADERSHIP	**90**
Senior executives provide personal leadership and involvement in creating and sustaining a customer focus and clear and visible quality values. Also examined is how the quality values are integrated into the company's management system and reflected in the manner in which the company addresses its public responsibilities and corporate citizenship.	
1.1 Senior executive leadership	45
1.2 Leadership system and organization, including assessments	25
1.3 Public responsibility/corporate citizenship	20
2.0 INFORMATION AND ANALYSIS	**75**
The scope, validity, analysis, management, and use of data and information to drive quality excellence and to improve operational and competitive performance. Adequacy of company data, information, and analysis system to support improvement of the company's customer focus, products and services, and internal operations.	
2.1 Management of (quality and performance) information and data	15
2.2 Competitive comparisons and benchmarking	20
2.3 Analysis and uses of company-level data	40
3.0 STRATEGIC PLANNING	**55**
The business strategy and planning process and how all key quality requirements are integrated into overall business planning. The company's short- and longer-term plans and how quality and operational performance are deployed to all work units.	
3.1 Strategy development	35
3.2 Strategy deployment	20
4.0 HUMAN RESOURCE DEVELOPMENT AND MANAGEMENT	**140**
The key elements of how the work force is enabled to develop its full potential to pursue the company's quality and operational performance objectives. Also examined are the company's efforts to build and maintain an environment for quality excellence conducive to full participation and personal and organizational growth.	

The criteria for the 1995 Baldrige Award are more future oriented and directed toward the business strategy and competitiveness requirements. The categories have been reduced by some 40 percent, while putting the emphasis on key business drivers. A major focus is on business development, coupled with more flexible and responsive organizations and work systems. The learning theme is strong in the following areas: strategy development (weak influence), customer

Examination categories/items	Point values

4.1 Human resource planning and evaluation	20	
4.2 High-performance work systems	45	
4.3 Employee education, training, and development	50	
4.4 Employee well-being and satisfaction	25	

5.0 PROCESS MANAGEMENT — **140**

Systematic processes the company uses to pursue ever-higher quality and company operational performance. The key elements are process management, R&D, design, management of process quality for all work units and suppliers, systematic quality improvement, and quality assessment.

5.1 Design and introduction of products/services	40
5.2 Process management: product/service production and delivery	40
5.3 Process management: support services	30
5.4 Management of supplier performance	30

6.0 BUSINESS RESULTS — **250**

The company's quality levels and improvement trends in quality, company operational performance, and supplier quality. Current quality and operational performance levels relative to competitors.

6.1 Product and service quality results	75
6.2 Company and operational results	130
6.3 Supplier performance results	45

7.0 CUSTOMER FOCUS AND SATISFACTION — **250**

The company's relationships with customers and its knowledge of customer requirements and of the key quality factors that drive marketplace competitiveness. Also, the company's methods to determine customer satisfaction, current trends, and levels of customer satisfaction and retention, and these results relative to competitors.

7.1 Customer and market knowledge	30
7.2 Customer relationships management	30
7.3 Customer satisfaction determination	30
7.4 Customer satisfaction results	100
7.5 Customer satisfaction comparison	60

TOTAL POINTS — **1000**

---

and market knowledge (heavy influence), employee development (weak influence), and information and analysis systems (medium influence). Many changes have been made in the criteria to strengthen key themes and to clarify, focus, and link requirements. The number of areas to address has been reduced from 91 to 54 and the application page limit reduced from 85 to 70. A major shift toward marketing and sales has begun to take place.

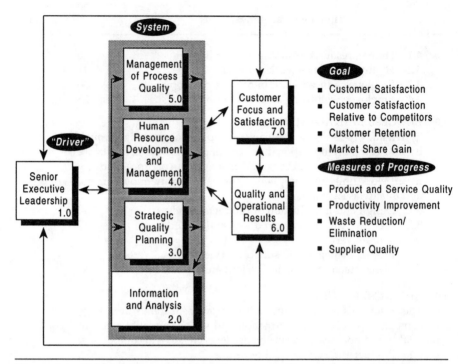

Figure 9.1 Baldrige Award Criteria Framework: Dynamic Relationships.

sures of progress provide a results-oriented basis for channeling actions to deliver ever-improving customer value and company performance. As stated in the award criteria, the measurement focuses on seven key areas of business performance:

1. Customer satisfaction/retention

2. Market share, new market development

3. Product and service quality

4. Productivity, operational effectiveness

5. Human resource performance/development

6. Supplier performance/development

7. Public responsibility/corporate citizenship

Most marketing plan formats include these areas in developing strategy, action plans, or monitoring the success of the strategy. As indicated in Table

9.2, customer focus and satisfaction, which is worth 25 percent of the total number of points, also offers the greatest potential for marketing contributions. All seven Baldrige categories provide opportunities for marketing expertise, as shown in Table 9.3. Let's examine the effect that achieving the Baldrige Award has had on past winners.

Horst Schulze, COO of the Ritz-Carlton Hotel Company, 1992 Baldrige Award recipient for the service sector, had the following to say at the Second International Congress on Customer Satisfaction: "We [Ritz-Carlton] did not enter the Baldrige Award competition just for quality, but, equally important, we did so to achieve our marketing objective, to be the number one supplier known for luxury properties that met Mobil's and AAA's highest standards."[1] Ritz-Carlton's service quality hallmarks include participatory executive leadership, information gathering and sharing, coordinated planning and execution, and a work force empowered to go to great lengths to satisfy customers. One of the tangible marketing outcomes for Ritz-Carlton as a result of pursuing the Baldrige Award was an improvement of its "marketing intelligence" system. For years, guest comment cards represented the only measure of customer satisfaction. Through its total quality process, Ritz-Carlton now routinely conducts mail and telephone surveys against best-of-breed competition and collects process-oriented market samples. Also, in keeping with the Baldrige criteria, Ritz-Carlton benchmarks such competitors as the Four Seasons Hotel Company.

Following the Baldrige Award criteria served as a difficult but achievable formula to outpace the competition. In 1991 alone, Ritz-Carlton received 121 quality awards from the travel industry. It is important to note that Ritz-Carlton did not become more concerned with winning the award in lieu of a real quality process. According to Patrick Mene, corporate director of quality at Ritz-Carlton, "People need to understand the economics of quality…when you don't satisfy all of the customers all of the time it can cost you a fortune. So we found that the benefits more than outweighed any problems. A quality approach to running a business is the most cost-effective, least capital-intensive path to profitability."

General Motors' Cadillac Division was much maligned when it applied for and won the Baldrige Award in 1990 but has since silenced its critics. For instance, sales of its redesigned Seville jumped from 150 to 600 in Japan in 1993 and earned accolades as one of Japan's top five imports of the year.

Texas Instruments attributes its turnaround to the adoption of many of the total quality principles. The company won the 1992 Malcolm Baldrige Award as a result of its success in following the Baldrige criteria in its defense business.

Eastman Chemical Company, 1993 Baldrige Award winner in the manufacturing sector, credits its success to a quality improvement process for sales and marketing efforts. Eastman's president of worldwide sales, George O.

Table 9.3 Potential Use of Marketing Expertise in the Baldrige Award (+ = modest potential, ** = high potential)

Baldrige Award category/item	ADVERTISING	CONSUMER BEHAVIOR	DISTRIBUTION	ENVIRONMENTAL SCANNING	MARKET ASSESSMENT	PERSONAL SELLING	PRICING	PRODUCT PLANNING	PROMOTION	PUBLICITY	RESEARCH METHODS
1.0 Leadership											
1.1				+							
1.2			+	+		+				+	**
1.3	+	+		**					+	+	+
2.0 Information and analysis											
2.1	**	**		**		**					**
2.2	**	**									**
2.3	**	**									**
3.0 Strategic planning											
3.1	**	**		**		**		+			**
3.2	+			+				+			**

4.0 Human resource development and management
4.1
4.2
4.3
4.4

5.0 Process management
5.1
5.2
5.3
5.4

6.0 Business results
6.1
6.2
6.3
6.4

7.0 Customer focus and satisfaction
7.1
7.2
7.3
7.4
7.5

Trabue, said, "we connect quality management and sales through a 'linking in' effort, known both internally and to our customers as the MEPS (Make Eastman the Preferred Supplier) program. The objective of the MEPS program is to identify ways to improve the processes that link us with our customers. We want to make those processes as simple and easy to use as possible, so that when a customer wants to do something, he thinks of us first." How has the MEPS program helped Eastman? The company's 500 salespeople are responsible for 7000 customers and over $4 billion in sales, and those salespeople are responsible for utilizing the MEPS system to coordinate the activities of 18,000 Eastman employees in team efforts focused on improving customer relationships. Eastman ranks as one of the fastest growing, most profitable companies in the chemical industry.

Measurement guidelines have proved beneficial to all of the Baldrige Award winners; however, not all have had the benefit of financial profitability. Wallace and Company, the 1990 Baldrige Award winner in the small business category, suffered the effects of the economic downturn in the oil and gas exploration industry. Wallace and Company, a manufacturer and servicer of pipeline equipment, found that winning the Baldrige Award meant continuous visits and requests from other interested firms, enough to disrupt its normal business practices and force the company to discontinue those activities and refocus on profitability.

Yet the award has its detractors. Deming saw little value in the Baldrige Award. During an interview before his death in 1993, Deming observed:

> Nothing could be worse than the [Baldrige criteria]. The evil effect of the Baldrige guidelines on American business can never be measured. The effect of training, for example. You may spend $20,000 to train six people in a skill. That benefit will come in the future. We'll never be able to measure that benefit. Never. So why do we spend that money for training? Answers are guided by theory. We believe that training will have its effect on future output. And though we cannot measure that output, we believe that it is positive.[2]

Others complain that it costs too much to apply for the award, that it can be bought by using high-priced consultants, and that it favors large companies. Further criticisms leveled at the Balridge Award are that it does not measure actual financial performance and that too few companies enter the competition to improve the quality of U.S. industry. Finally, there is the danger that companies focus so much on winning the prize that they lose sight of the process that guides this achievement.

No doubt these criticisms contain some truth, but there are strong counter-arguments as well. High-priced consultants certainly helped Xerox and IBM win the award, but were unable to help Intel win in 1991. While the actual number of Baldrige participants remains low, U.S. companies have requested more than 50,000 copies of the Balridge criteria and 10,000 presentations from Baldrige winners, examiners, and administrators. In the final analysis, the Baldrige has done more than any other program to lift U.S. businesses out of their complacency regarding quality. (For additional information, see Abstract 9.2 at the end of this chapter.)

THE DEMING PRIZE

The Deming Prize was instituted in December 1950 by the Union of Japanese Scientists and Engineers (JUSE) and is regarded as the highest form of industrial recognition in Japan. It was established in recognition of W. Edwards Deming's achievements in the introduction of statistical quality control. The award was also established to promote statistical quality control in Japan. Florida Power and Light won this coveted prize in 1989, the first company outside Japan to do so. In 1994, AT&T Power Systems became the second U.S. company to win the Deming Prize.

The Deming Prize and the Malcolm Baldrige Award are similar in that they both seek total involvement throughout the organization. They also share the same goal of continuous improvement of product and service quality.

Yet the emphasis of the two programs is different. The Baldrige Award places greater emphasis on customers than does the Deming Prize. The Deming Prize, in contrast, focuses more on the process used to apply statistical quality control. Also, the Deming guidelines are less specific than the Baldrige criteria and, as a result, are more dependent on the judges' interpretation. The Deming guidelines are provided in Table 9.4.

ISO 9000 STANDARDS OF QUALITY

Background

During World War I, approximately 200,000 soldiers were killed simply because their ammunition malfunctioned. This problem plagued the armed forces of many countries until a military tribunal authorized the adoption of military standards for all munitions manufacturers that supplied bullets and bombs to "free-world" armies.

Since World War I, these military standards have spread to most applications of products and services for both military and government agencies. The North American Treaty Organization (NATO) was the first group of countries to adopt shared standards in 1945, the same year that NATO was formed.

Table 9.4 Deming Prize Criteria

Item	Particulars
Policy	1. Policies pursued by management, quality and quality control 2. Method of establishing policies 3. Justifiability and consistency of policies 4. Utilization of statistical methods 5. Transmission and diffusion of policies 6. Review of policies and the results achieved 7. Relationship between short- and long-term planning
Organization and its management	1. Explicitness of scope of authority and responsibility 2. Appropriateness of delegations of authority 3. Interdivisional cooperation 4. Committees and their activities 5. Utilization of staff 6. Utilization of quality control circle activities 7. Quality control diagnosis
Education	1. Education programs and results 2. Degrees of understanding of quality control 3. Teach statistical methods and concepts 4. Grasp effectiveness of quality control 5. Educate related company (i.e., suppliers, distributors)
Collection/ dissemination and use of information on quality	1. Collection of internal information 2. Transmit information among divisions 3. Speed of information transmission 4. Statistical analysis of information and utilization of the results
Analysis	1. Selection of key problems and themes 2. Propriety of analytical approach 3. Linkage with proper technology 4. Quality analysis, process analysis 5. Utilization of statistical methods 6. Utilization of analytical results 7. Assertiveness of improvement suggestions
Standardization	1. Systematization of standards 2. Method for establishing, revising, and abolishing standards 3. Outcome of the establishment, revision, or abolition of standards 4. Contents of the standards

Table 9.4 Deming Prize Criteria (continued)

Item	Particulars
	5. Utilization of statistical methods 6. Accumulation of technology 7. Utilization of standards
Control	1. Systems for control of quality and related matters of cost and quantity 2. Control items and control points 3. Utilization of statistical control methods 4. Contribution to performance of quality control circle activities 5. Actual conditions of control activities 6. State of matters under control
Quality assurance	1. Procedure for the development of new products, services (analysis and upgrading of quality, checking design, reliability, etc.) 2. Safety and immunity from product liability 3. Process design, process analysis, and process control and improvement 4. Process capability 5. Instrumentation, gauging, testing, and inspecting 6. Equipment maintenance and control of subcontracting, purchasing, and services 7. Quality assurance system and its audit 8. Utilization of statistical methods 9. Evaluation and audit of quality 10. Actual state of quality assurance
Results	1. Measurement of results 2. Substantive results in quality, services, delivery time, cost, profits, safety, environment, etc. 3. Intangible results 4. Measures for overcoming defects
Planning for the future	1. Grasp the present state of affairs and the concreteness of the plan 2. Measures for overcoming defects 3. Plans for further advances 4. Linkage with long-term plans

Source: The Deming Prize Guide for Overseas Companies.

These quality assurance standards continued to evolve, with a global organization of standards issuers, the British Standards Organization, developing the British Standard (BS) 5750 in 1975. This became known as the "mother document" for the International Organization for Standardization, or ISO.

ISO is a worldwide federation of national standards bodies (ISO member bodies) that work to prepare international standards developed by their technical committees. ISO 9000 standards, a set of five technical standards, were established during the 1980s by the International Organization for Standardization to establish basic, uniform requirements for quality assurance systems. ISO 9000 standards are unique in that they apply to a very wide range of industries, encompassing both manufacturing and services.

To oversee that these standards are applied in a consistent fashion from business to business, a third-party system has evolved. An independent registrar assesses an organization to determine whether its quality program works as stated and documented. Basically, an organization is certified if its quality program meets ISO 9000 requirements.

In addition to the European Community (EC), NATO, and the U.S. Department of Defense, at least 51 countries around the world have endorsed the standards.[3] Despite the urgency to adopt ISO 9000 standards, many U.S. firms have not yet done so, nor do they plan to become certified any time soon. In a recent survey by Grant Thorton of 254 U.S. companies with annual sales between $10 million and $500 million, only 8 percent planned to become certified by the end of 1992 and 48 percent of senior executives polled had never even heard of ISO standards.[4]

Much of the credit for the ISO standards system becoming a worldwide effort goes to the impact of the EC 1992 agreement. Effectively, ISO 9000 marries the best of the British Standards (BS), the American National Standards Institute and American Society for Quality Control (ANSI/ASQC), and the European Standard (EN 29000). (For additional information, see Abstract 9.3 at the end of this chapter.)

Why Is ISO 9000 Important?

With the adoption of ISO 9000 standards comes the discipline imposed by the standards for processes that influence total quality programs. Pursuing ISO certification helps a company standardize its processes and provides a better platform for productivity analysis. Thus, firms should gain better control of their quality by virtue of applying the discipline required for ISO 9000 certification, even if they later decide not to register. A listing of the internal benefits of ISO 9000 registration is provided in Table 9.5.

Another important reason for considering ISO 9000 certification is that

Table 9.5 The Most Important Internal Benefits of Registration

Better documentation	201	32.4%
Greater quality awareness	159	25.6%
Positive "cultural" change	93	15.0%
Increased operational efficiency	56	9.0%
Enhanced intercompany communications	45	7.3%
Reduced scrap/rework expense	41	6.6%
Other	8	1.3 %
No answer	17	2.7%

Source: *Quality Systems Update*/Deloitte & Touche (QSU/D&T) survey of ISO 9000 registered companies (620 respondents from 1679 companies) in July 1993.

more and more companies worldwide are requiring their suppliers to become ISO 9000 registered, as the whole world is moving toward standards. ISO 9000 is fast becoming an admission ticket to compete in the global marketplace. Presently, ISO 9000 is becoming the de facto market requirement for doing business with the EC. One day, all companies that compete globally may well have ISO certification. When this happens, ISO registration will no longer represent a distinct competitive advantage.

ISO standards also provide a universally accepted method to communicate an organization's quality concepts and its processes for serving the customer. Once this system is accepted and certified by ISO representatives during an ISO audit, company adherence to those standards provides a sense of confidence and assurance to both the company's management and personnel and the company's customers.

Perhaps the most compelling reason for adopting ISO standards is the potential impact that it has from a marketing standpoint. Most companies that are ISO certified today use that certification as an image-building tool. John Harrleson, Alliance Account Executive for Dow Chemical Company, says the following regarding ISO: "If companies today truly desire to compete in the global market arena, they must be recognized as a global quality supplier. ISO certification provides customers that level of assurance. Companies attempting to compete globally, without the benefit of ISO, are missing a major portion of the 'global entry fee.'" The results of recently surveyed ISO 9000 registered companies are reported in Table 9.6. The survey found that "higher perceived quality" and "improved customer satisfaction" were the most important external benefits of ISO registration.

Table 9.6 The Most Important Internal Benefits of Registration

Higher perceived quality	208	33.50%
Improved customer satisfaction	165	26.60%
Competitive edge	133	15.00%
Reduced customer quality audits	53	8.50%
Increased market share	28	4.50%
Quicker time to market	41	0.60%
Other	6	1.00%
No answer	23	3.70%

Source: *Quality Systems Update*/Deloitte & Touche (QSU/D&T) survey of ISO 9000 registered companies (620 respondents from 1679 companies) in July 1993.

Understanding and Implementing ISO 9000

Unlike the Baldrige Award, the ISO 9000 series is not an awards program. Neither do ISO 9000 requirements refer to products or services, but rather to the systems that produce them. The standards are also generic and apply to all industries. They are meant to complement industry-specific product standards for quality assurance.

The standards cover everything that affects quality and provide a common measuring stick for gauging quality systems. The ISO series is also flexible in that quality levels are determined between customer and supplier. The ISO series serves as a means of accountability that a company's quality systems work as stated and documented. Yet companies pursuing ISO certification have considerable freedom as to *how* they will meet the certification criteria.

ISO 9000 consists of a series of criteria, or standards, numbered sequentially from 9000. A listing of those standards along with their applications is provided in Table 9.7.[5]

When implemented on an organization-wide basis, ISO 9000 can result in a significant improvement in the quality efforts of sales and marketing. The following are some of the key paragraphs in ISO 9001:

4.3 Contract Review: In this area of ISO 9001, systems must be in place to review contracts for nonstandard terms and conditions, such as special handling. There must be processes and procedures to consistently meet that special requirement of the customer.

Table 9.7 Summary of ISO 9000 Standards and Applications

Standard	Content	Application
ISO 9000	Provides definitions and concepts; explains how to select other standards for a given business	All industries including software development
ISO 9001	Quality assurance in design, development, production, installation, and servicing	Engineering and construction firms, manufacturers that design, develop, install, and service products
ISO 9002	Quality assurance in production and installation	Companies in the chemical process industries that are not involved in product design or after-sales service
ISO 9003	Quality assurance in test and inspection	Small shops, divisions within a firm, equipment distributors that inspect and test supplied products
ISO 9004	Quality management and quality system elements	All industries

4.5 Document Control: This area focuses on the salesperson's ability to develop a contract with the client. Document control would help ensure that the documents, such as the sales literature, are current and accurate. For example, quoting prices to a client would be predicated on timely and accurate sales literature.

4.9 Process Control: This involves putting procedures in place that everyone must follow. Marketing processes such as order processes, new product introductions, and delivery time are processes that can be documented and analyzed here. The goals are to reduce cycle time, reduce order defects, or improve time to market.

Perhaps the strongest support for including marketing in the quality process can be found in the ISO 9000 quality standards management guide. As stated in ISO 9004:

7.1 Marketing Requirements: "The marketing function should take the lead in establishing quality requirements for the product..."

7.2 Product Brief: "The marketing function should provide the company with a formal statement or outline of product requirements, e.g., a product brief..."

7.3 Customer Feedback Information: "The marketing function should establish an information monitoring and feedback system on a continuous basis..."

ISO certification simply calls for a quality documentation approach for any aspect of the business, including, but not limited to, manufacturing, R&D, product development, sales and marketing, finance, logistics, and even administration. Most companies take the approach of developing a quality manual to communicate information to employees and to impress customers with a system that exists to provide quality.

As a process, the suggested method for developing and documenting quality under ISO 9000 guidelines is as follows:

1. State your quality policy: Vision or mission statement defining the role of quality in your business (see Figure 9.2 for an example of a quality policy)

2. Describe the products or services, plants and facilities, and the organization

3. Develop a quality manual to:

   a. Say what you do

   b. Do what you say

   c. Demonstrate effectiveness

THE XYZ COMPANY

Quality Policy

*In all aspects of our business and in every task we perform,
we will each deliver to our internal and external customers
products and services that totally satisfy their requirements
the first time, on time, every time.*

All our products and services will be world class and known for quality and value

John Doe
Chairman and Chief Executive Officer

Date of issue: January 1, 1995

Figure 9.2 Example of a Quality Policy.

d. Monitor the process to make sure necessary changes are made

e. Make sure unauthorized changes are not made

Most managers today can agree on one thing when it comes to establishing procedures that comply with ISO 9000 standards: gathering input from all parties involved and then carrying out those procedures properly will provide more opportunities for success than a company that approaches activities on a "free-lance" basis.

Many companies leave the ISO certification process in the hands of manufacturing. An example of how Ethyl Corporation's marketing department adopted an ISO 9004 procedure for new product development is provided in Figure 9.3. Notice the level of multifunctional teamwork necessary for such a procedure to exist. More importantly, for those not currently involved in a marketing function, this ISO example provides an in-depth view of the level of interdepartmental involvement necessary to carry out the marketing function within a firm.

The British Standards Organization, the group responsible for developing ISO 9000 and related conformance criteria, probably envisioned some, but not all, of the competitive opportunities laid bare as a result of its efforts. Given the explosive global marketplace of the 1990s, marketers are looking at every potential advantage to demonstrate an edge within their global playing field. ISO certification, once a "seal of quality" for both U.S. and European firms, is now being touted by eastern European and Middle Eastern firms as well.

Once competitors match a company's offering, either in service or perceived quality, the marketing staff is charged with identifying the next level of differentiation. Most large U.S. corporations adopted ISO standards as a way to stand apart from their competition in the global marketplace during the mid to late 1980s. Quality experts now conclude that 60 percent of the *Fortune* 200 companies have achieved ISO certification, with EC companies averaging 90 percent ISO certification. What opportunities remain for a company not yet ISO certified?

Harwood Ritter, a global competition consultant who works with several U.S. and European-based companies, identified the key concepts that drive acceptance of ISO qualifications by firms today. According to Ritter, "ISO certification was once believed to be the utopia of companies interested in competing in the global marketplace. What has occurred as a result of the myriad of companies gaining ISO standards is that ISO as an edge no longer exists. What was once a luxury and a competitive advantage is now considered a requirement of entry into the marketplace. The companies that have invested time and resources to gain certification are now realizing that it must be maintained annually just to achieve the perception of parity by their customers."

I. SCOPE

Establish a procedure to bring developmental products into commercial, market-ready products for North American marketing operations.

II. RESPONSIBILITY

A. The Marketing/Product Managers (Business Management) are responsible for approval, pricing, and categorizing of all new products.

B. Sales Management is responsible for reviewing the market potential of any new product requests with Business Management.

C. Health and Environment personnel are responsible for assigning product code (HiTEC number) and researching and meeting product stewardship, E.P.A., and safety regulations.

D. The Pricing Administrator is responsible for insertion and maintenance of this product in the price and lead-time database.

E. Research and Development (R&D), Customer Technical Service, and Manufacturing Management, or their designates, will review with Business Management to determine what blend processes, manufacturing requirements, and product specifications are required.

III. PROCEDURE

A. A flowchart for the new product commercialization procedure is shown in Figure 9.4.

B. Sales Management and/or R&D will meet with Business Management to determine the requirements for a new product. Market general specifications and performance guidelines will be listed and sent to Customer Tech Service to issue a blend process.

C. If the product is to be utilized both internally and as a commercial product, then Manufacturing Management will assist Business Management in determining volume capacity and inventory requirements.

D. Customer Tech Service personnel will assign an "X" number to the product to identify it during the stages prior to receiving a HiTEC number.

E. Customer Tech Service personnel will provide general specifications and a blend process procedure for the product.

F. With acceptance by the business managers responsible for the product area, and coordination from Health and Environment, Customer Tech Service will identify the product with a HiTEC number.

G. Business Management will develop a product data sheet for the product and enter this information into the product data system via the Pricing Administrator.

Figure 9.3 Ethyl New Product Commercialization Procedure (Based on ISO 9004).

H. Business Management will develop both market general and customer-specific pricing guidelines for the product and report this information to the Pricing Administrator.

I. Business Management and Pricing Administrator, in conjunction with Manufacturing and Logistics, will develop a lead-time and minimum-order quantity requirement for this product.

J. A general announcement of the new HiTEC product will be made to all sales, marketing, logistics, customer service and order entry personnel, via cc:mail.

APPROVED BY: _____   DATE: _____

EFFECTIVE DATE: _____

Figure 9.3 (continued)

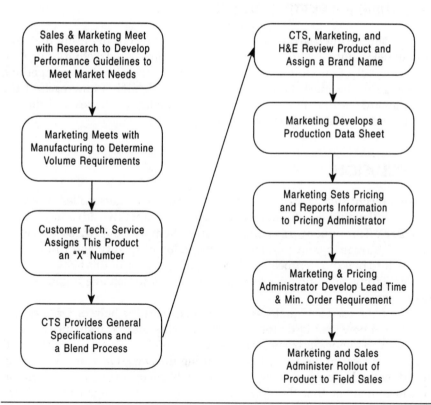

Figure 9.4 Ethyl New Product Development Flowchart.

Clearly, the image that ISO certification once provided has changed. What was once a banner of world-class quality is viewed today as simply the price of admission to compete globally.

Beyond its status as an admission ticket, ISO certification is important for two reasons: the customer requires it and it improves business. Customers are looking for a standard set of criteria to evaluate suppliers, and ISO 9000 has become the de facto standard for just that purpose. Customers value suppliers that can deliver consistent quality. ISO certification serves as a "badge" of quality assurance.

ISO certification also helps businesses improve by rethinking their marketing processes, especially as they relate to serving the customer. ISO 9000 certification should not be a goal unto itself, but rather a process of continually improving a company's business and marketing functions. (For additional information, see Abstract 9.4 at the end of this chapter.)

QUALITY STANDARDS COMPARED AND THEIR MARKETING VALUE

By using an internal quality program or adopting one of the international or national quality award or certification programs, a marketing group can instill a level of discipline within its activities to achieve a competitive advantage in the markets its serves. Table 9.8 highlights how each of the major award/certification programs utilizes quality processes and the impact of each award criterion on marketing.

CONCLUSION

In a recent survey, nearly 80 percent of U.S. managers polled indicated that quality would be a fundamental source of competitive advantage in the year 2000. Throughout this book, we have attempted to provide a foundation and format to better understand the value of quality and to integrate quality into marketing processes. In short, the purpose of this book is to help the marketing practitioner use quality practices to achieve a competitive advantage.

The Japanese took quality seriously and, with the help of Dr. Deming, established new standards for product reliability and performance in automobiles, consumer electronics, and heavy machinery. The quality "religion" began to spread in the United States during the early 1980s and was legitimized by the Malcolm Baldrige Award, established in 1987. Yet it is important to remember that the drive toward total quality began not with the

Table 9.8 Comparing Quality Standards and Their Marketing Value

Baldrige Award	Quality award criteria		Quality process	Marketing benefit
	Deming Prize	ISO		
Leadership	Organization and its management	Responsibility and authority	Vision/goal setting	Market focus and segmentation
Information and analysis	Collection and use of information/analysis	Standard 9001	Benchmarking	Market research and competitive analysis
Strategic quality and planning	Organization and its management	Quality system procedures and planning	Strategy	Strategy development and planning
Human resource development and planning	Education	Resources	Human resources training and effectiveness	Empowered sales and front-line workers
Quality and operational results	Standardization and control	Assurance Standard 9001/9003	Quality measurement	Performance measurements and reward systems

Baldrige Award, but with the consumer. Quality became an important issue because the customer said it was important.

As international competition intensifies, companies must recognize the importance of quality not just as a means of differentiation, but as the ticket into the global marketplace. Moreover, quality is now recognized as a minimum standard in competing for global business customers. The growing number of companies that have become or are becoming ISO 9000 certified was discussed in Chapter 9.

Whether you own a hot dog stand or manage a marketing function for a global business conglomerate, to borrow a phrase from "Forrest Gump," "quality is what quality does." That is, improving your core business processes will make your marketing functions more effective and more efficient. The upshot is that your organization's customers will benefit when quality is wrapped around core business processes such as delivery, order and transaction processing, and product development time.

DISCUSSION QUESTIONS

1. Compare the standards for each of the following quality awards. How are they similar? How do they differ?

   a. Deming Prize

   b. Malcolm Baldrige Award

2. Explain the role marketing plays in qualifying for the Baldrige Award.

3. Why is it important for U.S. firms to comply with ISO 9000?

4. Discuss the value of ISO certification as a global marketing tool.

ENDNOTES

1. Partlow, Charles. G. "How Ritz-Carlton Applies TQM." *The Cornell H.R.A Quarterly*, August 1993, p. 5
2. Stevens, Tim. "Management Doesn't Know What Its Job Is (the last interview with Dr. Deming)." *Industry Week*, January 17, 1994, p. 26.
3. Jackson, Suzan. "What You Should Know about ISO 9000." *Training*, May 1992, p. 48.
4. Miller, Cyndee. "U.S. Firms Lag in Meeting Global Quality Standards." *Marketing News*, February 15, 1993, p. 1.
5. Omachonu, V. and Ross, J. *Principles of Total Quality*, St. Lucie Press, Delray Beach, Fla., 1994.

ABSTRACTS

ABSTRACT 9.1
THE BALDRIGE: WHAT IT IS, HOW IT'S WON, HOW TO USE IT
TO IMPROVE QUALITY IN YOUR COMPANY

Hart, Christopher W.L. and Bogan, Christopher E.
McGraw-Hill, New York, 1992, 281 pp.

"The approach prescribed by this book," say the authors, "is based on the premise that the Baldrige is best used not to 'bag a trophy,' but as a process that helps a company learn more about its strengths and weaknesses, and then helps the company take steps to improve itself." The authors, a Baldrige examiner and a consultant who helped Federal Express win the Baldrige, have produced a very practical book, designed not only to describe how the Baldrige works, but to guide a company in the process of assessing itself and taking steps to improve. The book is divided into three parts:

1. **The Meaning of the Baldrige.** First, they describe the historical background to the Baldrige Award and the various review processes involved for applicants. Next, they give capsule summaries of companies which have won the Baldrige already. Then the authors discuss the pros and cons of five types of assessment: (1) using the criteria as the basis for discussions about organizational performance; (2) compiling surveys of managers based on the Baldrige criteria; (3) assessing, scoring, and evaluating the company using internal staff; (4) hiring others to score and evaluate data and reports compiled by the company; and (5) using outside experts to perform the entire assessment. Finally, the authors describe the scoring and evaluation process in some detail.

2. **The Seven Pillars.** This section discusses the Baldrige "mega-concepts," such as "involve everyone in the organization in quality" and "continuously improve." Then the authors discuss each of the seven sections ("pillars") of the Baldrige criteria. For each pillar, the authors give an introduction and a synopsis of the scoring ranges. Then they state the actual requirements, followed by several pages of discussion on the process to follow in meeting each requirement.

3. **The Baldrige Toolkit.** Chapter 15, "Executive Exercises," consists of 50 pages of worksheets designed to guide executives through developing vision statements, improving role model behavior and managerial effec-

tiveness, sharing success stories, managing employee development and retention, and managing for customer satisfaction. The final part of this chapter consists of a table which gives each requirement, examples of a successful company's compliance, examples of compliance by excellent companies (such as Motorola, Procter & Gamble, and Xerox), and space for a statement about the compliance of the executive's own company in this area. The remainder of this section lists resources on the Baldrige and where they may be obtained; other quality awards offered at the community, state, and national levels; and industry-specific awards. A brief quality glossary concludes the volume. (©*Quality Abstracts*)

ABSTRACT 9.2
INTEGRATING A BALDRIGE APPROACH INTO
A SALES DISTRICT'S MANAGEMENT SYSTEM

Cortada, James W.
National Productivity Review, Spring 1994

The author is a well-known business writer who presents a concise look at one of the key features of how to use the Baldrige criteria as standards for measuring, evaluating, and improving the performance of salespeople. He presents an approach whereby the sales organization can provide concrete direction for responding to the needs of the customers and the company as a whole. In 1991, a U.S. government study found that practitioners enjoyed average improvements of 8.6 percent in sales per employee, gained 13.7 percent in market share, and increased customer satisfaction by 2.5 percent. These are impressive credentials for the Baldrige followers in the marketing arena.

He points out that initially sales and marketing people think that the Baldrige is a waste of time and not applicable to them. As interest grows, they begin to use the criteria for self-evaluation, often scoring in the low 200s out of a possible 1000 points. He points out that during the evolution, quotas often change, with part of individual compensation coming from district–team performance instead of just one person's territory. He also introduces the concept of "top sheet" measurements, in which indicators beyond revenue or profit are used to measure business health. This is viewed by some as a watershed cultural change for most organizations. This approach is similar to the "Balanced Scorecard" approach and contains four main quadrants of measures: customer satisfaction, employee morale, quality, and financial contribution. He also argues that investing in technological aids, such as laptop computers and cellular telephones, becomes easier to justify because they improve speed of operations and responsiveness to customers. Caution must be taken, however, in that all sales organizations underestimate the amount of effort required to implement a Baldrige view of the business. This is a very worthwhile work, in spite of the absence of references.

ABSTRACT 9.3
BROKERING MARKETING INTO TOTAL QUALITY

Locander, William B.
Survey of Business, Summer 1989, pp. 31–35

In the future, the author writes, the marketing and sales functions will become the eyes and ears to the marketplace, especially for organizations seeking world-class quality and productivity levels. A critical core competency will be a "customer empathy" viewpoint, which is critical to becoming a market-driven company. Another important competency will be the ability to measure and develop indicators which are a part of a total quality management system. Indices such as dollar sales are global measures of how the system is operating.

Various suggestions are offered to help marketing and sales managers understand customer needs: Periodic market study and analysis, face-to-face customer contact, quality function deployment tools to capture the voice of the customer, and entry into the distribution channel to tap years of experience with the customer. The increasing importance of the logistics function in optimizing the value chain is also discussed, as is its relationship to customer-driven management. Limited references are provided.

ABSTRACT 9.4
YOU CAN EARN ISO 9002 APPROVAL IN LESS THAN A YEAR

Gasko, Helen M.
Journal for Quality and Participation, March 1992, pp. 14–19

Union Carbide's Taft, Louisiana plant—its Ethyleneamines Business (EA Business)—used a multifunctional team to help it gain ISO 9002 approval after only four months, reports the author. Since a large portion of the company's products are sold outside the United States, ISO registration was needed to compete in European Community member countries. A steering committee was formed to remove obstacles to progress, while day-to-day activities were left to accountable individuals. A preliminary evaluation and specific gap analysis was conducted, highlighting areas which needed correction. Then a three-tiered document system was adopted—with each document assigned to a different individual to write in parallel rather than sequentially—(a) a "Quality System Manual," which included a broad policy statement; (b) a "Facilities Quality Manual," which defined specific activities and assigned accountabilities to various plant functions; and (c) "Procedures and Systems," which detailed the standard operating practices for day-to-day operations. Since the writers kept in continual contact, nothing was written with which another could not comply. Some of the other insights the company gained concerning the completion of the ISO criteria were:

- Adapt, don't re-invent. Where different names are used for the ISO requirements, use your own jargon where you already comply.

- Entrust individuals with seeing their portion of ISO compliance through to completion without management interference.

- Use the people on the compliance team as quality auditors.

- Set an aggressive time frame to act as a catalyst.

- Allow each functional team to do whatever works for its particular area without bureaucratic rigidity.

- "Don't study it to death—just do it," became the motto.

"At Taft, we were able to do this because EA Business was already partially in compliance, and we recognized that we could adapt many procedures in place," says the author. "A more realistic target would be to aim for approval in less than a year." The article includes two sidebars: a brief description of each of the elements of the ISO 9000 series and the elements of the ISO 9002 standards dealing with production and installation. (©*Quality Abstracts*)

GLOSSARY

Abnormal variation: Changes in process performance that cannot be accounted for by typical day-to-day variation. Also referred to as nonrandom variation.

Acceptable quality level (AQL): The maximum number of parts that do not comply with quality standards.

Activity: The tasks performed to change inputs into outputs.

Adaptable: An adaptable process is designed to maintain effectiveness and efficiency as requirements change. The process is deemed adaptable when there is agreement among suppliers, owners, and customers that the process will meet requirements throughout the strategic period.

Appraisal cost: The cost incurred to determine defects.

Benchmarking: A tool used to improve products, services, or management processes by analyzing the best practices of other companies to determine standards of performance and how to achieve them in order to increase customer satisfaction.

Business objectives: Specific objectives which, if achieved, will ensure that the operating objectives of the organization are in alignment with the vision, values, and strategic direction. They are generally high level and timeless.

Business process: Organization of people, equipment, energy, procedures, and material into measurable, value-added activities needed to produce a specified end result.

Business process analysis (BPA): Review and documentation (mapping) of a key business process to understand how it currently functions and to establish measures.

Commercialization: The actions required to move a product from conception through design, creation, and marketing the finished good or service.

Competitive: A process is considered to be competitive when its overall performance is judged to be as good as that of comparable processes. Competitiveness is based on a set of performance characteristics (defects, costs, inventory turnaround, etc.) that are monitored and tracked against comparable processes within the corporation, the industry, and/or the general business community.

Competitive advantage: Generating and sustaining the greatest customer value over time that distinguishes one company from its competitors.

Competitive benchmarking: Comparing and rating the practices, processes, and products of an organization against the competition. Comparisons are confined to the same industry.

Conformance: Affirmative indication or judgment that a product or service has met specified requirements, contracts, or regulations. The state of meeting the requirements.

Continuous improvement: This is a principle used by W. Edwards Deming to examine improvement of product and service. It involves searching unceasingly for ever-higher levels of quality by isolating sources of defects. It is called *kaizen* in Japan, where the goal is zero defects. Quality management and improvement is a never-ending activity.

Control: The state of stability, or normal variation and predictability. It is the process of regulating and guiding operations and processes using quantitative data. Control mechanisms are also used to detect and avoid potential adverse effects of change.

Control charts: Statistical plots derived from measuring a process. Control charts help detect and determine deviations before a defect results. Inherent variations in manufacturing and non-manufacturing processes can be spotted and accounted for by designers.

Core business: The primary occupation of the business; the initial venture of an enterprise such as bakery products is for Sara Lee.

Corrective action: The implementation of effective solutions that result in the elimination of identified product, service, and process problems.

Cost of quality: The sum of prevention, appraisal, and failure costs, usually expressed as a percentage of total cost or revenue.

Critical success factors (CSFs): Areas in which results, if satisfactory, will ensure successful corporate performance. They ensure that the company will meet its business objectives. CSFs are focused, fluctuate, and are conducive to short-term plans.

Cross-functional: A term used to describe individuals from different business units or functions who are part of a team to solve problems, plan, and develop solutions for process-related actions affecting the organization as a system.

Cross-functional focus: The effort to define the flow of work products in a business process as determined by their sequence of activities, rather than by functional or organizational boundaries.

Culture (also vision): The pattern of shared beliefs and values that provides members of an organization rules of behavior or accepted norms for conducting operational business.

Customer: The recipient or beneficiary of the outputs of work efforts or the purchaser of products and services. May be either internal or external to the company.

Customer, internal: Organizations have both external and internal customers. Many functions and activities are not directly involved with external customer satisfaction, but their outputs provide inputs to other functions and activities within the organization. Data processing, for example, must provide an acceptable quality level for many internal customers.

Customer-focused teams: A group of employees assembled with the main objective to satisfy the business and/or individual needs of a specific customer account

Customer requirements (also called valid requirements): The statement of needs or expectations that a product or service must satisfy. Requirements must be specific, measurable, negotiated, agreed to, documented, and communicated.

Customer satisfaction: An emotional response to the difference between what customers expect and what they ultimately receive.

Customer/supplier model: The model is generally represented using three interconnected triangles to depict inputs flowing into a work process that, in turn, adds value and produces outputs that are delivered to a customer. Throughout the process, requirements and feedback are fed from the customer to the supplier to ensure that customer quality requirements are met.

Cycle time: The elapsed time between the commencement and completion of a task. In manufacturing, it is calculated as the number of units of work-in-process inventory divided by the number of units processed in a specific period. In order processing, it can be the time between receipt and delivery of an order. Overall cycle time can mean the time from concept of a new product or service until it is brought to market.

Defect: Something that does not conform to requirements.

Document of understanding (DOU): A formal agreement defining the roles, responsibilities, and objectives of all the parties to that agreement. The degree of detail is dictated by the nature of the agreement, but it should always clearly address the requirements of the work product in question.

Effective: An effective process produces output that conforms to customer requirements. The lack of process effectiveness is measured by the degree to which the process output does not conform to customer requirements (that is, by the level of defect of the output).

Effectiveness: The state of having produced a decided or desired effect; the state of achieving customer satisfaction.

Efficiency: A measure of performance that compares output production with cost or resource utilization (as in number of units per employee per hour or per dollar).

Efficient: An efficient process produces the required output at the lowest possible (minimum) cost. That is, the process avoids waste or loss of resources in producing the required output. Process efficiency is measured by the ratio of required output to the cost of producing that output. This cost is expressed in units of applied resource (dollars, hours, energy, etc.).

Employee involvement (EI): Promotions and mechanisms to achieve employee contributions, individually and in groups, to quality and company performance objectives. Cross-functional teams, task forces, quality circles, or other vehicles for involvement are used.

Employee well-being and morale: Maintenance of work environment conducive to well-being and growth of all employees. Factors include health, safety, satisfaction, work environment, training, and special services such as counseling assistance, recreational, or cultural.

Empowerment: Actions that a firm can take to give employees a greater sense of control and participation in the events and decisions affecting their business life.

Executive Quality Service Council (EQSC): Comprised of members of executive management and union leadership who oversee the quality effort from a corporate view and set strategic direction.

Facilitator: Responsible for guiding the team through analysis of the process. Also concerned with how well the team works together.

Failure cost: The cost resulting from the occurrence of defects (such as scrap, rework/redo, replacement, etc.).

Functional organization: An organization responsible for one of the major corporate business functions such as marketing, sales, design, manufacturing, or distribution.

Human resource management: Development of plans and practices that realize the full potential of the work force to pursue the quality and performance objectives of the organization. Includes (1) education and training, (2) recruitment, (3) involvement, (4) empowerment, and (5) recognition.

Implementer: An individual working within the process and who is responsible for carrying out specific job tasks.

Indicators: Benchmarks, targets, standards, or other measures used to evaluate how well quality values and programs are integrated.

Information system: A database of information used for planning day-to-day management and control of quality. Types of data should include (1) customer related, (2) internal operations, (3) company performance, and (4) cost and financial.

Inputs: Products or services obtained from others (suppliers) in order to perform job tasks. Material or information required to complete the activities necessary for a specified end result.

Involved managers: Managers who have responsibility for the day-to-day activities and tasks within the process.

Just-in-time (JIT): The delivery of parts and materials by a supplier at the moment a factory needs them, thus eliminating costly inventories. Quality is paramount because a faulty part delivered at the last moment will not be detected.

Kaizen: See Continuous improvement

Leadership: The category of the Baldrige Award that examines personal leadership and involvement of executives in creating and sustaining a customer focus and clear and visible quality values.

Management for quality: The translation of customer focus and quality values into implementation plans for all levels of management and supervision.

Marketing: Planning and executing the conception, pricing, promotion, and distribution of ideas, goods, and services to create exchanges which satisfy individual and organizational objectives.

Market orientation: Creating a culture within an organization that seeks to create superior value for buyers by increasing benefits relative to the cost of delivering those benefits.

Measurable outcomes: Specific results that determine, corporately, how well critical success factors and business objectives are being achieved. They are concrete, specific, and measurable.

Measurement: The methods used to achieve and maintain conformance to customer requirements. Measurement determines the current status of the process and whether the process requires change or improvement.

Mission: The core purpose of being for an organization. Usually expressed in the form of a statement 25 to 50 words in length.

Operating plans: Specific, actionable plans which, if carried out successfully, ensure that critical success factors are met, which in turn ensures that corporate business objectives are met. They are tied to critical success factors, are detailed, and contain measurements of success.

Operating Quality Service Council (OQSC): Comprised of activity management and their direct reports, and many include union and staff representation. The council oversees the quality effort within an activity and ensures that quality strategies support the corporate strategic direction.

Order fulfillment: Taking the order from a customer, creating the product or service, and delivering it to the customer.

Organization for quality: Structuring organizational activities to effectively accomplish the company's objectives.

Outputs: The specified end result, materials, or information provided to others (internal or external customers).

Pareto analysis (or Pareto chart): A statistical method of measurement to identify the most important problems through different measuring scales (for example, frequency, cost, etc.). Usually displayed by a bar graph that ranks causes of process variation by the degree of impact on quality (sometimes called the 80/20 rule).

Prevention activity: Elements of prevention activity include (1) education in

process quality management and (2) process management (ownership, documentation/analysis, requirements activity, measurements including statistical techniques, and corrective action on the process).

Prevention cost: Costs incurred to reduce the total cost of quality.

Process: The organization of people, equipment, energy, procedures, and material into the work activities needed to produce a specified end result (work product). A sequence of repeatable activities characterized as having measurable inputs, value-added activities, and measurable outputs. It is a set of interrelated work activities characterized by a set of specific inputs and value-added tasks that produce a set of specific outputs.

Process analysis: The systematic examination of a process model to establish a comprehensive understanding of the process itself. The intent of the examination should include consideration of simplification, elimination of unneeded or redundant elements, and improvement.

Process capability: The level of effectiveness and efficiency at which the process will perform. This level may be determined through the use of statistical control charts. Long-term performance level after the process has been brought under control.

Process control: The activity necessary to ensure that the process is performing as designed. Achieved through the use of statistical techniques, such as control charts, so that appropriate actions can be taken to achieve and maintain a state of statistical control.

Process elements: A process is comprised of activities and tasks. A process may also be referred to as a subprocess when it is subordinate to, but part of, a larger process. A subprocess can also be defined as a group of activities within a process that comprise a definable component.

Process management: The disciplined management approach of applying prevention methodologies to the implementation, improvement, and change of work processes to achieve effectiveness, efficiency, and adaptability. Critical to the success of process management is the concept of cross-functional focus.

Process model: A detailed representation of the process (graphic, textual, mathematical) as it currently exists.

Process owner: Coordinates the various functions and work activities at all levels of a process, has the authority or ability to make changes in the process as required, and manages the process end-to-end so as to ensure optimal overall performance.

Process performance quality: A measure of how effectively and efficiently a process satisfies customer requirements. The ability of a product or service to meet and exceed the expectations of customers.

Process review: An objective assessment of how well the methodology has been applied to the process. Emphasizes the potential for long-term process results rather than the actual results achieved.

Product life cycle: Portrays the distinct stages in the sales and profit history of a product; each stage requires different business, financial, and marketing strategies.

Quality function deployment (QFD): A system that pays special attention to customer needs and integrates them into the marketing, design, manufacturing, and service processes. Activities that do not contribute to customer needs are considered wasteful.

Quality Improvement Team (QIT): A group of people brought together to resolve a specific problem or issue identified by a business process analysis, individual employees, or the Operating Quality Service Council. A group of individuals charged with the task of planning and implementing process quality improvement. The three major roles in this task force are the team leader, team facilitator, and team members.

Quality management: The management of a process to maximize customer satisfaction at the lowest overall cost to the company.

Quality management system: The collective plans, activities, and events established to ensure that a product, process, or service will satisfy given needs. The infrastructure supporting the operational process management and improvement methodology.

Quality planning: The process of developing the quality master to link together all of the planning systems of the organization. The objective is to follow all areas of achievement of the vision, mission, and business objectives and to operationalize the strategy by identifying the requirements to achieve leadership in the market segments chosen. Includes key requirements and performance indicators and the resources committed for these requirements.

Quality tool: Instrument or technique that supports the activities of process quality management and improvement.

Reengineering: A complete re-thinking of the broad-based ways in which an organization develops and delivers its products. Reengineering often calls for radical, sometimes order-of-magnitude improvements in the cost, time, or quality of a process, rather than merely redesigning work flows or procedures.

Requirements: What is expected in providing a product or service. The *it* in "do it right the first time." Specific and measurable customer needs with an associated performance standard.

Resource allocation: A decision to allocate resources, capital, and people to support specific operating plans, tied to the budget process.

Results: Results are, quite simply, a measurement of how well corporate business objectives are being met. Results require that standards and goals for performance are set and the results of processes and performance tracked.

Robust design: Making product designs "production-proof" by building in tolerances for manufacturing variables that are known to be unavoidable.

ROI: Return-on-investment; often referred to as the "hurdle rate." The net profit from an enterprise divided by the amount invested to conduct that enterprise.

Root cause: Original reason for nonconformance within a process. When the root cause is removed or corrected, the nonconformance will be eliminated.

Sales territory: A geographic area or number of accounts that are managed by an individual salesperson.

Six-sigma: A statistical term that indicates a defect level. One-sigma means 68 percent of products are acceptable, three-sigma means 99.75, and six-sigma means 99.999997 percent perfect or 3.4 defects per million parts.

Sponsor: Advocate for the team who provides resources and helps define mission and scope to set limits.

Stakeholder: Individual or department who either has an effect on the process or is affected by it.

Statistical process control (SPC): The use of statistical techniques, such as control charts, to analyze a work process or its outputs. The data can be used to identify deviations so that appropriate action can be taken to maintain a state of statistical control (predetermined upper and lower limits) and to improve the capability of the process.

Statistical quality control (SQC): A method of analyzing measured deviations in manufactured materials, parts, and products.

Strategic quality planning: Development of strategic and operational plans that incorporate quality as product or service differentiation and the load-bearing structure of the planning process. Includes (1) definition of customer requirements, (2) projections of the industry and competitive environment for identification of opportunities and risks, (3) comparison of opportunities and risks against company resources and capabilities, (4) employee involvement, and (5) supplier capabilities.

Strategy: The overall philosophy that a company undertakes to compete and market its products or services.

Subprocesses: The internal processes that make up a process.

Suppliers: Individuals or groups who provide input. Suppliers can be internal or external to a company, group, or organization.

Taguchi methods: Statistical techniques developed by Genichi Taguchi, a Japanese consultant, for optimizing design and production.

Task: The basic work element of a process activity.

Test marketing: Offering a product in limited geographic areas and measuring how target markets and competitors respond to the marketing mix.

Time to market: The length of time involved from a product's initial concept to the finished good that is ready to sell.

Total quality management (TQM): The application of quality principles for the integration of all functions and processes of the organization. The ultimate goal is customer satisfaction. The way to achieve it is through continuous improvement.

Turbo-marketing: A term coined by marketing professor Phillip Kotler. It implies speeding up the processes of new products or reducing the time to market.

Variation: The degree to which a product, service, or element deviates from the specification or requirements. Quality in service organizations deals with identifying, measuring, and adjusting to variability resulting from interactions with customers, while manufacturing organizations are focused on bringing product variability under control.

Vision: The long-term future desired state of an organization, usually expressed in a 7- to 20-year time frame. Often included in the vision statement are the areas that the organization needs to care about in order to succeed. The vision should inspire and motivate.

INDEX